Contemporary Vietnam

Praise for Ian Jeffries' previous publications:

Socialist Economies and the Transition to the Market:

> This weighty tome can be unreservedly commended ... Students and their teachers can learn a great deal from this book ... Excellent! Ian Jeffries has done us all a service.
>
> (Alec Nove, *Europe-AsiaSt udies*)

The Countries of the Former Yugoslavia at the Turn of the Twenty-first Century: A Guide to the Economies in Transition:

> This massive volume ... should find a place in every university library.
>
> (Sabrina P. Ramet, *Europe-AsiaSt udies*)

North Korea: A Guide to Economic and Political Developments:

> Although it does not attempt to provide answers as to why events occurred as they did, it will be an indispensable source for any effort to do so.
>
> (Christopher Griffin, *Pacific Affairs*)

China: A Guide to Economic and Political Developments:

> This book is highly useful not only to casual China watchers ... but also to researchers and academics.
>
> (Marc Lanteigne, *International Affairs*)

This book provides full details of contemporary economic and political developments in Vietnam. It continues the overview of developments up to late 2005 which were covered in the author's *Vietnam: A Guide to Economic and Political Developments* (also published by Routledge, 2006). Key topics covered include Vietnam's success, in general, in maintaining high rates of growth in the face of problems such as inflation and the global financial crisis; continuing economic reforms; foreign trade and investment; battles against corruption; population growth; the determination of the Communist Party to maintain its hold on power; and Vietnam's response to public health problems such as AIDS, SARS and bird flu.

Ian Jeffries is Honorary Professor in the Department of Economics at Swansea University, UK. His recent publications include two volumes covering the economic and political developments in contemporary China (2010), alongside many books in the Routledge series *Guides to Economic and Political Developments in Asia*, covering China, North Korea and Mongolia.

Guides to economic and political developments in Asia

1 **North Korea**
   A guide to economic and political developments
   Ian Jeffries

2 **Vietnam**
   A guide to economic and political developments
   Ian Jeffries

3 **China**
   A guide to economic and political developments
   Ian Jeffries

4 **Mongolia**
   A guide to economic and political developments
   Ian Jeffries

5 **Contemporary North Korea**
   A guide to economic and political developments
   Ian Jeffries

6 **Political Developments in Contemporary China**
   A guide
   Ian Jeffries

7 **Economic Developments in Contemporary China**
   A guide
   Ian Jeffries

8 **Political Developments in Contemporary Russia**
   Ian Jeffries

9 **Economic Developments in Contemporary Russia**
   Ian Jeffries

10 **Contemporary Vietnam**
   A guide to economic and political developments
   Ian Jeffries

Contemporary Vietnam
A guide to economic and political developments

Ian Jeffries

LONDON AND NEW YORK

First published 2011 by Routledge

2 Park Square, Milton Park, Abingdon, Oxon OX14 4RN
711 Third Avenue, New York, NY 10017, USA

Routledge is an imprint of the Taylor & Francis Group, an informa business

First issued in paperback 2016

Copyright © 2011 Ian Jeffries

Typeset in Times by Wearset Ltd, Boldon, Tyne and Wear

All rights reserved. No part of this book may be reprinted or reproduced or utilised in any form or by any electronic, mechanical, or other means, now known or hereafter invented, including photocopying and recording, or in any information storage or retrieval system, without permission in writing from the publishers.

Notice:
Product or corporate names may be trademarks or registered trademarks, and are used only for identification and explanation without intent to infringe.

British Library Cataloguing in Publication Data
A catalogue record for this book is available from the British Library

Library of Congress Cataloging in Publication Data
Jeffries, Ian.
Contemporary Vietnam : a guide to economic and political developments / Ian Jeffries.
p. cm. – (Guides to economic and political developments in Asia)
Includes bibliographical references and index.
1. Vietnam–Politics and government. 2. Vietnam–Economic conditions.
3. Vietnam–Foreign economic relations. 4. Vietnam–Economic policy.
I. Title.
DS559.912.J44 2010
959.704'4–dc22   2010027435

ISBN: 978-0-415-60400-0 (hbk)
ISBN: 978-1-138-99171-2 (pbk)

Contents

Acknowledgements   vii

Introduction and summary   1

1   **Political developments**   10
Political background 10
A chronology of political developments since the Tenth Congress of the Communist Party held 18–25 April 2006 11
The Vietnam War: the human toll 83
Communist Party membership 85
The boat people 85
Religion 85
The internet 89
Demography 90
AIDS 91
SARS 95
Bird flu 100
Swine flu: influenza A(H1N1 or 2009 H1N1) 141

2   **The economy**   153
Economic background 153
The economic system 153
Financial and exchange rate policy: developments since October 2006 (including the global financial crisis) 154
The state sector 172
Privatization and stock markets 173
Foreign trade 181
Foreign debt and aid 192
Foreign direct investment 193

vi *Contents*

Agriculture 205
Economic performance 207

Postscript	209
Bibliography	230
Index	236

Acknowledgements

I am much indebted to the following individuals (in alphabetical order):

At Swansea University: Robert Bideleux; Siân Brown; Diane Darrell; Michele Davies; Chris Hunt; Nigel O'Leary; Mary Perman; Ann Preece; Paul Reynolds; Kathy Sivertsen and Chris West.

Professors: Nick Baigent, John Baylis; George Blazyca, Steve Brown, Mike Charlton, Steve Cook, Phillip Hanson, Paul Hare, Lester Hunt, Michael Kaser, Phil Murphy and Noel Thompson.

Russell Davies (Kays Newsagency).

At Routledge: Louise Collins, Emma Davis, Alan Jarvis, Tracy Morgan, Jillian Morrison, Eve Setch and Peter Sowden.

Copy-editor: Liz Jones.

At Wearset: Matt Deacon, Claire Toal and Allie Waite.

While Mark Axelby expertly renovated my house, I was free to write my books.

Ian Jeffries
Honorary Professor
Department of Economics and Centre of Russian and
East European Studies,
Swansea University

Introduction and summary

This is a follow-up book to *Vietnam: A Guide to Economic and Political Developments*, published in 2006. The postscript dealt with events as late as March of that year. So this book deals with subsequent events and supplementary material not available previously.

At the end of the Second World War in 1945 Vietnam was a classically poor country (with, for example, a low national income per head and most of the labour force working in agriculture) and a generally poorly endowed one in terms of natural resources.

Ho Chi Minh's resilience in seeing off, in turn, such powerful opponents as France (the original colonial power), Japan and the United States is truly remarkable. Vietnam went on to give China a bloody nose in the border war of February 1979 over Kampuchea. Equally impressive is the nation's capacity to forgive and forget. On the other hand, nobody is blind to the deficiencies of such a one-party state in terms of human rights (including those of ethnic minorities) and in terms of problems such as corruption. Like China, Vietnam is determined to remain a one-party state, seeing economic reform and development as a means of helping the Communist Party retain that control in a stable country.

The Vietnam War ended in 1975 and the reunited country faced the problem of how a poorer, planned economy in which state ownership and control dominated could successfully absorb a more advanced, capitalist economy. The two Vietnams were reunited in 1975 and the two Germanys in 1990 (with the West German economy effectively absorbing its poorer communist neighbour). But the two Koreas remain divided, with South Korea in a different economic universe compared with its (now nuclear-armed) twin.

By the time China started to introduce its economic reform programme in 1978, it had largely reoriented its trade away from Comecon – the communist trading bloc (after quarrelling with the Soviet Union in the early 1960s) – and was not aid-dependent. Vietnam, on the other hand, suffered from the collapse of communism.

Winning the war proved easier than winning the peace and after 1989 Vietnam felt compelled by the economic problems experienced to change course, specifically to adopt a market-orientated economic policy known as *doi moi* (usually translated as 'renovation'). Many of Victnam's 'renovations' have been influenced by China's economic reforms, e.g. China's Household Responsibility System. Vietnam's agriculture came to be based on the family farm (leasing state-owned land). There are many problems associated with such a system (such as the problem of the lack of firm property rights and the small size of the typical farm), but Vietnam became the world's number two exporter of rice.

Vietnam's attitude to economic reform has fluctuated. For example, the Asian financial crisis (which started in July 1997 with an attack on the Thai currency) dampened enthusiasm for a while. But generally the country has moved steadily in the direction of markets and greater non-state activity. Important bilateral trade agreements have been signed (including one with the United States). 'In 2009 the United States was the biggest importer of Vietnamese goods, absorbing about a fifth of the country's exports' (www.iht.com, 25 December 2009). Vietnam joined the WTO on 11 January 2007. Rising labour costs of late in the increasingly powerful Chinese economy are working in favour of even lower labour cost countries like Vietnam.

Some of the Vietnamese who fled to the United States and other countries (the Viet Kieu) are remitting substantial sums to the old country and some even investing in it.

Vietnam's economy has done well in recent years despite the global financial crisis, although inflation remains a problem.

> Over the past two years there have been violent swerves from austerity to stimulus and back again as the economy moved through inflation, the global crisis and now renewed signs of overheating. But for an economy that has relied on exports and foreign direct investment for much of its growth over the past decade, Vietnam has survived the global slowdown remarkably well.
>
> (*FT*, 5 January 2010, p. 7)

'Vietnam's government has coped well with the global crisis ... a new report by the World Bank says' (www.ft.com, 10 June 2009).

> Over the past twenty years Vietnam's economy has almost quadrupled in real terms. It has averaged 7.775 per cent annual growth and even last year, at the height of the financial crisis, managed 5.8 per cent. This year [2010] Vietnam expects to achieve another milestone, when GDP *per capita* passes $976 and it officially becomes a middle-income country.
>
> (*FT*, 1 June 2010, p. 22)

Despite problems such as inflation and corruption, Vietnam has generally coped well with the global financial crisis. Key developments are as follows:

'Vietnam's economy grew by around 8.5 per cent last year [2007], one of Asia's most impressive rates, having grown by an average of 7.5 per cent annually in the previous decade' (*The Economist*, 2 February 2008, pp. 61–2).

Inflation was in the 1980s peaked at 700 per cent in 1986. It peaked in the 1990s at 68.1 per cent in 1991. The inflation rate moved into single figures in 1996.

'In 2007 inflation had already reached a decade-high of 12.6 year on year. By February [2008] it reached 15.6 per cent ... Banks began to tighten purse strings, rejecting myriad loan applications' (Thuy 2008: 34–5).

> Vietnam's annual inflation rate has soared to 19.4 per cent year on year in March [2008], from 15.7 per cent in February, hitting double figures for a fifth consecutive month. Food price inflation, which holds around a 40 per cent weighting in the consumer price index and has been accelerating rapidly since mid-2007, continues to be the main factor driving up the general price level ... The government has begun to target consumer price inflation aggressively.
>
> (www.economist.com, 4 April 2008)

> The central bank of Vietnam said it will try to rein in inflation by limiting loans to consumers and investors in stocks and property ... Annual inflation rose to 21.42 per cent in April, among the highest rates since 1991 and among the highest in Asia.
>
> (www.iht.com, 5 May 2008)

'Vietnam's annual inflation rate accelerated to 25.2 per cent in May, its highest since 1992 ... Hanoi has said that fighting inflation is its top economic priority' (*FT*, 28 May 2008, p. 10).

'Vietnam yesterday [4 August] announced tough measures to contain rampant inflation' (*FT*, 5 August 2008, p. 5).

> With inflation rising to 27 per cent last month [July] – the highest in Asia – and food prices rising to 74 per cent above those of a year ago, Vietnam is suffering its first serious downturn since it moved from a command economy to an open market nearly two decades ago.
>
> (www.iht.com, 19 August 2008; *IHT*, 20 August 2008, p. 11)

> Vietnam has outlined a series of tax breaks and other measures as it fights to live up to its target of 6.5 per cent economic growth next year [2009] despite the slowdown in its main export markets. The government announced this week that it would expand a proposed $1 billion economic stimulus package largely through increasing tax breaks for importers, manufacturers and consumers. It also laid out further plans in a resolution passed last week, but released on Tuesday [16 December].
>
> (www.ft.com, 18 December 2008)

> Vietnam devalued the dong by 3 per cent in an attempt to keep its export-dependent economy afloat. The government said that 2008 economic growth had shrunk to 6.23 per cent from 8.5 per cent last year [2007] and there were signs it was likely to slow further in 2009 ... Hanoi's move comes after spending most of the year trying to maintain the currency's strength to slow spiralling inflation.
>
> (*FT*, 27 December 2008, p. 6)

4   *Introduction and summary*

> The government ... plans to boost spending this year [2009] by 23 per cent (almost $6 billion, about 6 per cent of GDP). Of this about $1 billion will subsidize loans to cash-strapped exporters ... An estimated 500,000 workers lost their jobs last year [2008] and the government reckons a further 400,000 may be laid off in 2009 ... [Vietnam] needs 1 million new jobs every year to absorb its growing work force, now around 45 million people ... GDP expanded by 6.2 per cent in 2008, the slowest rate for nine years ... Most observers, including the IMF, think it will be lucky to reach 5 per cent this year [2009]. Yet the government's target is still 6.5 per cent.
>
> (*The Economist*, 7 March 2009, pp. 62, 64)

'This week Vietnam increased import tariffs on dairy products, after raising duties on paper last month [February]' (*The Economist*, 14 March 2009, p. 67).

> Growth stumbled to its slowest rate in a decade in the first quarter [of 2009], falling to 3.1 per cent year-on-year as its export-driven economy is strangled by tumbling global demand and inward investment. The new estimate, released by the government on Thursday [26 March], represents a sharp slowing from growth of 7.4 per cent in the first quarter of last year [2008], and partially reflects both the 5 per cent fall in exports in the first two months of this year [2009] and rapidly diminishing foreign investment. FDI pledges fell 70 per cent in the first three months. The first quarter figures were lower than many analysts were expecting. The government is still hoping for annual growth of between 5 per cent and 6 per cent, down from its estimate of 6.5 per cent at the end of last year. Its estimates are in line with the World Bank's 5.5 per cent, and slightly above the IMF's recently revised estimate of 4.75 per cent growth ... Exports are forecast to contract by 7 per cent this year, down from growth of 2.6 per cent last year. But some analysts say that there might be a silver lining for Vietnam, one of the world's lowest cost producers. They believe that as consumers move down-market to save money, countries like Vietnam will be hit less hard than its more expensive export competition.
>
> (www.ft.com, 26 March 2009)

> Vietnam and India on Friday [28 March 2008] tightened limits on rice exports, joining India and Cambodia in trying to conserve scarce supplies for domestic consumption at the risk of triggering further increases in global prices, which have roughly doubled since the start of this year [2008] ... A plant virus has damaged the harvest in Vietnam ... Vietnam, the world's second largest rice exporter after Thailand, announced Friday that it would reduce rice exports by 22 per cent in the hope of curbing the rapidly accelerating inflation rates in the country.
>
> (www.iht.com, 29 March 2008)

'Vietnam extended its commercial loan subsidy programme, which was originally expected to last only until the end of this year [2009], to the end of 2011' (www.ft.com, 8 April 2009).

Elements of Vietnam's economic stimulus package have become clearer in recent weeks ... The package, which was announced earlier in 2009 ... is being implemented ... [at a] rapid pace ... One of the main components of the economic stimulus [is] a 4 percentage point interest rate subsidy ... Another component of the government's economic stimulus is a new credit-guarantee scheme to support commercial bank lending to small and medium-sized enterprises ... The government's latest announcement, on 18 April, presented a series of stimulus measures targeting the interest-free loans for purchases of farm equipment and subsidized loans for fertilizer and other agricultural inputs. Vietnam's agricultural sector employs more than two-thirds of the country's population and accounts for a major proportion of exports.

(www.economist.com, 22 April 2009)

Vietnamese exports have been fairly resilient. While economies such as Singapore and Taiwan have seen declines of 30 per cent or 40 per cent in shipments, Vietnam was down a modest 3.7 per cent in the first four months of this year [2009] against the same period in 2008.

(*FT*, 27 May 2009, p. 9)

Vietnam's government has coped well with the global crisis but needs to rein in its plans if it is not to overshoot, a new report by the World Bank says. The World Bank's 2009 GDP growth forecast of 5.5 per cent is at the optimistic end of the scale, but even the pessimists believe Vietnam's position as a low-cost producer, combined with an aggressive stimulus programme, will prevent it falling into recession.

(www.ft.com, 10 June 2009)

Vietnam has come through the worst of the economic crisis and the trial has provided new opportunities, according to Vu Van Ninh, finance minister. The national general statistics office on Wednesday [1 July] said GDP growth accelerated to a year-on-year rate of 4.5 per cent in the second quarter [of 2009] from 3.1 per cent in the first.

(www.ft.com, 1 July 2009)

'In Vietnam banks have been ordered to cap new lending to head off inflation' (*FT*, 28 July 2009, p. 5).

'Vietnam's economy is expected to expand some 5 per cent this year [2009]' (*FT*, 13 October 2009, p. 22).

'Vietnam plans to stop its interest rate subsidy scheme at the end of the year [2009], becoming the first Asian nation to start unwinding its post-crisis stimulus programme, the government announced on Wednesday [2 December]' (www.ft.com, 3 December 2009).

Vietnam's elegantly V-shaped recovery would be a terrible thing to spoil on the way to the Communist Party's Eleventh National Congress in early 2011. With that in mind, the government long denied any intention of devaluing the currency. On 25 November [however] ... the state bank lowered the official dong–dollar exchange rate by 5.2 per cent. In the same stroke Vietnam became the first country in Asia to increase interest rates since the financial crisis began, lifting the base rate from 7 per cent to 8 per cent in an attempt to slow credit growth and attract more dong-denominated deposits ... In the first half of 2008, when speculation and inflation threatened to surge out of control, the government was forced to rein in excesses. But it was to reverse itself only months later, as the global slowdown made itself felt. As the government followed the lead of other Asian nations trying to spend its way out of trouble – largely through a 17 trillion dong ($1 billion) interest rate subsidy programme – it began to build itself a new series of problems. Current account and budget deficits widened, foreign currency reserves shrank, and economists began to question the wisdom of a recovery based on government spending and cheap credit. Currency traders argued that its loose monetary policy would bring back inflation, which hit a six-month high of 4.35 per cent year-on-year in November. Their view was shared by many ordinary Vietnamese who, having been bruised by hyperinflation in the past, rushed to convert their dong-denominated savings into dollars and gold, the preferred stores of value in a country where only one person in ten has a bank account. Skittish foreign investors withdrew their money and cautious state-owned enterprises hoarded greenbacks; together, they created a persistent shortage of dollars. With too little hard currency to back it, in the past few months the dong went limp in the black market. The threat of a currency crisis loomed. Hence the government's volte-face. After lowering the exchange rate and tightening its monetary belt, it went on to egg state-owned enterprises into converting their stake in the dollar – estimated to be worth $10.3 billion – into the wilting dong to support its value and alleviate the shortage of harder currency ... This is Vietnam's third devaluation since the summer of 2008 ... Already 42 per cent of the total money supply is held in gold or dollars.

(www.economist.com, 10 December 2009)

Vietnam's strategy for competing in the global arena – and a relatively successful one until recently – had been to carve out niche markets where it could deliver, say, quality products like handicrafts or specialized clothing that China could not. But all of Vietnam's main export markets are heavily dependent on the United States. In 2009 the United States was the biggest importer of Vietnamese goods, absorbing about a fifth of the country's exports. Furniture companies, to take one industry, have had a huge drop in orders after the rapid downward spiral in sales of new homes in the United States ... Vietnam's economy grew 4.6 per cent for the first nine months of 2009, compared with the same period in 2008, according to the World Bank, in part because of government stimulus measures ... Vietnam in recent years had been able to sustain an average growth rate above 7 per cent ... In the first ten months of 2009 Vietnamese exports declined 13,8 per cent com-

Introduction and summary 7

pared with the period in 2008, the World Bank said ... In order to square off against China, many manufacturers try to rely on niche industries and specialties rather than competing on price or low labour costs ... As Vietnam's tourism market grows, particularly attracting new golf resorts and vacationers from nearby countries in South-east Asia and elsewhere, furniture manufacturers are turning to supply such resorts.

(www.iht.com, 25 December 2009)

Vietnam's economy grew at its fastest rate in two years in the fourth quarter [of 2009], helped by government spending. Hanoi's statistics office said economic growth expanded by 6.9 per cent in the final three months of the year. That compares to 6.04 per cent in the previous quarter. In a statement it said the economy 'had passed the most difficult period'. The government took measures worth about $8 billion to boost growth, including subsidies in order to encourage banks to lend. Overall in 2009 the rate of expansion slowed to 5.32 per cent, the lowest rate since 1999. That was put down to weaker demand for exports in the first part of the year. The government also said it must 'firstly continue to actively prevent the return of hyperinflation and the existing potential inflationary factors'. In November the central bank raised rates and devalued the currency in an attempt to control inflation, which ran at a rate of 6.52 per cent in December. Last year [2008] an overheating economy pushed it up to 28 per cent.

(www.bbc.co.uk, 31 December 2009)

Over the past two years there have been violent swerves from austerity to stimulus and back again as the economy moved through inflation, the global crisis and now renewed signs of overheating. But for an economy that has relied on exports and foreign direct investment for much of its growth over the past decade, Vietnam has survived the global slowdown remarkably well. Statistics released last week show the economy grew 5.32 per cent last year [2009], down from its average of more than 7 per cent over the preceding four years, but still substantially stronger than the expectations of many of its competitors ... [There is] a rising budget deficit that the World Bank estimates will hit 9.7 per cent of GDP this year [2010] after expenditure on a stimulus programme which the World Bank estimates has cost the country almost $4 billion, or 4 per cent of GDP.

(*FT*, 5 January 2010, p. 7)

[The] central bank said yesterday [10 February 2010] it was devaluing the dong for the second time since November [2009], slashing its reference rate by more than 3 per cent. Today the dong's mid-point reference rate will be 18,544 per cent, 3.36 per cent down from 17,941, where the State Bank of Vietnam has kept it since 10 December [2009].

(*FT*, 11 February 2010, p. 9)

The consumer price index rose by 2 per cent in February ... GDP grew by 5.3 per cent last year [2009] ... The government ... is believed to have spent over $1 billion in 2009 (over 1 per cent of GDP) to prop up the economy, mainly by subsidizing banks' loans to businesses. As a result the credit supply expanded by 37 per cent, driving up the black market price of dollars ... The loan-subsidy programme largely benefited well-connected state-owned enterprises ... On 10 February ... the central bank devalued the dong by 3.4 per cent, following a devaluation of 5.4 per cent in November [2009]. The aim was to entice holders of dollars to buy dong. A dollar shortage has been starving Vietnam's exporters of the currency they need to purchase imported parts and materials ... The government has reluctantly raised state-controlled commodity prices: petrol, electricity and coal are all to be more expensive ... The finance ministry has been circulating a draft decree that would allow the government to impose price controls on a wide range of essential goods. The European Chamber of Commerce has warned that such measures may well lead to nothing but 'shortages' and 'hoarding'.

(*The Economist*, 6 March 2010, p. 69)

'Russia's GDP grew the most of any major economy in dollar terms over the last decade, followed by Indonesia and Vietnam, according to a report released last week by Goldman Sachs' (www.iht.com, 11 January 2010).

Over the past twenty years Vietnam's economy has almost quadrupled in real terms. It has averaged 7.775 per cent annual growth and even last year, at the height of the financial crisis, managed 5.8 per cent. This year [2010] Vietnam expects to achieve another milestone, when GDP *per capita* passes $976 and it officially becomes a middle-income country.

(*FT*, 1 June 2010, p. 22)

The Ho Chi Minh City stock market caught fire, with the index reaching a peak of 1,170 in March [2007], up 140 per cent year on year ... On 25 March [2008] the stock market bottomed out at 496, a fall of 57 per cent off the peak of a year earlier.

(Pincus and Ahn 2008: 28)

It has been one of the worst ever stock market runs. Ho Chi Minh fell every trading day in May and early June ... By the time the stock market had finished its twenty-five-day slide last week the index was down 60 per cent from the start of the year [2008], making it the world's worst performer ... On four of the past five trading days Ho Chi Minh has risen, gaining nearly 4 per cent in total.

(*FT*, 19 June 2008, p. 40)

The plunge in the country's stock market has been as stunning as its ascent. The benchmark VN index surged 144 per cent in 2006 and an additional 56 per cent last year [2007] ... Since hitting a high of 1,179 in March 2007, the main index has sunk by more than 60 per cent, sinking to a two-year low of 370.45 last week.

(*IHT*, 17 June 2008, p. 16)

'[On 19 June] Vietnam's small market fell a further 2.4 per cent to take year-to-date losses to 60 per cent' (www.iht.com, 19 June 2008).

'Bao Viet, Vietnam's biggest insurer, has been given permission to list its shares on the Ho Chi Minh Exchange next week ... The share sales mark an important step in the revitalization of Vietnam's stalled privatization programme' (www.ft.com, 18 June 2009).

1 Political developments

Political background

Vietnam means 'land to the south' (of China).

'After years of intermittent rule by Chinese dynasties, Vietnam – often called the Land of the Blue Dragon – achieved independence in the tenth century' (*The Independent*, 14 November 2006, p. 25).

'Vietnam was a tributary state of China for 1,000 years and was invaded by China in 1979, and the two countries continue to joust for sovereignty in the South China Sea' (www.iht.com, 28 June 2009).

France began the colonial period for Vietnam in 1858 with the capture of present-day Da Nang, seized Saigon in 1861, and formed the protectorates of Annam and Tonkin by 1883.

'Vietnam has a consensual leadership. Its triumvirate of president [Nguyen Minh Triet], party boss [General Secretary Nong Duc Manh] and prime minister [Nguyen Tan Dung] must reach accommodations with an increasingly independent national assembly and a host of other forces' (*The Economist*, Survey, 26 April 2008, pp. 6, 15). 'A recent opinion poll by TNS and its affiliates found Vietnam's youthful population to be the most optimistic in Asia' (pp. 15–16). 'Party cells remain mandatory for all businesses, even private ones' (p. 15). 'The government insists that there are no political prisoners in its jails, though some detained dissidents have done nothing more than call for democracy' (p. 15).

'Vietnam wants to become a rich, high-tech country and has set a target date of 2020 for getting there' (*The Economist*, 26 April 2008, p. 16).

'Vietnam receives low marks in comparison to other East Asian countries on the various corruption perception surveys. For example, the World Bank's composite rankings place Vietnam below even China and far below Thailand and Malaysia' (Pincus and Ahn 2008: 31).

> A Vietnamese government report [on climate change] released last month [August 2009] says more than one-third of the [Mekong] Delta, where 17 million people live and where nearly half of the country's rice is grown, could be submerged if sea levels rise by 1 metre (3 feet) in the decades to come ... The risks to Vietnam go far beyond the Mekong Delta, up into the

Central Highlands, where rising temperatures could put the coffee crop at risk, and to the Red River Delta in the north, where large areas could be inundated near Hanoi.

(*IHT*, 24 September 2009, p. 8)

Top notch universities do little original research, and are rarely cited by scientific scholars, says a recent UN-financed study. Graduates are poorly prepared: as many as 60 per cent of new hires by foreign companies needed retraining, according to a Dutch report. Vietnam already spends more on education [as a percentage of GDP] than its neighbours [Malaysia, Thailand, Indonesia, the Philippines, Laos and Cambodia]. Literacy rates are high, and parents sacrifice much to put their children through college. Enrolment at Vietnamese universities rose from about 900,000 in 2001 to over 1.6 million by 2006. But most students study at lacklustre public universities or at private diploma mills. Those who can afford to go overseas. The best and the brightest ... rarely return. Efforts to reform public universities have floundered. So the government has seized on the idea of creating four new research-orientated institutions from scratch, with foreign universities as partners and, crucially, promises of autonomy. The first of the new breed, the Vietnamese German University (VGU), opened in 2008 in Ho Chi Minh City. A French-backed technology school in Hanoi will follow. VGU has around 220 students, enrolled in engineering and economics programmes, which are taught, in English, by visiting German professors. Within ten years it hopes to have 5,000 students. Its independent charter, a first for a Vietnamese university, allows it to hire professors and design its own courses ... For the moment VGU gets most of its money from Germany. Vietnam contributes a modest Euro 365,000 ($500,000) a year. But it must eventually bear the running costs, which are forecast to reach Euro 45 million to 50 million by 2030 ... Academics in both China and Vietnam are hemmed in by political dogma.

(www.economist.com, 30 September 2010;
The Economist, 2 October 2010, pp. 67–8)

A chronology of political developments since the Tenth Congress of the Communist Party held 18–25 April 2006

18–25 April 2006. The Tenth Congress of the Communist Party is held.

Nearly 1,200 party delegates to the event will set the political and economic course of the nation of 83 million people until 2010. Delegates representing 3.1 million party members will recommit to Marxism–Leninism, Ho Chi Minh thought and the twenty-year-old *doi moi*, or renewal, programme toward a 'market economy with socialist orientation' ... Party members [will] choose the new 160-member Central Committee and the elite Politburo with at least fifteen members.

(www.iht.com, 16 April 2006)

12 *Political developments*

'Party statistics show it has 3.1 million members in the population of 83 million people' (www.iht.com, 18 April 2006).

> The five-yearly ... week-long ... Communist Party Congress [is] starting Tuesday [18 April] amid a corruption scandal that has already claimed several government officials ... Transport ministry cadres [have] embezzled millions of dollars ... Transport minister Dao Dinh Binh resigned earlier this month [April] and his deputy was jailed over revelations that officials in the ministry's Project Management Unit 18 had taken funds earmarked for highways and other infrastructure. The scandal emerged in January with the arrest of the unit's chief, Bui Tien Dung, for betting $7 million, much of it from Japan and the World Bank, on European soccer matches. The state-controlled press has been allowed to report aggressively that officials took kickbacks, bought luxury homes and sought to pay off the police and officials for protection ... 'There is now a serious crisis of trust among our people and in our party,' a former interior minister, General Mai Chi Tho, was quoted as [saying] ... General Vo Nguyen Giap, who led Vietnamese forces to victory against French and US troops, said ... that 'the party has become a shield for corrupt officials'.
>
> (www.iht.com, 16 April 2006)

> Within Vietnam's ministry of transport Project Management Unit 18 handled more than $2 billion allocated for road and bridge building and other infrastructure ... Much of the cash [was] from low interest loans and grants by the World Bank and the Japanese government. Bui Tien Dung [was] the powerful civil servant who ran the unit ... In January [he] confessed to betting $7 million of ministry money on European football matches ... A Swedish-funded study by the Communist Party's internal affairs committee found 69 per cent of Vietnam's businesspeople and 64 per cent of the general public considered corruption the country's most serious problem ... In 2004 the then deputy trade minister was arrested for selling garment export quotas. Senior officials from Vietnam Airlines' petroleum subsidiary were arrested for illegally exporting oil to Cambodia. In November [2005] the National Assembly adopted legislation requiring government officials and close relatives to file asset declarations. A purge took place at PetroVietnam, the state-owned oil and gas company. The general director and his deputy were sacked for misconduct while tendering for Vietnam's first oil refinery ... Three months after Mr Dung's confession his patron, Nguyen Viet Tien, deputy transport minister and former head of the planning unit, was also arrested and charged with negligence and breaking laws of economic management. Dao Dinh Binh, transport minister, was pressed to resign.
>
> (*FT*, 18 April 2006, p. 6)

> An office computer log showed almost 200 [transport] ministry employees followed suit [after Bui Tien Dung] and wagered online with government

funds earmarked for bridges and roads ... Sports gambling is now an obsession across Vietnam, not just in government offices.

(*The Independent*, 20 April 2006, p. 31)

[The] Communist Party opened its congress on Tuesday [18 April] vowing to choose new leaders 'with talent and morals' to fight corruption and accelerate economic reforms ... [The government] will for the first time give each of the 1,176 delegates the right to recommend candidates for the top post of general secretary ... In the past the elite Politburo alone chose the general secretary ... Officials announced changes in the method of choosing the general secretary after a special plenum in the past few days to discuss personnel selection following the corruption scandal ... The incumbent general secretary, Nong Duc Manh, acknowledged in his opening speech that corruption was 'one of the risks that threaten the survival of our regime' ... Manh said the eight-day congress wanted 'to further accelerate' Vietnam's change from a centrally controlled economy to a market-orientated one ... Manh: 'In the next five years it is our policy to continue to improve market economy status with socialist orientation and to speed industrialization and modernization in close relation with developing a knowledge-based economy.'

(www.iht.com, 18 April 2006)

'General Secretary Nong Duc Manh told more than 1,100 delegates that the party's Central Committee must "seriously make a self-criticism" for allowing corruption to "threaten the survival of our regime"' (*The Independent*, 20 April 2006, p. 31).

Correspondents say the gathering has been overshadowed by the corruption scandal ... Senior transport ministry officials are accused of using state funds to bet on football matches and buy luxury cars ... General Secretary Nong Duc Manh warned party members the issue was threatening 'the survival of our regime'. He stressed the party aimed to 'build a clean and strong leadership and management, to overcome a huge risk'.

(www.bbc.co.uk, 24 April 2006)

On Sunday [23 April] 1,176 delegates elected a new Central Committee and 160 of its members will choose the fifteen to seventeen people for the powerful Politburo. Analysts expect that both President Tran Duc Luong, sixty-eight, and prime minister Phan Van Khai, seventy-two, will announce their retirements during the congress. However, the sixty-five-year-old General Secretary Nong Duc Manh is seen as likely to stay on. The front-runner for the premier's job is deputy prime minister Nguyen Tan Dung, fifty-six. Ho Chi Minh City party chief Nguyen Minh Triet, sixty-four, is seen as the top contender for the presidency. If the two southerners are chosen, correspondents say the move would mark a departure from the formula that kept the top three positions evenly distributed between the north, centre and south of Vietnam. The new line-up will reportedly be announced on Tuesday [25 April] at the close of the tenth congress – and must then be approved by the National Assembly.

(www.bbc.co.uk, 24 April 2006)

Vietnam's Communist Party announced ... during the closing session of the eight-day National Party Congress in Hanoi [on 25 April] ... that Nong Duc Manh will be reappointed as its general secretary for another five-year term ... Other key positions, such as those of prime minister and president, have yet to be appointed ... Other key roles, including those of president, prime minister and chairman of the National Assembly have yet to be decided, but correspondents say they should become clear once the National Assembly, Vietnam's parliament, meets next month [May] ... The newly elected Politburo ... has been half replaced by younger members. Current premier Phan Van Khai, President Tran Duc Luong and the National Assembly chairman Nguyen Van An all announced they would not seek to continue their positions after age limitation has been reinforced ... The congress has agreed on ambitious economic targets, including the maintenance of a high growth rate of 7.5 per cent to 8 per cent a year, and for Vietnam to achieve the status of an industrialized country by 2020.

(www.bbc.co.uk, 25 April 2006)

Nong Duc Manh, fifty-six ... a member of the Tay ethnic minority ... while affirming the Communist Party's central role in policy and continued state ownership of the country's major strategic industries, said economic reforms would be pursued 'in a stronger, more comprehensive manner and develop with a faster and sustainable pace' ... Manh said his main goal was to raise living standards in a nation where the gap between rich and poor has grown wider and to make Vietnam an industrialized nation by the year 2020, with the number of people living in poverty cut to 10 per cent. *Per capita* is now only $640 a year, with 75 per cent of the population living in the countryside ... [Vietnam] plays host to dozens of world leaders in November at an annual meeting of the Asia-Pacific Economic Co-operation forum. President George W. Bush is expected to attend, following in the footsteps of Bill Clinton, who in 2000 was the first US president to visit postwar Vietnam ... A new fourteen-member Politburo ... was also announced [on 25 April] ... The party congress also mandated a change in the three top government positions: president, prime minister and chairman of the National Assembly ... who are to be voted in at a separate meeting of the National Assembly ... The age of ... the Communist Party's ... leaders is dropping.

(www.iht.com, 25 April 2006)

On 22 April Bill Gates, the founder of Microsoft, visits Hanoi University.

Prime minister Phan Van Khai and President Tran Duc Luong had earlier taken time away from the ... National Congress, the most important event on the political calendar, to meet Mr Gates. Under an agreement signed

Saturday [22 April] Vietnam's finance ministry became the country's first government office to use completely licensed Microsoft software. A statement said the agreement 'reaffirms the government's commitment in copyright protection as the country integrates into the international community'.

(www.bbc.co.uk, 22 April 2006)

'Bill Gates landed in Hanoi for a one-day visit and was received as a conquering hero ... [He] was given a red carpet welcome at the dilapidated Hanoi University of Technology' (*FT*, 24 April 2006, p. 7).

The most important Communist Party meeting in five years was under way. And the star of the show was ... Bill Gates. The president, the prime minister and the deputy prime minister all excused themselves from the party meeting to have their pictures taken with the man who has more star power in Vietnam than any of them. When they heard he was in town hundreds of people climbed trees and pushed through police lines to get a glimpse of him. He was the top story in the next morning's newspapers ... About half the population of 83 million was born after the war with the United States that ended thirty-one years ago. This is a country that is very much looking toward the future, not to the past. Reaching out in an unprecedented way the party published its draft documents for public discussion early this year [2006] and received, by Nong Duc Manh's count, tens of thousands of comments, suggestions and criticisms ... This is the first party congress since the meetings began in 1951 that has not invited delegations from foreign communist parties.

(Seth Mydans, *IHT*, 27 April 2006, pp. 1, 7)

As Vietnam has opened its economy to the rough and tumble of the free market, officials have spoken often of the need to combat corruption. But investigations and prosecutions have never publicly touched the highest ranking members of the party and government ... Over the years the government has repeatedly tried to address the problem and hundreds of midlevel officials have been investigated and arrested ... Most wounding was a comment from Vo Nguyen Gap, the former general who is an icon of Vietnam's victories over both the French and the Americans. In a widely quoted comment he said: 'The party has become a shield for corrupt officials' ... Even Nong Duc Manh's predecessor as general secretary, Le Kha Phieu, has talked of the limits to what even the most powerful leaders can do ... [Le Kha Phieu, 2005]: 'We should say frankly to each other that corruption is still widespread at a serious level. Myself and Vo Van Kiet, the former prime minister, knew of some particular cases but could not unravel them and make them public. Corruption is guarded by the perpetrators and even defended by outside sources. This really is a fierce battle in which, if we wish to win, the party and the state must take a close look at themselves.'

(*IHT*, 5 May 2006, p. 2)

16   *Political developments*

'The party congress approved a law letting its members engage in business ... In truth, many party bosses are already up to their necks in capitalism' (*The Economist*, 29 April 2006, p. 68).

> The new five year plan, approved at April's congress of the ruling Communist Party, is laden with targets for increasing output and improving infrastructure, with the objective of making Vietnam a modern, industrial nation by 2020 ... The government is racing to build enough power stations, roads and railways to keep the economy moving.
>
> (*The Economist*, 5 August 2006, p. 50)

16 May 2006.

> Prime minister Phan Van Khai told reporters on the opening day of the National Assembly that he had asked to step down from his post ... Khai was appointed prime minister in 1997 amid the Asian financial crisis ... [He said that] he had nominated as his successor deputy prime minister Nguyen Tan Dung ... fifty-six ... a one-time central bank governor who has been groomed for the job for years ... [and who] has had responsibility for overseeing the economy in recent years ... The National Assembly is expected to confirm Dung as well as new replacements for the posts of president and National Assembly chairman during its month-long session.
>
> (www.iht.com, 16 May 2006)

> [The] National Party Congress chose Nguyen Tan Dung as prime minister and Nguyen Minh Triet as president. Dung and Triet support economic change but are political diehards who favour the Chinese model; economic transition to open markets with firm Communist Party political control, analysts say.
>
> (www.iht.com, 19 June 2006; *IHT*, 20 June 2006, p. 2)

4–5 June 2006. US Secretary of Defence Donald Rumsfeld visits Vietnam.

> Donald Rumsfeld and his Vietnamese counterpart ... Pham Van Tra ... agreed Monday [5 June] to bolster military exchanges ... Vietnamese military leaders also said they would try to do more to help the United States recover the remains of Americans missing in action in the Vietnam War [in Vietnam, Laos and Cambodia] ... There are 1,805 US troops unaccounted for from the war, including 1,376 in Vietnam ... US military ties with Hanoi ... have warmed gradually with ship visits.
>
> (www.iht.com, 5 June 2006)

> The United States and Vietnam agreed Monday to increase their military contacts and to discuss ways to broaden their defence co-operation ... One step in the still evolving relationship is to be taken this month [June] when two Vietnamese officers are scheduled to begin English language training at a US military language school in Texas.
>
> (*IHT*, 6 June 2006, p. 4)

27 June 2006.

The National Assembly ... on Tuesday [27 June] elected Communist Party chief for Ho Chi Minh City, Nguyen Minh Triet, as the country's new president in a continuing leadership shuffle. Triet, sixty-three, an economic reformer and the sole candidate for the job, won overwhelming backing from the National Assembly with 94 per cent of the vote ... [In 2001] he was at the helm when underworld kingpin Truong Van Cam, known as Nam Cam, was arrested. Nam Cam was the star of the country's biggest ever criminal trial in 2003. The proceedings involved 155 defendants, including police officers and high-ranking government officials. Nam Cam was convicted of murder and bribery and was executed by firing squad along with four of his associates ... Triet, in turn, nominated deputy prime minister Tan Dung, fifty-six, to become the next prime minister. Over the weekend the lawmaking body cleared the way for the new leaders after approving the resignation of prime minister Phan Van Khai, seventy-two, President Tran Duc Luong, sixty-nine, and National Assembly chairman Nguyen Van An, sixty-nine. On Monday [26 June] the assembly elected Nguyen Phu Trong, sixty-two, Communist Party chief for Hanoi, as the new chairman of the legislature ... Triet ... from the southern province of Binh Duong ... was appointed party chief of southern Song Be province in 1992 and guided the largely agricultural province into one of the most attractive places for foreign investors ... The National Assembly was expected to vote on the new prime minister later Tuesday. The legislators are expected to approve the appointments of six other positions, including the ministers of defence, foreign affairs and transport, before wrapping up its six-week session on Thursday.

(www.iht.com, 27 June 2006)

Vietnam's legislature confirmed a new prime minister with a record of fostering economic growth and a president known for his aggressive approach to fighting corruption ... Nguyen Tan Dung [is] a former central bank governor from the southernmost province of Ca Mau ... He served as central bank governor from May 1998 to December 1999, when the country's banking system was in turmoil ... The general secretary of the Communist Party, Nong Duc Manh, was appointed in April to a second five-year term ... The reshuffle has been expected since April, when the Politburo did not re-elect the three leaders. Their terms were due to expire in July 2007, but the early change will allow the new leaders to host the Asia-Pacific Economic Co-operation summit meeting in Hanoi in November as well as usher Vietnam into the WTO, which they are expected to do later this year [2006].

(www.iht.com, 27 June 2006)

Vietnam's legislature has approved a new prime minister and president, both of which are seen as economic reformers ... Nguyen Tan Dung, fifty-six, became the country's youngest prime minister since unification in 1975 ... Both Mr Dung and Mr Triet are from the south of Vietnam and this will be the first time the government has been headed by two southerners since 1975. Mr Dung, who has a military and police background, was formerly deputy prime minister and has been groomed for years to replace seventy-two-year-old Phan Van Khai … As sole candidates for the job, Mr Triet won 94 per cent of the National Assembly vote, while Mr Dung received 92 per cent of the vote. Vietnam's president is the third most powerful figure in the country after the head of the Communist Party – Nong Duc Manh – and the prime minister.

(www.bbc.co.uk, 27 June 2006)

30 August 2006.

Pham Hong Son, a high-profile dissident convicted of espionage, was released from jail Wednesday [30 August], but will remain on probation for three years … Son was freed as part of an amnesty gesture made in advance of Vietnam's National Day celebrations, which take place Saturday [2 September]. But Son will remain under surveillance and will be limited by travel restrictions during his three-year probation … Son's case attracted international attention when he was arrested on espionage charges for having translated and circulated over the internet a document titled 'What is democracy?' The original article was from the website of the US Department of State. In 2003 Son was sentenced to thirteen years for spying, but the term was then reduced to five years on appeal … On Monday [28 August] Le The Tiem, vice minister of public security, announced that Son was among more than 5,000 inmates that would be released in a general amnesty.

(www.iht.com, 30 August 2006)

13 November 2006. 'The United States dropped Vietnam on Monday [13 November] from its list of nations that severely violate religious freedom, citing improvement in its tolerance for religious expression' (www.iht.com, 14 November 2006).

The United States has removed Vietnam from a list of countries which it says severely violate religious freedom. The list is published annually by the State Department and includes China, North Korea, Iran and Sudan. Vietnam was removed just days before President George W. Bush travels to Hanoi for a meeting of the Asia-Pacific Economic Co-operation (Apec) forum … The US State Department said there had been 'significant improvements toward advancing religious freedom' in the country … While Vietnam has been taken off the US list of Countries of Particular Concern (CPC) regarding religious freedoms, Uzbekistan has been added … The State Department said Burma, China, North Korea, Eritrea, Iran, Saudi Arabia and Sudan would remain on the list.

(www.bbc.co.uk, 14 November 2006)

In April [2006] America praised the country's advances in several areas, such as releasing some political dissidents and signing an agreement on religious freedom. As a result, on 13 November, it removed Vietnam from a blacklist of countries that suppress religion. The same day Vietnam sent back to America a Vietnamese-American democracy activist it had detained for fourteen months for 'terrorist activities'.

(*The Economist*, 18 November 2006, p. 65)

17 November 2006. 'President George W. Bush has arrived in Vietnam for the annual Asia-Pacific Economic Co-operation (APEC) summit ... He is only the second US president [after Bill Clinton] to visit Vietnam since [the end of the Vietnam War]' (www.bbc.co.uk, 17 November 2006).

20 November 2006.

Russia and Vietnam agreed Monday [20 November] to step up economic co-operation and work together to combat terrorism during a visit by the Russian president, Vladimir Putin ... [his first since 2001] after a weekend summit of Pacific Rim leaders ... Russia could extend co-operation in the energy sector to include nuclear power, Putin said ... The joint pledge on fighting terrorism and the spread of weapons of mass destruction was among six agreements between the two governments, most of which focused on co-operation in energy and finance ... The main focus of Putin's visit was on business ... Co-operation has been most active in the energy sector ... The agreements signed Monday included a deal between the Russian company Gazprom and PetroVietnam on building up gas infrastructure and developing offshore gas fields. Gazprom is already working with the state-owned Vietnamese energy company to explore a section of the offshore Hanoi shelf ... The two countries also signed two agreements on co-operation in the banking sector. Putin presided Sunday [19 November] over the launching of a Russian–Vietnamese joint venture bank, Vietnam–Russia Bank. The state-owned Bank for Investment and Development Bank of Vietnam, the country's third biggest commercial bank, holds a 51 per cent share of the venture and Vneshtorgbank, Russia's second largest, a 49 per cent stake. The bank is meant to facilitate trade: Vietnam hopes to double bilateral trade with Russia to $2 billion by 2010 from $1 billion.

(www.iht.com, 20 November 2006)

27 December 2006.

A Vietnamese bank [has decided] ... to order the immediate closure of all accounts linked to Pyongyang. East Asia Commercial Bank made the move even as diplomats tried to make progress during six-party nuclear talks last week ... East Asia Commercial Bank in Vietnam, which acts as a 'correspondent bank' for customers wanting to remit money into and out of North Korea, last week told Pyongyang-based customers, including a foreign joint venture bank, to close their accounts by yesterday [27 December] ... Hank Paulson, the US Treasury Secretary, in September [2006] thanked Vietnam for co-operating with the crackdown by investigating North Korean bank accounts. Pyongyang-based Tanchon Commercial Bank, which the United States labelled the primary financial facilitator of North Korea's ballistic missile programme, hastily shut its accounts after Vietnam's Military Bank said it would go through the transactions ... North Korean banks cannot transfer funds electronically so have to carry large amounts of cash to correspondent banks for remittance.

(*FT*, 28 December 2006, p. 5)

5 February 2007.

Vietnam plans to build a high-speed railroad with aid from Japan at an estimated cost of $33 billion in a project that would cut travel time by two-thirds between Hanoi and Ho Chi Minh ... The railroad [is] to be built over a six-year period ... Seventy per cent of the funding will come from the government, mainly in the form of Japanese official development assistance. Vietnam Railways will raise 30 per cent of the cost from loans ... Japan is the biggest country donor to Vietnam. It has pledged $890 million in aid for the country this year [2007] or 6.5 per cent higher than the 2006 level of $835.6 million. International governments and agencies have pledged a record $4.45 billion in aid to Vietnam this year [2007].

(www.iht.com, 6 February 2007)

28 March 2007.

Vietnam has abolished a measure used to hold dissidents without trial, a government official said Wednesday [28 March]. However, analysts said the move could prove to be largely symbolic. President Nguyen Minh Triet signed a decree last week to abolish 'administrative probation', used to hold people suspected of national security crimes, a National Assembly official said ... Vietnam first raised the possibility of abolishing administrative probation in August 2006 ... Analysts and Western diplomats praised the president's move, but said the authorities still had ways to harass and detain pro-democracy activists ... The detention practice was first included in a piece of 1997 legislation known as 'Decree 31'. It allowed provincial governors to impose administrative probation for up to two years on those who 'violate the laws, harming national security, but not so serious as to justify prosecution'. Nearly 200 people are thought to have been held under the measure, including Thich Quang Do and Thich Huyen Quang, leaders of the outlawed Unified Buddhist Church of Vietnam. Vietnamese courts will still be allowed to impose house arrest on people convicted of national security crimes. The government has recently come under increasing criticism for starting a crackdown on the country's small number of political dissidents. A Roman Catholic priest, Nguyen Van Ly, goes on trial this week, charged with undermining the government by trying to organize an independent political organization. On 6 March the police arrested and jailed two Hanoi human rights lawyers, Nguyen Van Dai and Le Thi Cong Nhan, accusing them of distributing information harmful to the state. Human Rights Watch said the three had been targeted in one of the worst crackdowns on Vietnamese dissidents in twenty years.

(www.iht.com, 28 March 2007)

The National Assembly this week urged the government to press on with building a market economy ... Vietnam has a corruption problem but is taking serious steps to tackle it. A former deputy trade minister was jailed last week for fourteen years for bribery – the latest among dozens of top officials given stiff penalties for dishonesty, The armed forces, such a baleful influence in some countries, are fairly clean, Many Asian economies are sucked dry by entrenched, predatory elites. In Vietnam, although collectivist economics have gone, the government remains collective and consensual. Leadership is shared between the party boss, president and prime minister. No personality cults are allowed, other than the one idolizing Ho Chi Minh, the revolutionary leader, who died in 1969 ... The National Assembly, once a rubber stamp, has become a forum for debate and scrutiny. Serious criticisms of the government are aired and reported in the press. A record number of self-nominated candidates are standing in the Assembly elections due in May. However, the party remains terrified of the slightest challenge to its monopoly on power. The press is to remain party-run and independent candidates must still be party-approved. The government claims no one is arrested for political views, but in reality it treats pro-democracy activists as common criminals, jailing them for supposed spying or sabotage. In February charges were laid against Nguyen Van Ly, a dissident priest who found Bloc 8406, a new and widely supported group which last year [2006] issued a manifesto for democracy.

(*The Economist*, 31 March 2007, pp. 75–6)

'Vietnam last month [March] issued a decree requiring legislators and senior officials to declare their assets' (*The Economist*, 21 April 2007, pp. 69–70).

30 March 2007.

Father Nguyen Van Ly ... a Catholic priest [and] a prominent democracy activist ... has been jailed for eight years in Vietnam on charges of disseminating information to undermine the state ... The sixty-year-old has been under house arrest since early February [2007] ... Four co-defendants received prison terms ranging from eighteen months suspended to six years ... Father Ly has already spent fourteen of the past twenty-four years in prison ... He was last jailed in 2001 after he urged the United States to link its trade policy with Vietnam's human rights record. He was released as part of an amnesty in 2005. Father Ly is a founding member of Bloc 8406, a pro-democracy movement launched last April [2006]. He is also a member of the Progression Party. Leading members of both groups have been detained in recent months ... State media has accused Father Ly and other pro-democracy activists of trying to undermine the Communist Party by forming illegal parties to field candidates in National Assembly elections in May. Only the Communist Party is allowed to stand, although a small number of seats are reserved for non-party members.

(www.bbc.co.uk, 30 March 2007)

Father Nguyen Van Ly, a sixty-year-old priest who previously served about fifteen years in prison for criticizing the government, was convicted of 'conducting propaganda against the state'... He was a founding member of 'Bloc 8406', a group that last April [2006] launched an internet petition signed by 118 pro-democracy advocates calling for an end to one-party rule and greater respect for human rights. In September [2006] he launched the Vietnam Progression Party, which has been outlawed by authorities. Another four members of the VPP were also convicted, with punishments ranging from an eighteen-month suspended sentence to six years' imprisonment ... Human Rights Watch called the trial part of 'the worst crackdown' on dissent in nearly twenty years in Vietnam ... Authorities in recent months arrested two of Vietnam's few practising human rights lawyers and several members of a new independent trade union, the United Workers–Farmers Organization of Vietnam. Other free speech activists were detained and questioned.

(www.ft.com, 30 March 2007)

The communist rulers of Vietnam want to send a zero-tolerance message to advocates of a multi-party system by putting several political activists on trial this week, analysts and diplomats say. They note that the trials come as the governing party prepares for elections on 20 May [2008] of 500 delegates to the National Assembly ... In March an outspoken Roman Catholic priest, Reverend Thadeus Nguyen Van Ly, was sentenced to eight years in prison. He was jailed along with four others after a four-and-a-half hour trial ... and some of the other defendants facing trial this month [May] are members of 'Bloc 8406', named after the 8 April 2006 date when it revealed itself with a 'Manifesto for Freedom and Democracy'. Diplomats and analysts describe the block as the closest thing Vietnam comes to having a dissident movement. Amnesty International and other groups have recorded more than twenty arrests since November [2006], when Hanoi was host to an Asia-Pacific meeting, won approval to join the WTO and was removed from a US religious rights blacklist. Farm worker organizers, lawyers, writers and religious people are among those detained.

(www.iht.com, 6 May 2007)

12 April 2007.

Vietnam, said Thursday [12 April] that a BP-led $2 billion natural gas field and pipeline project in the South China Sea ... [a] co-operation project between PetroVietnam and BP ... was within the bounds of its sovereignty, after Beijing accused Hanoi of infringing on China's territory. China,

Vietnam and Taiwan claim all of the Spratly Islands ... while Malaysia and the Philippines claim parts of them ... The planned $2 billion gas field and pipeline project ... is adjacent to the BP-led Lan Tay–Lan Do gas fields that have been producing gas for power generation since 2002.

(www.iht.com, 12 April 2007)

10 May 2007.

Three dissidents have been jailed for up to five years for spreading anti-communist propaganda. They were found guilty of being members of a banned political party and having links to a Vietnamese-American activist, expelled from Vietnam last year [2006]. The authorities have recently stepped up a campaign to silence dissent, and several activists have been jailed ... The three jailed activists were said to be members of the banned People's Democratic Party, which campaigns for a multi-party system of government. Le Nguyen Sang, forty-eight, was sentenced to five years in jail, Nguyen Bac Truyen, thirty-nine, received four years and Huynh Nguyen Dao, thirty-nine, was given three years. They were found guilty of violating Article 88, which bans disseminating information harmful to the state. Prosecutors said that they had 'carried out activities that aimed to end the leadership of the Communist Party of Vietnam, demanding pluralism and a multi-party system'. The three were also accused of collaborating with Cong Thanh Do, who emigrated from Vietnam to the United States in the 1980s. Do was arrested while on holiday in Vietnam and deported last September [2006] by the authorities, who accused him of plotting to overthrow the government ... Two prominent human rights lawyers in Hanoi are expected to go on trial on Friday [11 May], also accused of defaming the state. Another lawyer faces the same charge at a court hearing scheduled for next week in Ho Chi Minh.

(www.bbc.co.uk, 10 May 2007)

The sentences were issued a day after a political prisoner, Phan Van Ban, was released after twenty-two years in prison ... Hanoi released Ban – a former police officer from the city of Dalat – and allowed him to fly to the United States to be reunited with his family. Ban had been imprisoned since 1985 after he joined an organization calling for political change. He flew Wednesday [9 May] to the United States ... President Nguyen Minh Triet granted a pardon on 25 April, citing his advancing age and desire to be reunited with his family ... Ban was born in 1937. Ban's release came amid an ongoing crackdown against dissidents ... On Friday [11 May] two well-known human rights lawyers, Nguyen Van Dai and Le Thi Cong Nhan, will go on trial for spreading information intended to undermine the government. Another dissident, Tran Quoc Hien, is to go on trial in Ho Chi Minh City next week on charges of spreading propaganda against the state and disrupting public security.

(www.iht.com, 10 May 2007)

11 May 2007.

> Two human rights lawyers have been jailed ... Nguyen Van Dai and Le Thi Cong Nhan were sentenced to five years and four years respectively ... They were found guilty of spreading propaganda intended to undermine Vietnam's communist government ... Both Mr Dai and Ms Nhan were arrested on 6 March, accused of collaborating with overseas pro-democracy advocates and using the internet to spread their views ... Another dissident, Tran Quoc Hien, is scheduled to go on trial next week.
>
> (www.bbco.uk, 11 May 2007)

20 May 2007.

> Vietnam is voting for new members to the National Assembly ... The vast majority of the candidates are Communist Party members and the rest have been screened by the authorities ... More than 500 new deputies are being chosen from a field of almost 900 candidates, only 150 of whom are not ruling party members ... It is compulsory for the 50 million-strong electorate to cast their ballots ... The assembly has shown some independence in investigating laws and ministers ... The legislative assembly has made a priority of cracking down on corruption.
>
> (www.bbc.co.uk, 20 May 2007)

> The 875 candidates for 500 seats include 150 who are not Communist Party members but who have the party's approval to run. Thirty candidates were allowed to enter on their own with their nominations approved by colleagues and neighbours. Electoral law calls for all seats in 182 constituencies to be contested, but in practice many are not ... The National Assembly is no longer seen as purely a rubber stamp for the party. Delegates question ministers and scrutinize policy more than they did in the past, although the party does not allow unsupervised challenge to its rule.
>
> (www.iht.com, 20 May 2007)

10 June 2007.

> The Vietnamese authorities have released leading dissident Nguyen Vu Binh from prison. A former journalist who used the internet to criticize the government, he was sentenced to seven years in prison for spying in 2003 ... Mr Binh was arrested in September 2002 for writing an online article criticizing a border agreement between Vietnam and China. He also planned to create an alternative political party.
>
> (www.bbc.co.uk, 10 June 2007)

13 June 2007.

> Bracing himself for criticism over the Vietnamese human rights record, President Nguyen Minh Triet said Wednesday [13 June] that he would keep an eye firmly on trade and investment when he visits the United States next week. The first Vietnamese head of state to visit Washington since the Vietnam War

ended thirty-two years ago, he is a longtime proponent of his country's economic liberalization and integration into the world economy ... He said: 'We really want the United States to increase its investment in terms of high technology in Vietnam and we want the United States to create favourable conditions for Vietnamese goods in the United States market' ... Triet is seen as one of the most outward-looking members of the Vietnamese hierarchy. A southerner who was party chief in Ho Chi Minh City, he is known for his innovations in supporting private enterprise and foreign investment. He made his reputation as the chief of what is now Binh Duong province, a landlocked area just north of Ho Chi Minh City that has few advantages for development. By relaxing conditions for private and foreign investment at a time when these were new and controversial policies he created what is now one of the most prosperous regions in the country, a magnet for both business and labour ... The United States is the largest Vietnamese trading partner, with an increasing two-way trade that rose to $7.8 billion in 2005 from $1.5 billion in 2001, according to Vietnamese government figures ... But last year [2006] Vietnam listed the United States as only its eleventh largest investor, with licensed projects whose total capital was $1.7 billion ... Vietnam has carefully balanced its relations between the United States and China, and in advance of his trip to Washington Triet visited Beijing last month [May] ... The Vietnamese prime minister and defence minister have both visited the United States.

(www.iht.com, 13 June 2007; *IHT*, 14 June 2007, p. 2)

22 June 2007.

President George W. Bush yesterday [22 June] hailed the rapid growth in economic ties between the United States and Vietnam but warned that the broader bilateral relationship risked being soured by Hanoi's recent clampdown on pro-democracy activists. Mr Bush delivered the message during a meeting with President Nguyen Minh Triet at the White House, as part of the first visit by a Vietnamese head of state since the Vietnam War. The United States is Vietnam's biggest trading partner, with two-way trade from the year before amounting to nearly $10 billion. The former enemies this week signed a trade and investment pact intended to further deepen the relationship. But Mr Triet's six-day visit has been overshadowed by protests about recent arrests and sentencing of several Vietnamese dissidents ... Other items on the agenda included US support for the fight against AIDS in South-east Asia and co-operation in the search for the remains of US soldiers missing in Vietnam ... Human rights groups have described Hanoi's crackdown on dissidents as the most severe for years, reflecting efforts by the communist regime to prevent economic growth from weakening its grip on political life ... Mr Triet has sought to keep the focus of his visit on trade and investment ... [The United States] described the trade and investment framework deal signed this week as an important step forward in ties. The pact is widely viewed as a first step towards a possible bilateral trade deal.

(*FT*, 23 June 2007, p. 7)

2 August 2007.

The National Assembly approved a smaller cabinet Thursday [2 August] that is charged with pushing forward reforms in Vietnam's rapidly expanding economy. The chamber elected a new central bank chief and nine new ministers and reconfirmed twelve for a total of twenty-two ministries and ministerial-rank agencies, down from the previous twenty-six ... The assembly elected two new deputy prime ministers, bringing the total to five. Former industry minister Hoang Trung Hai was promoted to deputy prime minister, as was Nguyen Thien Nhan, who will also run the education and training ministry ... The assembly re-elected three deputy prime ministers, Nguyen Sinh Hung, Pham Gia Khiem and Truong Vinh Trong. Nguyen Tan Dung was re-elected as prime minister last week to run a government that is expected to be more business-friendly and tougher on graft. Nguyen Van Giau, a southerner who had been a deputy central bank governor, was re-elected to run the State Bank of Vietnam ... The new cabinet includes three new ministries covering industry and trade, information and communications, and culture, sports and tourism. The agriculture ministry had absorbed the fisheries ministry. Last week the assembly confirmed Nguyen Phu Trong as its chairman and Nguyen Minh Triet as state president.

(www.iht.com, 2 August 2007)

7 August 2007.

Nine people have been sentenced over a high profile gambling and bribery scandal that led a senior government minister to resign in 2006. Former transport ministry official Bui Tien Dung was jailed for thirteen years, seven others for up to seven years and one received a suspended sentence. They were accused of embezzling funds to place illegal bets on football, although Dung said he used family cash ... Dung, the former director of a ministry of transport infrastructure body known as PMU-18, was sentenced to six years' jail for illegally gambling $760,000 on European football games between 2005 and 2006. He received a further seven-year sentence for bribery over attempts to cover up the bets ... Gambling is illegal in Vietnam ... Six others – including state officials, former police officers and businessmen – were jailed for seven years on gambling and bribery charges. One received a two-year suspended sentence for gambling ... The scandal led to the resignation of former transport minister Dao Dinh Binh in April 2006. His deputy, Nguyen Viet Tien, was arrested in connection with the case but has not been charged. Ministerial resignations are extremely rare in Vietnam.

(www.bbc.co.uk, 7 August 2007)

20 August 2007.

Vietnamese who live abroad can enter Vietnam without visas from 1 September [2007] ... Many of the 3 million Vietnamese living abroad are from families that left in 1975 at the end of the war. A visa exemption certificate

– allowing multiple entries and a stay of up to three months at a time – will be issued once applicants provide documentary proof they are ethnically Vietnamese.

(*FT*, 21 August 2007, p. 6)

17 September 2007.

Nearly 4 kilograms of highly enriched uranium have been returned to Russia from Vietnam under a Russian–US programme to secure nuclear materials that could be used to make weapons [it was announced on Tuesday 17 September] ... The transfer of the uranium from a research reactor in the Vietnamese city of Dalat was completed at the weekend ... It was conducted with help from the International Atomic Energy Agency ... Under the programme Russian-produced fuel located in former Soviet-allied countries is sent back to be blended down to a concentration no longer suitable for making weapons.

(*FT*, 18 September 2007, p. 8)

16 October 2007.

Libya and Vietnam ... were elected overwhelmingly to two-year terms on the United Nations [fifteen-member] Security Council beginning 1 January [2008]. Also named in secret balloting of the 192-member General Assembly were Burkina Faso, Costa Rica and Croatia ... The Security Council has five veto-bearing permanent members – Britain, China, France, Russia and the United States ... Vietnam and Croatia will be council members for the first time.

(*IHT*, 17 October 2007, p. 4)

'Vietnam, which was endorsed by the Asian group, ran unopposed' (www.iht.com, 16 October 2007).

('In October the [Vietnamese] Communist Party's [General Secretary] Nong Duc Manh got the red carpet treatment from North Korea's Kim Jong Il on a visit to Pyongyang': *The Economist*, Survey, 26 April 2008, pp. 14–15.)

14 December 2007.

Plans for a four-lane highway from Hanoi to Kunming [in China] are expected to clear the last hurdle Friday [14 December] when the board of the Asian Development Bank gives the green light to a loan that will underwrite the Vietnamese side of the project ... The board is expected to approve its biggest single-project loan – $1.1 billion – to finance the start of work next year [2008] on a 244-kilometre, or 152-mile, stretch of the highway from Hanoi to Lao Cai on the border ... The Vietnamese government is contributing $100 million to the low-interest loan, to be paid off over thirty-two years ... The existing Hanoi-to-Kunming road [is] narrow, dangerous and congested ... The route follows a southern branch of the ancient Silk Road ... The highway is [expected to be] completed] ... by 2012 ... The construction will add a section to the ambitious Asian Highway programme under which twenty-seven Asian countries have pledged to build a 140,000-kilometre network of roads that meet minimum uniform standards ... The Vietnamese section of the project will be designated Asian Highway No. 14. It will link up with a highway under construction on the Chinese side of the border at Lao Cai ... The highway [is] one of the several transport infrastructure projects that are integrating the economies of northern Vietnam with southern China.

(www.iht.com, 13 December 2007; *IHT*, 14 December 2007, p. 8)

'Vietnam will get a $1.1 billion loan from the Asian Development Bank to build a highway linking Hanoi with mainland China' (www.bbc.co.uk, 14 December 2007).

('Thousands of Vietnamese held demonstrations earlier this month [December] outside the Chinese embassy in Hanoi over Beijing's establishment of the new Sansha municipality in Hainan province, which will have jurisdiction over three islets Vietnam claims in the Spratly and Paracel archipelagos: *IHT*, 21 December 2007, p. 8.)

('[In] December Vietnamese students held "spontaneous" anti-Chinese protest in Hanoi, after reports that China was creating a new municipality incorporating ... the Spratlys and the Paracels (to the Vietnamese the Truong Sa and the Hoang Sa)': *The Economist*, Survey, 26 April 2008, p. 13.)

22 January 2008.

The US immigration authorities reached an agreement with Vietnam that cleared the way for Vietnamese immigrants under deportation orders to be sent back to their home country. Under the memorandum of understanding, signed Tuesday [22 January] in Hanoi, Vietnam agreed to accept the return of Vietnamese immigrants ordered deported by the United States, many of whom are convicted criminals ... Previously Vietnam had generally refused to issue travel documents for the deportees. The agreement immediately affected about 1,500 Vietnamese immigrants who went to the United States after diplomatic relations were restored in 1995.

(*IHT*, 24 January 2008, p. 4)

8 February 2008.

One of Vietnam's best-known dissidents, Hoang Minh Chinh, has died at the age of eighty-five after a long illness ... Hoang Minh Chinh was once a leading figure in the Communist Party, holding several senior positions ... [including] vice-minister of education, vice-director of the Nguyen Ai Quoc Communist Party School and director of the Marxist–Leninist Philosophy Institute ... But he became disillusioned with the communist ideology and began calling for more democracy. He spent many years in jail and under house arrest ... He was considered one of the great ideologists of the regime until the 1960s, when he began criticizing some of the ruling party's decisions ... [He] restarted the Vietnam Democratic Party two years ago ... In 2006 he took part in the establishment of the largest democratic campaign to date, Bloc 8406.

(www.bbc.co.uk, 8 February 2008)

('In April 2006 a new dissident group, Bloc 8406, emerged with a "manifesto on freedom and democracy". An exile-backed political party, Viet Tan, is sending members back home to recruit members and agitate for change and several have been detained or expelled. When Hoang Minh Chinh, the leader of another group, the Democratic Party of Vietnam, and one of the founders of Bloc 8406, died in February, hundreds of activists turned up for his funeral in Hanoi': *The Economist*, Survey, 26 April 2008, p. 16.)

March 2008. 'In March Vietnam's ambassador to the UN announced that Vietnam was preparing for some involvement in peacekeeping missions' (*The Economist*, Survey 2008, p. 14).

28 April 2008.

> Vietnam will end a baby adoption agreement with the United States after being accused of allowing corruption and baby selling, government officials said Monday [28 April]. The agreement was being considered for renewal but the two sides remained far apart over revisions, said Vu Duc Long, director of Vietnam's International Adoption Agency. The agreement is due to expire on 1 September [2008]. The decision was made after the US embassy in Hanoi released a report earlier this month [April] alleging pervasive corruption and baby selling in Vietnam's adoption system. The report listed cases in which infants were sold or birth mothers were pressured to give up their babies. It also described brokers going to villages in search of babies who could possibly be put up for adoption. The report also said some American adoption agencies have been paying orphanage directors for referrals. Others have bribed orphanage officials by taking them on shopping sprees and junkets to the United States in return for a supply of babies ... Vietnamese officials denied the charges, calling the allegations 'unfair' ... In a letter sent to the US embassy in Hanoi on 25 April Vietnam said it will stop taking adoption applications from American families after 1 July [2008], although it will continue to process applications of families matched with babies before 1 July. The decision will also lead to the closure of forty-two US adoption agencies operating in Vietnam, Vu said ... Vietnam suspended all adoptions with foreign countries in 2003 as part of its efforts to improve the legal system governing adoption and prevent rampant corruption. A bilateral agreement between the United States and Vietnam was resumed in 2005. Since then adoptions from Vietnam have boomed with more than 1,200 Vietnamese children being adopted over the eighteen months ending 31 March [2008]. In 2007 alone Americans adopted 828 Vietnamese children.

(www.iht.com, 28 April 2008)

A recent report from the US embassy in Hanoi cited cases in which children had allegedly been sold and families pressured to give up their babies. Vietnam dismissed the claims, which it described as unfair. Vu Duc Long (director of Vietnam's International Adoption Agency): 'The US report includes a lot of distorted information; it is untrue' ... The report said the embassy had received 'credible' accounts that some adoption agencies gave $10,000 for each child that was referred. It also detailed brokers travelling to look for babies. The report was drawn up after US officials noticed a rapid increase in the number of 'abandoned' babies offered for adoption ... The programme attracted media attention when Hollywood actress Angelina Jolie adopted a child from Vietnam last year [2007]. Though China is still the most popular country for US families adopting from abroad ... adoptions from Vietnam – which had fewer restrictions – had been rising.

(www.bbc..co.uk, 28 April 2008)

29–30 April 2008.

The [Chinese] Olympic torch arrived in Ho Chi Minh City in Vietnam [on 29 April] for the final international stop ... The parade [on 30 April] is expected to pass off fairly smoothly ... But a group of activists have promised demonstrations linked to a territorial dispute with Beijing ... Some activists say they will rally against China's claim to the disputed Spratly Islands ... After Vietnam the torch goes to Hong Kong to begin the domestic leg of the relay. International protests have turned the torch's celebratory tour of twenty countries into what analysts describe as a public-relations disaster for Beijing.

(www.bbc.co.uk, 29 April 2008)

30 April 2008.

The US-based Freedom House organization ... [issued a report which said that] Vietnam had reversed some of the gains in press freedom that had been made in 2006, with a crackdown on dissident writers. It said the fledgling community of online pro-democracy writers was targeted by the government – with six cyber-dissidents imprisoned within one week in May [2008].

(www.bbc.co.uk, 30 April 2008)

11 June 2008.

Vo Van Kiet, a former prime minister and major force behind the country's economic reform, died at the age of eighty-five. Mr Kiet became prime minister in 1991 and held office until he stepped down in favour of Phan Van Khai in 1997. He was considered a key architect of the *doi moi* market reforms of the late 1980s ... He had been in poor health and died at a Singapore hospital.

(www.bbc.co.uk, 11 June 2008)

Among the grey ranks of Vietnam's communist leadership Mr Kiet was one of the few figures to have stood out. Credited as the author of the reforms known as *doi moi* ... he was a rarity among senior officials in speaking out publicly against the failings of the communist system ... After the communist victory in 1975 he became party secretary of Saigon, and quietly defied hardline official policy by trying to work with officials and businesses associated with the defeated government. As prime minister Mr Kiet presided over a period of dramatic economic growth and foreign investment ... There have been signs recently that Mr Kiet's reformist allies have been losing their influence.

(www.bbc.co.uk, 15 June 2008)

11 July 2008.

The funeral of leading Vietnamese Buddhist dissident Thich Huyen Quang has gone ahead under tight security ... Mr Quang, who was eighty-seven, had spent most of the last three decades in prison or under house arrest. He led the outlawed Unified Buddhist Church of Vietnam, which refused to submit to communist government control ... Thich Huyen Quang was first arrested in 1977 after he publicly criticized the communist regime for suppressing religious freedom. He spent most of the next thirty years under house arrest, but continued to call for human rights and political reforms in Vietnam. Thich Huyen Quang's Unified Buddhist Church was banned in 1981 after refusing to join the religious movement sanctioned by Vietnam's Communist Party leaders.

(www.bbc.co.uk, 11 July 2008)

12 September 2008.

US Deputy Secretary of State John Negroponte, on a visit to Vietnam, has lauded the 'close partnership' between the two countries. He praised Vietnam's 'economic miracle' and its goodwill toward its former foe, but also called for more political and legal freedoms. Mr Negroponte is visiting Vietnam for the first time since as a young official during the war in 1973 ... His trip comes two years after that of US President George W. Bush and Secretary of State Condoleezza Rice, and follows the visit of prime minister Nguyen Tan Dung to Washington in June ... Two days before Mr Negroponte's arrival in Hanoi, an internet writer and activist was sentenced to thirty months in prison for tax fraud. Nguyen Hoang Hai, whose pen-name is Dieu Cay, had criticized his government's handling of disputes with China over the Spratly and Paracel Islands in the South China Sea. His imprisonment was condemned by Human Rights Watch as part of a broader crackdown on democracy activists in Vietnam.

(www.bbc.co.uk, 12 September 2008)

19 September 2008.

Tensions are high in Hanoi after authorities began construction work on land claimed by the Catholic church ... The disputed site [is] at Nha Chung street. Crowds of priests and believers soon gathered outside. The site, which once served as the Vatican ambassador's residence, was the centre of a month-long protest by Hanoi Catholics earlier this year [2008]. They only learned that their claim to the land had been turned down the previous afternoon, when the authorities announced via the state media that it would become a park ... The church has called on all believers to join in protests, as well as pray for the Catholic claim to more disputed land in Hanoi, this time at Thai Ha. This second land grievance has been going on for more than a month, attracting hundreds of believers for prayer and protest every day. The Vietnamese government maintains that all land belongs to the state and land claims should be submitted to the law courts for consideration.

(www.bbc.co.uk, 19 September 2008)

15 October 2008.

A journalist was sentenced Wednesday [15 October] to two years in prison for writing inaccurate stories about one of the country's most high profile cases. Nguyen Viet Chien, fifty-six, was convicted of 'abusing freedom and democracy' at the end of a two-day trial ... The presiding judge said before announcing the verdict that Chien included fabricated information and that he 'damaged the prestige of some high ranking officials and cause negative public opinion'. Fellow reporter Nguyen Van Hai, thirty-three, was given two years of re-education without detention on the same charges. Hai was given a lesser sentence for his 'active co-operation with investigators and remorse' ... The two reporters worked for two of the country's most popular newspapers. Also standing trial with the two journalists were Major General Pham Xuan Quac of the police and Dinh Van Huynh, an investigator, who were charged with 'deliberately revealing state secrets'. Quac, sixty-two, who has retired, was given a warning while Huynh received one year in prison. The case involved a major corruption and gambling scandal that erupted in 2005 at a division of the transportation ministry.

(www.iht.com, 15 October 2008)

Reporters Nguyen Van Hai and Nguyen Viet Chien work for two of Vietnam's largest dailies and are known for their aggressive reporting on corruption ... [The charge of] 'abusing freedom and democracy' carries a maximum jail term of seven years ... Media groups have called for their release and say their arrests will discourage reporting on corruption. The two journalists were arrested on 12 May for unspecified inaccuracies in their reporting [of the scandal].

(www.iht.com. 14 October 2008)

Nguyen Viet Chien insisted he was innocent ... Another journalist, who had pleaded guilty, was deemed to have served out a suspended sentence and freed. The case attracted criticism from abroad, with one human rights group calling it 'revenge' against daring journalists revealing state corruption ... Nguyen Van Hai, from *Tuoi Tre* newspaper, was the only accused to plead guilty ... He asked for leniency while accepting that some of his reports contained errors, saying his mistakes were 'professional accidents' ... Nguyen Viet Chien, from *Thanh Nien* newspaper, always maintained his innocence. The two journalists were arrested in May for 'abusing their professional power and position'. The charge was changed last month to 'abusing freedom and democratic rights'. The two former police officers, Major General Pham Xuan Quac and Senior Lt Col Dinh Van Huynh, were charged with 'deliberately disclosing investigative secrets' ... Media watchdog Reporters Without Borders has condemned the trail, calling it the Vietnamese government's 'revenge' against 'daring journalists who revealed embarrassing cases and brought greater freedom to the Vietnamese press'.

(www.bbc.co.uk, 15 October 2008)

The US embassy in Hanoi called the verdict 'disappointing' and counterproductive in combating the 'social scourge' of corruption ... The Paris-based organization Reporters Without Borders: '[The trial was a] terrible step backwards for investigative journalism in Vietnam. The fragile basis of a press capable of playing its role of challenging established authority has been badly shaken' ... In 2006 the two journalists helped expose a corruption scandal in the transport ministry, which resulted in the resignation of the minister and the arrest of several high ranking officials. But the tide appeared to turn against the journalists earlier this year [2008], as a deputy minister was cleared of wrongdoing over the matter, and attention turned to alleged failures in the journalists' coverage ... [At] the Tenth Communist Party Congress in April 2006 new leaders were being elected ... According to the leaked official indictment, prosecutors accused the two reporters of 'abusing democratic freedoms to infringe the interests'. The prosecutors added: '[This had] serious consequences, negatively affecting the ideology, morale and psychology of the public at a sensitive time ... [They] exploited their position as journalists to write sensitive, false information ... Hostile forces took advantage to attack and distort the Party Congress, negatively affecting the preparation of the congress.'

(www.bbc.co.uk, 16 October 2008)

6 December 2008.

Voters in the US state of Louisiana have elected the first Vietnamese-American member of Congress. Anh Joseph Cao ... a Republican ... was born in Saigon, now Ho Chi Minh City, and came to the United States with his family at the age of eight, after the end of the Vietnam War ... His father was an officer in the South Vietnamese army who spent seven years in a communist prison before moving to the United States.

(www.bbc.co.uk, 7 December 2008)

24 December 2008.

Vietnam has tightened restrictions on internet blogs, banning bloggers from raising subjects the government deems inappropriate. Blogs should follow

34   Political developments

Vietnamese law and be written in 'clean and wholesome' language ... Internet service providers will be held accountable for the contents of blogs they host. More than 20 million Vietnamese use the internet – a quarter of the population ... The new rules, drawn up by the ministry of information and communications, require internet service providers to report to the government every six months and provide information about bloggers on request. The rules ban posts that undermine national security, incite violence or disclose state secrets. It is unclear whether the new regulations will apply to international companies such as Google or Yahoo; currently the most popular blogging host in Vietnam is Yahoo! 360.

(www.bbc.co.uk, 24 December 2008)

The government has cracked down on the country's vibrant cyber community, closing websites and imprisoning those who use the internet to challenge the Communist Party. For year the internet has been relatively free of government control pervasive elsewhere in Vietnam. But several recent decrees have curtailed free speech by the country's fast growing number of bloggers ... Vietnam was a latecomer to the online age, but the extraordinary economic growth of the past few years has triggered an explosive growth in internet use. Best estimates say some 24 million of the country's 88 million people regularly use the web ... The vast majority of Vietnamese bloggers use platforms created by Yahoo and Google ... A law passed last year [2008] requires all service providers established under Vietnamese law to provide information on users who violate the prohibitions set out by the information ministry.

(*FT*, 30 January 2009, p. 12)

'In December 2008 Vietnam's government issued regulations holding internet service providers responsible for ensuring that blogs they host do not include content deemed "undesirable"' (www.feer.com, 2 May 2009).

31 December 2008.

China and Vietnam say they have resolved a long-running border dispute. The two countries announced they had completed the demarcation just hours before a midnight deadline. Government teams from both sides had worked for years planting stones to mark the line of the frontier which stretches 1,350 kilometres (840 miles) ... Neither side mentioned any progress on a separate unresolved maritime dispute. The Spratly Islands, a strategic string of rocky outcrops in the middle of the South China Sea, are claimed by several nations including China and Vietnam ... The two countries normalized relations in 1991.

(www.bbc.co.uk, 31 December 2008)

Vietnam and China have completed the demarcation of their long-disputed land border ... The two countries signed a land border agreement in 1999, but it took them nine years to demarcate the 1,350-kilometre, or 840-mile,

Political developments 35

frontier ... China backed the Vietnamese communists during the Vietnam War but sent troops to invade Vietnam in early 1979 for ousting the Khmer Rouge from Cambodia. The Khmer Rouge was backed by Beijing. Vietnam and China normalized relations in 1991 and have since maintained annual high level visits. The two sides, however, did not resolve their dispute over the Spratly Islands, the largely uninhabited islands and surrounding waters that are believed to have large oil and natural gas reserves. They straddle busy sea lanes and are rich fishing grounds. Taiwan, the Philippines, Malaysia and Brunei also claim sovereignty over all or some of the Spratlys. The dispute touched off a rare anti-China street protest in Vietnam late last year.

(www.iht.com, 1 January 2009)

The settlement of the dispute – which covered the land border between the two countries – came during a 28–31 December meeting in Hanoi ... The border dispute arose after China ... invaded its southern neighbour in February 1979 – two months after Vietnam invaded Cambodia and ousted the pro-Beijing Pol Pot regime. The twenty-nine-day incursion ended with the last Chinese troops leaving on 19 March – and without having forced the Vietnamese out of Cambodia. During the next two decades both sides stationed hundreds of thousands of troops along the border until the 1999 China–Vietnam land boundary treaty.

(www.cnn.com, 2 January 2008)

The two largest pro-reform newspapers ... *Thanh Nien* and *Tuoi Tre* ... lost their chief editors in the last hours of 2008 ... Vietnamese media reports confirm that two other newspapers, *Legalit* and *Saigon Business People*, also lost their editors-in-chief in December 2008. Just two months earlier ... a veteran journalist and the editor of *Dai Doan Ket*, was 'disciplined' and sacked for publishing a letter by General Vo Nguyen Giap criticizing the current leadership's handling of a public construction project. But the year 2008 ended most unfortunately for *Thanh Nien* and *Tuoi Tre* because their reporters, Nguyen Viet Chien and Nguyen Van Hai, had been picked to stand trial in October for a vigorous reporting of a major corruption case. They seem to fall victim of a new policy pursued by the Communist Party to tighten control over the flow of news and information, both in the state-run media and the private blogosphere, that has been booming in Vietnam in the last two years. For the government commercialization of the 20 million web-user media market in Vietnam requires more adequate regulations ... A new law in 2009 explicitly bans bloggers from discussing politically sensitive and demands that all journalists reveal their source of information. Those who dare to break these rules set by the Party would face to $12,000 in fines or twelve years in jail.

(www.bbc.co.uk, 2 January 2009)

This month [January 2009] two leading reformist newspaper editors, Nguyen Cong Khe, of *Thanh Nien* (Young People), and Le Hoang, of *Tuoi*

Tre (Youth Daily), were told that their contracts would not be renewed ... Their papers have assiduously uncovered official corruption, most notably with a joint exposé in 2006 about a crooked transport ministry road-building unit. The journalists behind that story were punished by a Hanoi court last October [2008] for 'abusing democratic freedoms' ... Despite some highly publicized successes, critics contend that only low-ranking officials have so far been charged under a 2005 anti-corruption law.

(*The Economist*, 17 January 2009, p. 53)

12 January 2009.

On the heels of its attention-grabbing trip to North Korea last February [2008] the New York Philharmonic is planning another high profile visit for next season: to Vietnam. The stop [is] part of an Asian tour in October ... The New York Philharmonic has been to fifty-nine countries, by its count, but never Vietnam, nor, for that matter, North Korea before February ... Zarin Mehta [is] the orchestra's president.

(www.iht.com, 13 January 2009)

15 January 2009.

A well-known anti-corruption journalist ... [is] among more than 15,000 prisoners to be released before term. The Lunar New Year amnesty is one of Vietnam's largest ever. President Nguyen Minh Triet signed on 15 January the decision to free Nguyen Viet Chien, of *Thanh Nien* newspaper. His release is set for Saturday [17 January]. He had been given a two-year jail term for his reporting on a major corruption case, causing an international outcry. Mr Chien was arrested last May [2008] and brought to trial in October for 'abusing freedom and democratic rights' while covering the so-called PMU-18 scandal, on which government officials were accused of misusing large amounts of public funds. Announcing his early release, vice minister of public security Le The Tiem said the reporter had showed 'regret and remorse' ... The trial of Nguyen Viet Chien and another colleague, Nguyen Van Hai, last May drew huge criticism from rights organizations and foreign governments alike ... The case relates to a corruption scandal in Vietnam's ministry of transport that first came to light in 2006. Both journalists pursued the story, which claimed several high level scalps, but their reportage was later condemned by authorities as inaccurate and harmful ... Mr Hai pleaded guilty at the beginning of the trial and was awarded a lenient sentence of two years of re-education without detention. But Mr Chien always maintained that he was innocent and received a harsher punishment.

(www.bbc.co.uk, 16 January 2009)

20 January 2009. Barack Obama is sworn in as the forty-fourth US president, having won the 4 November 2008 election.

May–June 2009. 'Recently there was the news that Vietnam is to buy six submarines and twelve SU-30 fighters from Russia for $2.3 billion' (www.iht.com, 2 June 2009).

8 June 2009.

> Vietnam has called on China to stop preventing Vietnamese fishermen from working in what Hanoi says are its territorial waters ... This is the second time in three weeks that Vietnam has spoken out over the fishing ban and the increase in arrests and fines by Chinese naval patrols ... The tensions have been stoked by rival claims to parts of the South China Sea. China has been enforcing an annual fishing moratorium since 1999 in order to conserve stocks, but this year's has been seen by many as extremely tough ... Witnesses have been quoted as saying that their boats were chased and attacked by foreign vessels ... The latest incident reportedly took place two weeks ago, when a Vietnamese fishing boat was hit and sunk, but the fishermen escaped.
>
> (www.bbc.co.uk, 8 June 2009)

13 June 2009.

> Authorities have arrested a high profile lawyer for allegedly conspiring against the government. Le Cong Dinh, forty-one, one of Vietnam's most respected lawyers, has defended a number of pro-democracy activists. He was allegedly to have been found with a copy of a new constitution he wrote aiming to replace the current one. The police say they will charge Mr Le with Article 88 of the Criminal Code for distributing anti-government materials ... [It is claimed that] Mr Le and his accomplices had also libelled Vietnam's top leaders, including prime minister Nguyen Tan Dung, in published documents ... In recent years Mr Le defended some of Vietnam's leading human rights and democracy activists, such as fellow lawyers Nguyen Van Dai and Le Thi Cong Nhan, who have also been jailed for anti-government activity.
>
> (www.bbc.co.uk, 14 June 2009)

> Le Cong Dinh was arrested on 13 June on charges of 'distributing propaganda against the state' ... the police said they will charge Mr Dinh with Article 88 of Vietnam's criminal code for distributing anti-government materials ... The Paris-based Reporters Without Borders reported several sources saying his arrest could be linked to a complaint filed by several Vietnamese lawyers against the government about the granting of a bauxite mine concession to a Chinese company, a case which has caused an outcry in Vietnam ... Le Cong Dinh has [also] defended ... the renowned blogger Dieu Cay.
>
> (www.bbc.co.uk, 16 June 2009)

12 August 2009.

> In a surprise move China has decided to free twenty-five Vietnamese fishermen arrested months ago [twelve on 16 June and thirteen on 1 August].

They were held off the Paracel Islands, which are claimed by both countries. Until recently, the Chinese authorities were demanding thousands of dollars for their release. But the Vietnamese government requested the fishermen be returned unconditionally, saying they were operating within Vietnam's territory ... Vietnam and China have been involve in a long territorial dispute over the islands, as well as over the Spratly Islands located further south. China took the Paracels by force in 1974 after a bloody battle in which fifty soldiers from the then South Vietnamese Saigon government were killed. But Vietnamese fishing boats continue to operate near the islands in what they call their traditional fishing fields. This year [2009] Beijing has toughened its three-month fishing ban in the South China Sea, leading to attacks on Vietnamese boats and arrests of fishermen.

(www.bbc.co.uk, 12 August 2009)

4 September 2009.

Vietnam has released a blogger and a journalist who were critical of government policies towards China. The releases came ahead of a visit by Nong Duc Manh, Communist Party General Secretary, to Australia and New Zealand this week. Police told blogger Bui Thanh Hieu he was being freed because of the 'cancellation of preventative measures' on him. Pham Doan Trang, a journalist for news website VietnamNet, was released on Friday [4 September].

(*FT*, 7 September 2009, p. 6)

Two well-known bloggers and an online reporter have been detained after the police uncovered an apparent attempt to print T-shirts opposing Chinese investment in a controversial new bauxite mining project in Vietnam's central highlands and casting doubts on China's claims to disputed islands in the South China Sea. The trio, who had written critically about Vietnam–China relations on the internet, were detained on suspicion of 'abusing democratic freedoms' to undermine the state. By the middle of this week Bui Thanh Hieu, a blogger who used the pen name Nguoi Buon Gio ('Wind Trader'), and Pham Doan Trang, a journalist who works for VietnamNet, a news site, had been freed without charge after several days in detention. Nguyen Ngoc Nhu Quynh, who blogged as Me Nam ('Mother Mushroom'), was still in custody. These are the latest arrests in a continuing crackdown against bloggers and journalists. Ahead of a congress of the ruling Communist Party in 2011, when the country's top three political posts will be up for grabs, the government is keen to rein in more outspoken commentators. Last December [2008] it imposed new restrictions on bloggers, making it illegal for them to publish under a pseudonym or to write about politics. Policing these rules will be hard. More than 21 million people, a quarter of the population, use the internet, according to government figures. Estimates of the number producing blogs range from a low of 1 million to as many as 4 million. The vast majority are personal diarists, not socio-political activists, but the spectacular growth of blogs and the difficulty of regulating them make the government, used to exercising total control of the media, twitchy. Bloggers who have found themselves in the dock include some who have exposed government corruption or made negative remarks about the former Soviet Union. But the government seems particularly anxious about criticism of China. Many Vietnamese remain hostile to their northern neighbour, after 1,000 years of imperial domination and a bloody border war in 1979. But the country runs a large trade deficit with China and needs its investment more than ever. This explains the government's eagerness to push ahead with the Chinese bauxite mining project, despite widespread criticism from scientists and generals (as well as bloggers). They have questioned Chinese companies' environmental records and expressed their fears for national security.

(*The Economist*, 12 September 2009, p. 70)

12 September 2009.

> The police released a gadfly blogger on Saturday [12 September] after holding her more than a week [nine days] on the grounds of state security ... The release of the blogger, Nguyen Ngoc Nhu Quynh, came a week after the police freed two others, Bui Thanh Hieu and Pham Doan Trang, who were detained in late August ... Ms Quynh, who blogged under the name Me Nam, or 'Mother Mushroom', had written critically of a government plan to exploit bauxite reserves with the help of a state-owned Chinese company and of China's claims to sovereignty over islands in the South China Sea. Mr Hieu and Ms Quynh were also involved in plans to print and distribute T-shirts to major Vietnamese cities with slogans against the bauxite plan and in support of Vietnam's claims to the Spratly and Paracel Islands. A foreign ministry spokeswoman said Thursday [10 September] that the two bloggers and Ms Trang had been detained for investigations into possible violations of national security, although she did not elaborate. Mr Hieu and Ms Trang were released on the eve of a visit to Australia and New Zealand by the Vietnamese Communist Party chief, Nong Duc Manh.

(www.iht.com, 13 September 2009)

A blogger ... Nguyen Ngoc Nhu ... has said she was freed after promising she would quit writing her blog ... A foreign ministry spokesman said the three had been arrested legally for national security reasons ... On 27 August blogger Bui Thanh Hieu, also known as Nguoi Buon Gio, was arrested ... A day later a journalist, Pham Doan Trang, who worked for one of the most visited semi-official news websites in the country, VietnamNet, was also detained by the security police. She too ran a well-read personal blog. [There are] more than 2 million personal blogs in Vietnam ... The government ... has also been pursuing a crackdown on political dissidents that saw dozens interrogated and detained in the last couple of months.

Among them are human rights lawyer Le Cong Dinh, businessman Tran Huynh Duy Thuc and democracy activist Nguyen Tien Trung.

(www.bbc.co.uk, 14 September 2009)

24 September 2009.

Nine North Koreans, including a nineteen-year-old girl who travelled through China to join her mother and brother who had already defected to South Korea, entered the Danish embassy in Hanoi on Thursday seeking political asylum and eventual transit to Seoul, South Korean activists said. The group, which also included a forty-two-year-old doctor and his wife, as well as a thirty-eight-year-old woman and her daughter, entered Vietnam from China in recent weeks through smuggling routes, said Kim Sang Hun, a leader of the International Network of North Korean Human Rights Activists who assisted in the North Koreans' escape to Vietnam. The International network said the defectors carried a message in English: 'We are now at the point of such desperation and live in such fear of persecution within North Korea that we have come to the decision to risk our lives for freedom rather than passively await our doom. The only power we have left is to appeal to you on our knees and with tears' ... About 20,000 North Koreans have defected to the South since the 1950–3 Korean War, nearly all of them in the past fifteen years. Since twenty-five North Koreans barged into the Spanish embassy in Beijing in 2002 human rights activists have often copied the tactic and sent defectors into diplomatic missions in South-east Asia ... Human rights activists have complained that the South Korean embassy in Vietnam, unlike other South Korean missions in Asia, was especially reluctant to accept North Korean refugees ... Both Hanoi and Seoul were put in a diplomatically awkward position in 2004 when there were so many North Korean refugees in the South Korean embassy in Hanoi it had to hire a chartered plane to airlift 468 of them to Seoul ... South Korea said it would never attempt such a large-scale refugees transfer again. Hanoi maintains a diplomatic balance between South Korea, Vietnam's main investor, and North Korea, a ideological ally. Since the 2004 airlift the South Korean embassy has turned away North Korean refugees, said Kim Hee Tae, a Seoul-based activist who has been rescuing North Korean refugees in South-east Asia. To pressure the embassy, activists helped a total of nine North Korean refugees to enter the Danish and Indonesian embassies in Hanoi in 2007. They were eventually allowed to fly to South Korea. Mr Kim said: 'Before today's operations, we called the South Korean embassy in Hanoi and asked for help, but we were again rejected' ... The number of defectors arriving in the South rose to 2,809 last year [2008] ... The activists' group said that earlier this month [September] the Chinese police arrested six North Korean refugees who were trying to cross into Vietnam, including two women who had been abused by human traffickers in China. The detainees now face the prospect of being returned to North Korea, where they could face severe penalties in labour camps, it said.

(www.iht.com, 24 September 2009; *IHT*, 25 September 2009, p. 5)

The [nine] North Koreans said in a statement they had fled their country 'in search of food and freedom from oppression' ... The group's statement said: 'Some of us were caught by Chinese police and were then subjected to forced deportation to North Korea. After repatriation, some of us endured months of detention in North Korea that can only be described as atrocious. We are now at the point of such desperation and live in such fear of persecution within North Korea that we have come to the decision to risk our lives for freedom rather than passively await our doom' ... The group of defectors included six women and three men ... [A] Danish foreign ministry spokesman said ... that Copenhagen was working with Hanoi 'to find a safe and dignified solution' ... Thousands of people have fled North Korea in recent years, and at least 14,000 of them have found asylum in South Korea. Many of them seek passage to South Korea via China and other countries in the region. Because China repatriates North Koreans, refugees often attempt to reach foreign embassies in third countries.

(www.bbc.co.uk, 24 September 2009)

More than 200 North Koreans arrived in South Korea Tuesday [27 July 2004] behind a wall of secrecy in the biggest influx yet of defectors from the North. Officials said the mass arrival was 'sensitive' and refused to discuss details, disclosing only that an Asiana Airlines flight had airlifted the North Koreans from a South-east Asian nation they would not specify ... The unification ministry, which handles South Korea's ties with the North, said the unusually secretive reception for the defectors was organized at the request of the third country ... [South Korean] officials denied that Seoul imposed a blanket of secrecy on the influx of defectors to appease the North ... 'The main reason is that the third country in South-east Asia strongly insisted that they want to keep this matter very low profile,' said a ministry official ... Another batch of more than 200 refugees from the same country, bringing the total to around 450, is expected Wednesday [28 July]. In the first six months of the year 760 North Koreans arrived, mostly via China, where tens of thousands of North Koreans are said to be in hiding. Hundreds more are believed to be gathering in various South-east Asian nations, including Vietnam, Thailand and Cambodia ... Under an accord with Beijing Pyongyang insists that all defectors who escape into China are repatriated to North Korea, where they face severe punishment including internment in camps for political prisoners ... Under the accord Beijing refuses to grant North Korean defectors refugee status and considers them illegal economic agents.

(www.iht.com, 27 July 2004)

The first of two planes carrying refugees – part of the largest single group ever – touched down ... 'There are about 230 people arriving today [27 July]' ... [said the head of] a group of missionaries helping North Korean defectors ... About 70 per cent of the new arrivals are women, because more women than men cross the border into China, drawn by rumours that it is easier for them to find jobs ... Sources in Vietnam said North Korean refugees had been gathering in southern Ho Chi Minh City after trickling over the border from China for months ... Government sources [are quoted] as saying the sheer number of refugees who were crammed into safe houses and their long wait drove many of them to threaten suicide unless their cases were resolved. The threats prompted Seoul to intervene officially in May and ask the country to allow 'every one of them' to go to the South.

(*IHT*, 28 July 2004, p. 3)

'Seoul is said to have stepped in when the country [Vietnam] threatened to send the refugees back to China' (*FEER*, 5 August 2004, p. 10).

[The] 229 North Koreans ... [constituted] the largest single group of defectors since the 1953 armistice ... Another group of 260 was expected in Seoul today [28 July] ... [There are] an estimated 300,000 [North Korean defectors] in China alone ... Refugees are fleeing to third countries from China, especially Vietnam, Thailand and Cambodia.

(*The Independent*, 28 July 2004, p. 28)

Those that are caught [in China] are repatriated to North Korea, where they face punishments ranging from a few days in re-education camps to the death penalty, depending on their rank and the extent to which they are considered to have damaged national security. Many stay close to the border, setting up secret camps in the densely wooded mountains. Desperate and vulnerable, many of the men become bandits and countless women are sold as brides or prostitutes ... In South Korea they are guaranteed citizenship, a resettlement payment of 28.3 million won (£13,000), and a monthly stipend of 540,000 won ... South Korea is struggling to cope with the influx ... The rising financial burden prompted the government to announce last week a 40 per cent cut in the resettlement payment from next January [2005].

(*Guardian*, 28 July 2004, p. 11)

[There has been a] shift from poor individuals to better-off families ... Pyongyang appears to be dealing less harshly with those returned by China. Beijing, in turn, looks less zealous in its pursuit of the escapees, who, with the help of South Korean and Korean-American missionary groups, traverse China for a third country.

(*Daily Telegraph*, 28 July 2004, p. 21)

China and Vietnam ... have burgeoning trade links with South Korea, which is using its new-found stature to win concessions for the refugees. South Korean officials said on Monday [26 July] that they were close to signing a deal to buy 100,000 tonnes of Vietnamese rice ... In recent months increased controls in northern China have meant that instead of heading for Mongolia, escapees must first make a difficult journey across China to reach South-east Asia ... Sixty Chinese security troops raided the city of Nanking near the Vietnamese border in November [2003] and hauled away 270 North Koreans.

(*The Times*, 28 July 2004, p. 13)

North Korea issued multiple propaganda attacks on the United States on Tuesday [27 July], demanding that Washington reduce its troops from the South and saying US human rights policies raised doubts about nuclear crisis talks ... A statement ... criticized human rights legislation passed last week by the US House of Representatives ... The North Korean Human Rights Act ... calls for the United States to support North Korean refugees and to lead international pressure on the North to safeguard human rights and ensure aid transparency ... The bill was 'full of lies and fabrications' designated to subvert the North, it [the North Korean statement] said ... The [North Korean] foreign ministry repeated Pyongyang's rejection on Saturday [24 July] of US calls for North Korea to follow Libya and trade its nuclear arms programmes and other dangerous weapons for better diplomatic and economic ties with the West.

(www.iht.com, 27 July 2004)

'The North Korean Human Rights Act also authorized funds to promote democracy and a market economy in North Korea' (*IHT*, 28 July 2004, p. 3).

'The North Korean Human Rights Act ... called on the administration to actively encourage refugees, with the help of an annual budget of $22 million' (*Guardian*, 28 July 2004, p. 11).

US Congress representatives voiced their desire for action last week by unanimously passing a bill that, if approved by the Senate, would allow North Korean to claim asylum in America and force the State Department to put the refugee issue at the heart of diplomacy in north-east Asia ... [There are] up to 300,000 North Koreans at large in China and neighbouring countries, many seeking ways to reach the South ... Those caught by Chinese police risk repatriation to North Korea, where they face imprisonment and sometimes execution in brutal labour camps. Despite the dangers most defectors remain in north-east China, living in constant fear of capture ... China and South Korea are nervous that offering asylum to North Koreans could spark a mass exodus, threatening Kim Jong Il's regime with collapse.

(*FT*, 31 July 2004, p. 8)

'Less than a decade ago ... South Korea viewed anyone from the North as the agent of an enemy state and turned away applicants from its embassy doors' (*The Economist*, 31 July 2004, p. 54).

More than 200 North Koreans arrived in South Korea on Wednesday [28 July], the second day of a secretive operation that spirited the largest number of refugees ever from [North Korea] ... In all an estimated 460 people arrived on Tuesday and Wednesday, the largest single group to reach the South ... The new arrivals followed a similar number that reached South Korea on Tuesday [27] ... They had all been airlifted from Vietnam ... [where they] had been staying in safe houses provided by sympathetic South Koreans in [Ho Chi Minh City] ... South Korea declined to confirm where the flights had originated from ... Among refugees who were waiting to enter South Korea there was a backlog of more than a year, and some had threatened to commit suicide over conditions in safe houses.

(www.iht.com, 28 July 2004)

'The latest arrivals [amount to] 468 people in all' (*The Times*, 28 August 2004, p. 19).

North Korea has called this week's defection of nearly 460 of its citizens to South Korea a 'planned kidnapping' and on Thursday [29 July] lashed out at Seoul and other parties involved in the operation ... [The statement said]: 'This is an organized and planned kidnapping, as well as a terror crime that took place in broad daylight. The South Korean government will be [held] fully responsible for the outcome of this situation, and other forces that co-operated in this affair will also pay a big price' ... The Vietnamese government has refused to acknowledge any role in the airlift – a move that is intended to avoid straining relations with Pyongyang and Seoul, according to analysts and diplomats. Fears of a further influx of refugees, and concern over the inevitable international fallout had the asylum seekers been deported, has also prompted Hanoi to remain firmly in the shadows, they said.

(www.iht.com, 29 July 2004)

'North Korea ... characterized Seoul's actions as "abduction and terrorism"' (*IHT*, 30 July 2004, p. 5).

'[North Korea described South Korea's actions as] "premeditated abduction and terrorism"' (*The Times*, 30 July 2004, p. 19).

Lost in the news of the two planeloads of refugees who arrived in Seoul is a report from the *Dong-A Ilbo* on how quickly some North Korean refugees are managing to reach safety ... According to the paper, in June, 'for the first time, defectors arrived in the South only eight days after escaping from the North. There are as many as six recent cases of them arriving in the South within a month.' It also said that 32 per cent of arrivals in April spent less than six months in a third country – that is, China – and that among arrivals in May the figure was 25 per cent. The quicker pace of escape is credited to a more developed underground railroad that is opening new paths out of China – the first stop for most defectors.

(*FEER*, 12 August 2004, p. 6)

North Korea boycotted cabinet-level talks with South Korea on Tuesday [3 August], angry over the defection of hundreds of North Koreans to the South last week. North Korea described the mass defection as an act of 'kidnapping and terrorism committed by South Korean authorities in broad daylight' ... Cabinet-level talks are the highest level of current dialogue between the two Koreas. They were started after a North–South summit meeting in 2000 ... The two Koreas have been at odds over the defections and Seoul's earlier refusal to let pro-unification activists visit Pyongyang for the tenth anniversary of the death of Kim Il Sung on 8 July. North Korea also scrapped maritime and military talks with South Korea in retaliation ... [South Korea] said the work to remove loudspeakers and propaganda billboards along the border has been suspended since military talks scheduled for 19 July had not taken place. The two Koreas had agreed to eliminate the loudspeakers and billboards by 15 August ... Because of the delay ... [South Korea] said it would be difficult to meet the deadline ... [South Korea] said it planned to buy 100,000 tonnes of rice from Vietnam as part of a package of food aid for North Korea ... [South Korea] said the North Koreans had arrived in small groups over the past few years, and that their number reached a level that the host country could no longer sustain, compelling Seoul to bring them to South Korea. As many as 300,000 North Koreans are said to be hiding in China, according to some estimates, and hundreds are believed to be gathering in various South-east Asian countries. Most are waiting a chance to reach South Korea.

(www.iht.com, 3 August 2004)

North Korea has called off talks with South Korea, angered by a recent mass defection of its people to the South ... [North Korea] blamed the United States for instigating last week's arrival of 460 North Koreans ... [A North Korean statement said]: 'The United States seems to calculate that it can use the issue of defectors for bringing down the DPRK' ... [North Korea] also rebuked fellow communist state Vietnam – which has denied knowledge of the refugee operation – for 'discarding elementary sense of obligation and morality to aid a plot conceived by the United States to topple North Korea'.

(*FT*, 4 August 2004, p. 9)

More than 100 North Korean refugees have been expelled from South-east Asia to China and face deportation to the North ... The refugees had been captured and sent back across the border from Vietnam and were being held in a prison in southern China ... Aid workers estimate that 100,000 refugees – and possibly double that number – are in hiding, mostly in China.

(www.iht.com, 11 August 2004)

North Korea has recalled its ambassador to a South-east Asian country to protest the defection of 468 North Koreans to the South in July ... Some observers worry that Pyongyang's actions could pressure Seoul to downplay assistance to defectors. On 15 August the [South Korean] minister of unification ... asked activist groups to exercise restraint and not encourage defections ... Seoul has not named the country for diplomatic reasons, but it is widely thought to be Vietnam. The North demanded that the country apologize and ensure against any similar incident, threatening to withdraw its embassy if demands were not met ... Also on Tuesday [31 August] the North refused to attend inter-Korean economic talks scheduled for this week in Seoul.

(www.iht.com, 31 August 2004)

46   *Political developments*

9 October 2009.

> A court in Vietnam has sentenced six democracy activists to up to six years in prison for 'spreading propaganda' against the government. The six men are the latest to be tried in a clampdown that has seen dozens investigated or arrested for alleged anti-government activities ... [The six] were accused of hanging political banners, distributing leaflets and disseminating anti-government materials via the internet. Their banners bore pro-democracy slogans and were hung in August last year [2008] over a bridge on the Hanoi–Haiphong highway. All of them were arrested in September 2008. The men were also accused of being associated with Bloc 8406, a pro-democracy network inside Vietnam. The prosecutors said their actions were 'harmful to national security'. Their sentences ranged from two to six years in prison. Writer Nguyen Nghia, sixty, considered the leader of the group, received the harshest sentence: six years in prison plus four years of house arrest. He was accused of receiving money from 'reactionary sources overseas' to 'organize anti-government activities' ... Earlier this week three people were sentenced to three to four years in jail for propaganda against the state. Other well-known dissidents, including lawyer Le Cong Dinh, await trial ... Observers say Vietnam is tightening up security ahead of the next Communist Party congress, to be held in early 2011.
>
> (www.bbc.co.uk, 9 October 2009)

26 November 2009.

> International scholars are meeting in Vietnam to discuss territorial disputes in the South China Sea ... China and six other nations (Vietnam, Malaysia, Indonesia, Brunei, Singapore and the Philippines) claim sovereignty to areas in the South China Sea ... Smaller claimants have been especially alarmed by recent developments such as the establishment of a Chinese submarine base on Hainan Island and increasing Chinese naval activities. Beijing always maintains that territorial disputes in the South China Sea are bilateral issues that should be dealt with by individual countries. But the two-day meeting in Hanoi is sending out clear signals that smaller claimants may have embarked on a different approach.
>
> (www.bbc.co.uk, 26 November 2009)

16 December 2009.

> Vietnam has signed billion-dollar contracts to buy submarines and fighter jets from Russia, prime minister Nguyen Tan Dung has announced in Moscow ... [It is reported that] Hanoi was to buy six diesel-electric Kilo-class submarines worth $2 billion. Vietnam is already awaiting the delivery of eight Sukhoi Su-30 MK2 fighter jets from Russia in 2010. It is considering ordering twelve more.
>
> (www.bbc.co.uk, 16 December 2009)

22–23 December 2009.

Intensifying a crackdown on dissent in advance of a Communist Party Congress, Vietnam has charged a prominent American-educated human rights lawyer and at least two associates with the capital crime of subversion, the official press reported Wednesday [23 December]. The lawyer, Le Cong Dinh, was arrested in June along with four other pro-democracy campaigners. All had at first faced the more common and less severe charge brought against dissidents of spreading anti-government propaganda. In an unsettling display two months later, Mr Dinh was shown on Vietnamese television in a shaky hand-held video sitting in his shirtsleeves at a small, bare table and reading out a handwritten confession as his jailers shuffled around noisily off camera. Mr Dinh said, looking at his text: 'I regret my wrong actions. I wish the state to consider clemency for me' ... Mr Dinh's televised confession in August, along with similar confessions by other dissidents, was a very public illustration of a crackdown that human rights groups say has included dozens of arrests and prison terms. In October nine people were sentenced to prison terms ranging from two to six years for hanging banners that called for multi-party democracy. Diplomats and political analysts say the high-profile arrests are meant not only to punish but to set out the boundaries for discussion in advance of a five-yearly Communist Party Congress scheduled for early 2011 ... The restrictive atmosphere has also included tighter limits on press freedom and on internet discussion sites including political blogs. Access to the file-sharing site Facebook has recently been restricted ... The restrictions and arrests come at a time of fluidity, as factions struggle over the wording and substance of the policies that will emerge from the next party congress ... Among the accusations against Mr Dinh was that in March he had attended a three-day training course in Thailand sponsored by an overseas Vietnamese political group, at which two Serbians made presentations about methods of peaceful change ... Mr Dinh and his colleagues are expected to go to trial soon under Article 79 of the Penal Code, 'carrying out activities aimed at overthrowing the people's administration'. Mr Dinh, who studied at Tulane University in New Orleans for two years on a Fulbright scholarship, has often met with diplomats and other foreigners. He has served as vice chairman of the Ho Chi Minh bar association and practised on behalf of the government several years ago when he successfully represented Vietnamese catfish farmers in a dispute with American fishermen. More recently his activities have taken on a political tone, and he has published pro-democracy essays on the internet and defended human rights lawyers accused of anti-government propaganda. Among other things, according to the charges against him, Mr Dinh used his platform as a defence lawyer to speak out about human rights.

(www.iht.com, 23 December 2009; *IHT*, 24 December 2009, p. 5)

Authorities have charged ... Le Cong Dinh ... with working to overthrow the state – a more serious charge than he initially faced. Le Cong Dinh,

48   *Political developments*

arrested in June, was first accused of a lesser charge of spreading anti-government propaganda ... The new prosecution charges, announced on Tuesday [22 December] and reported by state media on Wednesday [23 December] are against Mr Le, internet activist Nguyen Tien Trung, and fellow defendants Tran Huynh Duy Thuc and Le Thang Long ... The fourth suspect, Le Thang Long, was also charged with subversive activities but as an accomplice ... The *Thanh Nien* newspaper quoted the indictment as saying Mr Le and his associates 'colluded with Vietnamese reactionary groups and hostile forces in exile' to form a political organization 'aimed at overthrowing the people's government through non-violent means'. The defendants have also been accused of links with the Democratic Party of Vietnam, a group earlier linked to the Vietnamese Communist Party but now banned. A fifth defendant, Tran Anh Kim, is to be tried separately in the northern province of Tahi Binh ... Mr Le was also accused of participating in a three-day training course for non-violent struggle organized by Viet Tan, a California-based pro-democracy group that Vietnam considers a terrorist organization.

(www.bbc.co.uk, 24 December 2009)

28 December 2009.

The first in a series of trials of dissidents in Vietnam concluded Monday [28 December], when a court convicted a former army officer of subversion for pro-democracy activities and sentenced him to five-and-a-half years in prison. The conviction of the former officer, Tran Anh Kim, comes as the government is tightening controls on dissent in advance of a Communist Party congress in early 2011. Mr Kim is one of five activists who were arrested in June [2009] and at first faced the less serious charge of spreading anti-government propaganda. But this month [December] Mr Kim and at least two others were charged with the capital crime of subversion. Prosecutors asked for a lighter sentence in view of the military background of Mr Kim, a wounded veteran. Sentences in political cases are generally determined in advance, and the trial took just four hours. The other four campaigners are to go on trial next month [20 January 2010]. The most prominent among them is Le Cong Dinh ... The others are Nguyen Tien Trung, who recently studied engineering in Paris, Tran Huynh Thuc and Le Thang Long ... In court the defiant Mr Kim acknowledged his membership in the Democratic Party of Vietnam, an outlawed group of small affiliated parties and opposition factions ... He also said he had joined Bloc 8406, a group of petitioners calling for democratic elections and a multi-party state. The petition was originated on 8 April 2006 – hence its name – but Mr Kim was not one of the original 118 signatories. A principal architect of Bloc 8406, a Catholic priest, Nguyen Van Ly, was convicted and sentenced along with four other dissidents in March 2007. He received an eight-year prison term for 'overtly revolutionary activities' and 'conspiring with reactionary forces', according to the official Vietnam News Agency ... Judge Tran Van

Loan said Mr Kim had participated in what he called an organized crime against the state, co-operating with 'reactionary Vietnamese and hostile forces in exile'. The judge said: 'This was a serious violation of national security' ... Ardent critics of the government [include] the writer Duong Thu Huong, whose banned novel *Paradise of the Blind* was a searing description of life in postwar Vietnam, and Thich Quang Do, a Buddhist monk who has been a critic of the communist regimes for decades.

(www.iht.com, 28 December 2009; *IHT*, 29 December 2009, p. 8)

Kim Anh Kim was arrested in July [2009] on charges of conducting propaganda against the state. He was later indicted with the more serious crime of 'conducting activities to overthrow the people's administration' – charges that carry a maximum penalty of death. He said: 'I joined the Democratic Party of Vietnam and Bloc 8406 to fight for democratic freedom and human rights for the Vietnamese nation through peaceful dialogue and non-violent means.'

(www.bbc.co.uk, 28 December 2009)

December 2009–January 2010.

China, Taiwan and Vietnam have competing claims on the Paracels, while all three countries and the Philippines, Malaysia and Brunei have claims on the Spratlys or the nearby waters ... In December Vietnam asked China to return fishing boats and other equipment seized from Vietnamese fishermen detained by the Chinese military near ... Hoang Sa, the Vietnamese name for the Paracels. One Vietnamese news organization has estimated that China detained seventeen fishing vessels and 210 fishermen last year [2009]. Also in December the Vietnamese prime minister signed an arms agreement in Russia that official Russian news organizations said included the purchase of six submarines for $2 billion. The submarines are expected to be used to defend Vietnamese interest in the South China Sea. China has agreed to continue talks with Vietnam, but it is willing to discuss only joint development of the area, not sovereignty rights. And it refuses to negotiate with relevant South-east Asian nations in a multilateral way ... Tensions arose last month [January 2010] after China announced plans to develop tourism in the Paracels, an area the Chinese military has controlled since 1974 ... The Vietnamese foreign ministry strongly denounced China's move ... Vietnam is pushing hard behind the scenes to bring more foreign players into the negotiations so that China will have to bargain with all South-east Asian nations that have territorial claims in the South China Sea ... In the last two years China has been more aggressive in asserting control over the area, as it detained Vietnamese fishermen, increased sea patrols and warned foreign oil companies against working with Vietnam ... Just last month Japan protested Chinese plans to develop gas fields in the East China Sea ... This year [2010] Vietnam takes over the chairmanship of Asean. Vietnam is expected to use its position to persuade the countries to come together in territorial negotiations with China, analysts say. In November [2009] Vietnam held a conference in Hanoi, where fifty scholars and officials from across Asia discussed disputes in the South China Sea – a first start to its new strategy, analysts say.

(*IHT*, 5 February 2010, p. 8)

20 January 2010.

The trial of Le Cong Dinh and three other democracy activists for subversion has begun ... The subversion charge carries a minimum sentence of twelve years and a maximum sentence of execution ... It has been a long time since the communist regime tried anybody on a subversion charge.

(www.bbc.co.uk, 20 January 2010)

Le Cong Dinh, one of the country's best known lawyers, is among three defendants on trial who could be sentenced to the firing squad ... The fourth defendant, who is being tried as an accomplice, could face fifteen years ... The main issue to be determined at trial involves the length of the sentence. They have been charged under Article 79 of Vietnam's criminal code with 'carrying out activities aimed at overthrowing the people's administration'. The first to testify was Le Cong Dinh, who acknowledged violating Article 79 by joining the Democratic Party of Vietnam [DPV]. He said: 'The purpose of the party was to call for a multi-party system, political pluralism and a new state. During my studies overseas, I was influenced by Western attitudes toward democracy, freedom and human rights' ... [He] acknowledged receiving a draft of a proposed new Vietnamese constitution from DPV leaders and attending a three-day seminar in Thailand on non-violent political change organized by Viet Tan, an international pro-democracy network with members inside and outside Vietnam. Vietnam's government considers Viet Tan a terrorist organization, but US officials say there is no evidence to support that view ... During closing arguments at a 2007 human rights trial in Hanoi, Le Cong Dinh made a highly unusual public plea for freedom of expression. In recent months Vietnam has arrested several bloggers and blocked the popular social networking site Facebook. Last month [December 2009] authorities convicted democracy advocate Tran Anh Kim of subversion and sentenced him to five-and-a-half years in prison for violating Article 79. In October [2009] nine others were convicted of violating Article 88, a lesser charge that prohibits spreading propaganda against the state ... The trial comes during one of Vietnam's crackdowns against dissent, amid speculation that the latest move is the result of jockeying among political factions in advance of next year's Communist Party congress.

(www.guardian.co.uk, 20 January 2010)

'The four men received sentences of up to sixteen years ... Tran Duy Thuc, an internet entrepreneur, received the longest sentence' (www.bbc.co.uk, 20 January 2010).

Four pro-democracy campaigners were convicted Wednesday [20 January] of trying to overthrow the state ... Their sentences ranged from five years for Le Cong Dinh ... to sixteen years in prison for a well-known internet entrepreneur and blogger, Tran Huynh Duy Thuc ... All but one of the defendants had been charged with the capital crime of subversion, an unusually severe charge ... During the one-day trial in Ho Chi Minh City, Mr Dinh admitted he had broken the law by meeting with foreign groups and advocating multi-party democracy. He said: 'From the bottom of my heart I myself and these three other defendants had no intention to overthrow the government. During my studies overseas I was influenced by Western attitudes toward democracy, freedom and human rights' ... Mr Thuc, the blogger, denied the charges, saying he had only been campaigning against corruption and trying to improve the political system. He acknowledged organizing a study group that prosecutors said was dedicated to undermining the government but said the group was intended to study issues and make constructive suggestions to the government.

(www.iht.com, 20 January 2010)

A court in Ho Chi Minh City sentenced four democracy activists to jail terms ranging from five to sixteen years ... Le Cong Dinh and Nguyen Tien Trung are among the country's best-known criminal defence lawyers and had previously studied and lived abroad ... Last year [2009] the authorities detained Mr Dinh and Mr Trung along with two internet entrepreneurs who had posted political articles online and dared to organize a political discussion group. In August all four read out confessions on national television and then were charged with conspiring to overthrow the government. Two of the men later recanted the confessions during a trial, saying they had been coerced into making them. One of them Tran Huynh Thuc, was handed a sixteen-years entence.

(www.economist.com, 22 January 2010)

('A court has rejected appeals by Le Cong Dinh ... and Tran Huynh Duy Thuc ... Le Thang Long had his jail term cut by a year and a half ... Tran Nguyen Tien Trung did not appeal': www.bbc.co.uk, 11 May 2010.)

29 January 2010.

A democracy campaigner who criticized the government was sentenced Friday [29 January] to four years in prison on charges of spreading propaganda against the state ... The defendant, Pham Thanh Nghien was also given three years' probation ... Ms Nghien was the fifteenth democracy advocate to face charges in the last three months.

(*IHT*, 30 January 2010, p. 4)

'Writer Pham Thanh Nghien ... [was] convicted ... of "conducting propaganda against the state" ... [She was sentenced] to four years in prison, followed by three years of house arrest' (*FT*, 30 January 2010, p. 7).

52   *Political developments*

A writer and democracy activist has been jailed for three-and-a-half years for attacking two men during a parking dispute in Hanoi. Tran Khai Thuy and her husband, Do Ba Tan, had denied the charges, saying they had been the victims of the attack and not the perpetrators ... The Hanoi court sentenced Thuy to forty-three months in prison, including time served since October [2009]. Tan was given a two-year suspended sentence and forty-seven months under probation ... At least sixteen activists have been jailed in recent months.

(www.bbc.co.uk, 5 February 2010)

25 April 2010.

Members of the World Bank agreed on Sunday [25 April] to support a $5.1 billion increase in its operating capital, the largest increase in general financing since 1988, and give developing countries a greater say in running the anti-poverty institution. Under the changes China will become the World Bank's third largest shareholder, ahead of Germany, after the United States and Japan. Countries like Brazil, India, Indonesia and Vietnam will also have greater representation ... The World Bank's 186 members also agreed a reform package that calls for greater openness and disclosure of information and improvements in managing risks and measuring results. The World Bank has made $105 billion in financial commitments since July 2008 in response to the global economic turmoil ... The World Bank president ... Robert Zoellick ... devised the capital increase and voting changes to be adopted together. The $5.1 billion in so-called paid-in capital, which the bank can use for day-to-day operations, will bring the bank's cash on hand to about $40 billion. Of the $5.1 billion, developing countries will contribute $1.6 billion in connection with a shift in representation that will give them 47.19 per cent of voting power, up from 44.06 per cent. The actions fulfil a pledge the bank's members made in Istanbul in October [2009] ... In 2008 the bank's members approved a smaller shift of 1.46 per cent of voting power to the developing countries from the wealthy ones ... All told, the cumulative shift of 4.59 per cent of voting power amounts to the greatest alignment in representation at the World Bank since 1988 ... The bank's members approved on Sunday an $86.2 billion general capital increase, bringing the bank's total subscribed capital, not counting about $26 billion in reserves, to $276.1 billion ... Mr Zoellick ... said ... that the less wealthy countries were leading the global economic recovery.

(www.iht.com, 26 April 2010)

'The United States, which holds the largest voting share in the World Bank at 16.4 per cent, would not seek any increase in that' (www.bbc.co.uk, 26 April 2010).

The World Bank increased the voting power of developing and transition countries among its 186 members, raising the total for that block to 47.2 per cent, from 44.6 per cent in 2008. China's voting share was raised to 4.42 per cent, vaulting it ahead of European countries and leaving it behind only the United States and Japan ... World Bank shareholders (2010): United States, 15.85 per cent; Japan, 6.84 per cent; China, 4.42 per cent; Germany, 4.00 per cent; France, 3.75 per cent; Britain, 3.75 per cent; India, 2.91 per cent.

(www.economist.com, 29 April 2010; *The Economist*, 1 May 2010, p. 8)

30 April 2010.

Vietnam has marked thirty-five years since the end of its war by staging a re-enactment of the fall of Saigon ... The Vietnam War claimed the lives of 3 million Vietnamese and some 60,000 US soldiers ... The ceremony in Ho Chi Minh City ... was attended by leaders and dignitaries from Cuba, Russia, Laos and Cambodia ... President Nguyen Minh Triet used the event to praise the country's economic development since the war. He said: '[The] economy has steadily grown while socio-economic stability and national defence have been guaranteed. The country's status in the international arena has been lifted while its people's lives increasingly improved.'

(www.bbc.co.uk, 30 April 2010)

4–6 June 2010.

An annual Asia security summit [was] held between 4 and 6 June in Singapore ... Tensions are rising over sovereignty and navigation rights in the contested South China Sea ... a vital shipping lane and home to the Paracel and Spratly Islands, which several littoral countries claim as their own and which are believed to sit atop sizeable oil and gas deposits. China's rapid naval build-up has stirred fears among neighbours of a future territorial grab ... China's officials have begun describing the South China Sea as one of its 'core interests', on a par with Taiwan and Tibet. It has stepped up military exercises from its naval base on Hainan. That is worrying for Vietnam, which has sparred with China over undersea drilling by Western oil companies. In 2008 China reportedly browbeat ExxonMobil and BP into stopping exploration in Vietnamese waters ... US Defence Secretary Robert Gates said American firms should not be blocked from 'legitimate economic activity'. Vietnam would like the ten-member Asean, whose rotating chairmanship it holds, to stick together on the South China Sea issue, lest China pick off the weaker members. Vietnam's defence chief told the forum that he hoped maritime disputes could be resolved with 'good-neighbourliness, friendship, co-operation and brotherhood'.

(*The Economist*, 12 June 2010, pp. 71–2)

29 June 2010.

The United States said Tuesday [29 June] that it had begun a $5 million project to clean up contamination caused by the defoliant Agent Orange at a former US air base in Vietnam. The project will focus on contamination at Bien Hoa airport on the outskirts of Ho Chi Minh City.

(*IHT*, 30 June 2010, p. 5)

14 July 2010.

> The [US] Senate Foreign Relations Committee on Wednesday [14 July] released more than 1,100 pages of previously classified Vietnam-era transcripts that show senators of the time sharply questioning whether they had been deceived by the White House and the Pentagon over the 1964 Gulf of Tonkin incident ... [Transcripts included those of a] March 1968 closed session of the Foreign Relations Committee ... Historians said the transcripts, which are filled with venting by the senators about the Johnson administration and frustrations over their own ineffectiveness, added little new to the historical record. Even at the time there was widespread scepticism about the Gulf of Tonkin incident, in which the North Vietnamese were said to have attacked American destroyers on 4 August 1964, two days after an earlier clash. President Lyndon B. Johnson cited the attacks to persuade Congress to authorize broad military action in Vietnam, but historians in recent years have concluded that the 4 August attack never happened ... Robert J. Hanyok ... National Security Agency historian ... concluded in 2001 that NSA officers had deliberately falsified intercepted communications in the incident to make it look like the attack on 4 August 1964 had occurred, although he said they acted not out of political motives but to cover up earlier errors. Many historians say that President Johnson might have found reason to escalate military action against North Vietnam even without the Gulf of Tonkin crisis, and that he apparently had his own doubts. Historians note that a few days after the supposed attack he told George W. Ball (the Under Secretary of State): 'Hell, those dumb, stupid sailors were just shooting at flying fish.'
>
> (www.iht.com, 15 July 2010)

22–23 July 2010.

> US Secretary of State Hillary Clinton expressed concern on Thursday [22 July] about what she called the Vietnamese government's intolerance of dissent as she started a two-day visit to mark fifteen years of normalized relations between Vietnam and the United States ... The United States normalized diplomatic ties with Vietnam in 1995 while Bill Clinton was president, and Mrs Clinton spoke of the 'poignant' memories that the country evoked for her and her husband. She last visited as first lady with Mr Clinton in late 2000, in the waning days of his presidency, a few weeks after she had been elected a senator from New York ... Noting Vietnam's recent jailing of democracy activists, attacks on religious groups and curbing of internet social-networking sites, Mrs Clinton said she raised the status of human rights in a meeting with deputy prime minister Pham Gia Khiem ... She devoted most of her remarks to promises that the United States would increase co-operation on trade and investment, and would do more to help Vietnamese suffering lingering effects from Agent Orange, a chemical the American military used as a defoliant during the Vietnam War ... [Mrs

Clinton is undertaking a] weeklong trip to Pakistan, Afghanistan, South Korea and Vietnam ... In addition to promoting Vietnamese–American ties, Mrs Clinton is in Hanoi to attend a regional security meeting sponsored by the Association of South-east Asian Nations (Asean). North Korea is likely to be high on the agenda. An international investigation led by South Korea concluded that the North was responsible for torpedoing a South Korean warship, killing forty-six sailors. Asean issued a statement deploring the attack but declining to point a finger at the North as the culprit. Mrs Clinton is also expected to raise the issue of Myanmar, also known as Burma ... She said the United States was concerned about the shipments of military equipment and material to Myanmar from North Korea, as well as unconfirmed reports that Burma is seeking help from North Korea to develop its own nuclear weapons programme.

(www.iht.com, 22 July 2010)

Secretary of State Hillary Clinton chided Vietnam on Thursday [22 July] for intolerance of dissent and infringement of internet freedom, even as she celebrated fifteen years of normalized relations with the United States, a step taken by her husband, Bill Clinton, when he was president ... She said: 'The United States will continue to urge Vietnam to strengthen its commitment to human rights and give its people a greater say over the direction of their lives. But our relationship is not fixed on our differences. We have learned to see each other not as former enemies, but as friends.'

(*IHT*, 23 July 2010, p. 4)

The United States said on Friday [23 July] that it was ready to step into a tangled dispute between China and it smaller Asian neighbours over a string of strategically sensitive islands in the South China Sea. US Secretary of State Hillary Clinton, speaking in Vietnam at a meeting of Asean, said: 'The United States has a national interest in freedom of navigation, open access to Asia's maritime commons and respect for international law in the South China Sea' ... The United States, she said, was prepared to facilitate multinational negotiations to settle competing claims over the islands – among them the Spratly and Paracel islands – something sought by Vietnam, which has had deadly clashes with China over them. In 1988 warships from China and Vietnam traded fire in the Spratly Islands, sinking several Vietnamese boats and killing dozens of sailors ... China has long laid claim to islands in the South China Sea because they are rich in oil and natural gas deposits. And it has put American officials on notice that it will not brook foreign interference in the waters off its south-eastern coast, which it views as a 'core interest' of sovereignty ... In March [2010] senior Chinese officials pointedly warned their American counterparts that they would brook no interference in the South China Sea, which they called part of the 'core interest' of sovereignty ... For decades China has sparred with South-east Asian nations over control of 200 tiny islands, rocks and spits of sand that dot these waters ... Many of the islands are just rocks or spits of sand, but they are rich in oil and natural gas deposits, and China views them as important outposts of its territorial waters far in the busy shipping lands in the sea ... In 1974 China seized the Paracel Islands from Vietnam, and in January [2010] it announced plans to develop the islands for tourism – ratcheting up tension with Vietnam, which has never recognized China's territorial claims. Vietnam's strategy is to 'internationalize' the dispute by bringing in other players and forcing China to negotiate in multinational forums. Mrs Clinton's announcement that the United States would be willing to play a part was a significant victory for the Vietnamese ... In recent months, administration officials said, China has harassed fishing boats and leaned on energy companies that have tried to make offshore deals with other countries.

(www.iht.com, 23 July 2010, and 24 July 2010)

Mrs Clinton stressed that the United States was not changing its longstanding neutrality on the competing claims. But China has been adamant that the disputes be resolved through one-on-one negotiations, and the administration's decision to get involved angered China's foreign minister, Yang Jiechi ... twelve of the twenty-seven countries at the meeting spoke out in favour of a new approach to the South China Sea, prompting Mr Yang to observe that the American effort seemed orchestrated.

(*IHT*, 24 July 2010, p. 8)

US Secretary of State Hillary Clinton [attended] the Asean Regional Forum in Hanoi ... where she enraged Chinese officials by offering US support to a 'collaborative diplomatic process by all claimants for resolving the various territorial disputes without coercion' ... Foreign ministers from twelve of the twenty-seven countries in attendance in Hanoi were outspoken in agreement –insisting that territorial issues be resolved multilaterally, rather than the Beijing-preferred bilateral method of picking off one claimant at a time.

(www.iht.com, 30 August 2010)

US Secretary of State Hillary Clinton said a peaceful resolution of overlapping territorial claims in the South China Sea was a 'national interest' of the United States. She said: 'The United States supports a collaborative diplomatic process by all claimants for resolving the various territorial disputes without coercion. We oppose the use or threat of force by any claimant' ... This runs counter to China's restated 'indisputable' claim to the entire South China Sea, and its desire to reach bilateral deals with each South-east Asian claimant, rather than a multilateral agreement. Mrs Clinton's comments backed a recent letter from Indonesia to the United Nations which called for a resolution of the region's territorial disputes to be settled according to the Law of the Sea.

(www.bbc.co.uk, 3 August 2010)

China, Vietnam, Malaysia, the Philippines, Brunei, Taiwan and Indonesia lay claims to all or part of the body of water that extends from China's

Hainan Island to Borneo. The areas with the most overlapping claims are mainly near the Spratly and Paracel islands. In 2002 China and Asean signed a declaration of conduct, under which all parties pledged to exercise restraint in the disputed waters. But Asean members feel that the accord has become meaningless, and observers speak of a new Chinese assertiveness in the area, while disputes between fishing vessels and naval forces are on the rise ... Indonesia is leading efforts to try to forge a regional consensus. In a recent letter to the UN, Jakarta said China's attempt to use isolated islets to establish its legal claim to sovereignty 'clearly lacks international legal basis', and to allow it would undermine the UN Convention on the Law of the Sea – the framework for establishing sovereignty ... Vietnam, and to a lesser extent Malaysia, have also begun to push back against what some see as Chinese bullying ... China claims virtually all of the South China Sea.

(*FT*, 4 August 2010, p. 8)

26 July 2010.

The Chinese government reacted angrily on Monday [26 July] to an announcement by US Secretary of State Hillary Clinton that Washington might step into a long-simmering territorial dispute between China and its smaller neighbours in the South China Sea ... Foreign minister Yang Jiechi of China: 'What will be the consequences if this issue is turned into an international or multilateral one? It will only make matters worse and the resolution more difficult' ... An editorial Monday in the Communist Party-run *People's Daily* newspaper: 'American hopes to contain a China with growing military capabilities' ... *Global Times* (an English language tabloid published by the *People's Daily*): 'China will never waive its right to protect its core interest with military means' ... Until Mrs Clinton made her remarks, the dispute over the South China Sea islands had remained a largely regional concern. The area of contention, which spans 1.2 million square miles, is an increasingly important conduit for a third of the world's maritime trade and much of the region's energy supplies. Just as compelling are the enormous deposits of oil and natural gas thought to be under the ocean floor ... American officials have reacted with growing concern over China's naval ambitions, a new strategy that Chinese admirals have described as its 'far sea defence'. Beyond refusing to cede any ground on sovereignty in the South China Sea, China has announced plans to deploy aircraft carriers, and it has strengthened its armada with nuclear powered submarines capable of firing ballistic missiles. In March [2010] China warned two visiting American officials that it would not tolerate any interference in the South China Sea, an area it described as its 'core interest', much like Tibet and Taiwan. China's neighbours have reacted by bolstering their own naval forces. In recent years Vietnam, Singapore and Malaysia have acquired submarines. On Sunday [25 July] Japan announced plans to increase its submarine fleet for the first time in more than three decades. Mrs Clinton's announcement on Friday [23 July] was essentially a nod to

Vietnam, which has been seeking support for multilateral negotiations as a bulwark against China's stance on sovereignty.

(www.iht.com, 26 July 2010; *IHT*, 27 July 2010, p. 5)

The United States, by declaring in Hanoi that it has an interest in freedom of navigation in the South China Sea and the settlement of disputed claims by international law, has put itself firmly in the camp of Vietnam, the Philippines, Malaysia and other nations with stakes in the outcome. Although China owns only about one-fifth of the coastline, Beijing claims almost all the islands, resources and navigation rights. It bolsters its claims with a Sino-centric version of history that ignores the fact that ethnic Malay seafarers, the ancestors of today's Malaysians, Indonesians, Filipinos and the Chams of Vietnam, dominated commerce in those waters centuries before the Chinese. Vietnam has recently been showing more determination than the other claimants – Malaysia, the Philippines and Brunei – to talk back to China, strengthening its island defences and ordering six submarines from Russia. US power and Vietnamese resolve have now made other claimants willing to support internationalization of the issue rather than, like the Philippines, be sucked into bilateral discussions and oil exploration joint ventures with China. Asean has proved a poor vehicle for pressing the South-east Asian claims because only half its members are concerned about the issue. Nor have the claimants shown much willingness to compromise among themselves and present China with a united front.

(Philip Bowring, www.iht.com, 2 August 2010; *IHT*, 3 August 2010, p. 3)

A large airborne military exercise is underway in China's central and eastern provinces and seas. Fighter jets, spy planes and helicopters, along with 2,000 soldiers are taking part in the drill. It is one of several announced in official media in recent weeks. The exercise follows verbal sparring between the United States and China over conflicting territorial claims by China and many South-east Asian nations in the South China Sea. It also comes after China protested against major US–South Korea military exercises last month [July] in the Sea of Japan. China's five-day exercise, called Vanguard 2010, is taking place over the central province of Henan and the eastern coastal province of Shandong, which borders the Yellow Sea ... China was also angry at US–South Korean military drills in late July.

(www.bbc.co.uk, 3 August 2010)

The United States is said to be negotiating an agreement with Vietnam to provide nuclear fuel and technology, without the usual constraints on enriching uranium to prevent proliferation. The deal has been under discussion for several months, following Hanoi's announcement of plans to build fourteen nuclear power stations over the next twenty years. Washington has required several other countries, most recently the United Arab Emirates and Jordan, to agree to source all their nuclear fuel on the international market and to renounce the right to enrich uranium as a requirement for assistance in developing nuclear power. Vietnam signed an initial memorandum of understanding on nuclear power with the Bush administration in 2001. But the Obama administration has accelerated talks in recent months as Vietnam reaches agreements with other countries, including Russia, which has been contracted to begin a light-water reactor for $8 billion in 2014. The United States and Vietnam signed a new memorandum of understanding in April [2010] over broad co-operation on nuclear power including access to 'reliable sources of nuclear fuel'. An agreement would allow US companies such as General Electric and Bechtel to sell nuclear reactors and other equipment to Vietnam. But the talks have drawn criticism that Washington is setting a different standard for Vietnam than some other countries.

(*Guardian*, 6 August 2010)

8 August 2010. 'The United States and Vietnam demonstrated their blossoming military relations Sunday [8 August] as an American nuclear supercarrier cruised in waters off Vietnam' (*IHT*, 9 August 2010, p. 8).

The United States and Vietnam are conducting joint naval exercises in the South China Sea, a sign of increasing military ties between the two former enemies. The week-long activities focus mainly on non-combatant exercises and are part of the fifteenth anniversary of diplomatic ties between Washington and Hanoi ... The United States has described the exercises as a 'series of naval engagement activities' which focus mainly on damage control and search and rescue. The US Navy on Sunday [8 August] hosted Vietnamese military and government officials on the USS *George Washington*, which is on its way back from naval exercises with South Korea in the Sea of Japan. Its strike force of three destroyers are also in the South China Sea, while the USS *John S. McCain* is due to call at the Vietnamese port of Danang later on Tuesday [10 August] ... Last week the Vietnamese foreign ministry said that Chinese ships which were carrying out seismic studies in the Paracels zone – a disputed area – had breached Vietnam's sovereignty.

(www.bbc.co.uk, 10 August 2010)

17 August 2010. 'Officials from Vietnam and the United States met on Tuesday [18 August] to discuss defence issues for the first time ... They talked about disaster relief, search and rescue, international peacekeeping and maritime security' (*IHT*, 18 August 2010, p. 5).

26 August 2010.

China said Thursday [26 August] that it had used a small, staffed submarine to plant the national flag deep beneath the South China Sea, where it has tussled with other nations in territorial disputes. The vessel achieved the feat during seventeen dives from May to July [2010], when it went as deep as 12,330 feet [3,759 metres], state media reported.

(www.iht.com, 27 August 2010)

21 September 2010.

> Sharply raising the stakes in a dispute over Japan's detention of a Chinese fishing trawler captain, the Chinese government has blocked exports to Japan of a crucial category of minerals used in products like hybrid cars, wind turbines and guided missiles. Chinese customs officials are halting shipments to Japan of rare earth elements, preventing them from being loaded aboard ships this week at Chinese ports, three industry officials said Thursday [23 September] … China mines 93 per cent of the world's rare earth minerals, and more than 99 per cent of the world's supply of some of the most prized rare earths … Japanese companies are now setting up rare earth processing factories in northern Vietnam, partly to use small reserves of rare earth elements found there but also to process rare earth elements smuggled across from southern China. But the Chinese government has been rapidly tightening controls on the industry in the last four months to try to limit smuggling. Rare earth elements are already in tight supply and prices are soaring after the Chinese government announced in July that it was cutting export quotas by 72 per cent for the remainder of the year [2010].
>
> (www.iht.com, 23 September 2010; *IHT*, 24 September 2010, pp. 1, 18)

> Chinese customs officials stopped exports of rare earth minerals to Japan on Tuesday [21 September] as tensions mounted over the captain's detention. While Beijing has denied imposing a ban, Chinese exporters were still waiting Sunday [26 September] for permission to resume shipments … Rare earths are important for the automotive, electronics and clean-energy industries … China mines 93 per cent of the world's tonnage of rare earths, and more than 99 per cent of some of the least common and most valuable rare earths. The halt in exports has caused considerable dismay in Japan, where rare earth users from a variety of industries have gone on television to warn of the importance of access to supplies … The Chinese commerce industry … denies that it imposed a ban on exports of the minerals to Japan. A commerce ministry spokesman said on Saturday [25 September]: 'According to the information we know, we did not make any restrictions [on exports of the minerals]' … Japanese companies have been accumulating stockpiles of rare earths over the past two years in case of shortages … Industrial Minerals Co. of Australia, a rare earths consulting firm, estimated that Japanese companies had stockpiled enough of the minerals to last six to nine months without further supplies from China. But there is no national system for sharing stockpiles among companies, and the number of months' worth of supplies kept in warehouses varies widely from company to company and among the seventeen different rare earth elements.
>
> (www.iht.com, 26 September 2010)

> Rare by name, though not by nature, seventeen elements in the periodic table – the 'rare earths' – are among the most sought-after materials in

modern manufacturing. In tiny amounts, their unique magnetic and phosphorescent properties make them vital ingredients in a host of gadgets and components, ranging from hard drives to lasers. Though abundant in nature, extracting them is difficult, costly, time-consuming and dirty. China is the world's largest (and for some of them the only) producer of rare earths ... Japan, with its electronics and car industries, uses a fifth of the global supply, making it the world's biggest importer of rare earths ... The Chinese dominance comes from heavy investments in the 1980s. Deng Xiaoping later said that rare earths would be to China what oil was to the Middle East. As Chinese production came on stream, prices plummeted and other producers closed. Since 2006 China has behaved in a way that resembles OPEC, the oil producers' cartel, cutting exports by 5 per cent to 10 per cent a year. In July [2010] the export quota was cut by 40 per cent. Prices have soared: the cost of cerium oxide (often used as a catalyst) has increased six-fold since the start of the year, and is twenty times higher than in 2005. The squeeze comes as a surge in demand for high-tech equipment has sent the demand for rare earths soaring. In 2003 some 85,000 tonnes were shipped, valued at $500 million. This year's sales are expected to total 125,000 tonnes, worth nearly $2 billion. Demand is forecast to increase by around two-thirds over the next five years. For now, China's position is strong. It holds 35 per cent of global reserves but supplies more than 95 per cent of demand, of which 60 per cent is domestic, according to Industrial Minerals Company of Australia (IMCOA). In 'heavy' rare earths such as dysprosium, which helps magnets keep their properties at high temperatures, its market share is nearly 100 per cent. China cites environmental concerns to justify its export curbs. The real reason is probably to persuade foreign firms to move manufacturing to China before non-Chinese mines are on stream and its market control ebbs. Market forces should be providing an answer already. But they face peculiar snags. The quantities of rare earths used in technology components are so tiny that higher prices are invisible in the cost to consumers. Recycling is tricky: just half a penny's worth of neodymium helps a mobile phone vibrate. In the next four years new production is starting in Australia and in California (where it ceased in 2002). Capacity is being increased at mines in India and Vietnam. The newcomers will shrink China's market share by 15 per cent, says ... IMCOA. The only existing producer outside Asia not dependent on Chinese ores is Silmet, a rare earth metal firm in Estonia, which says it is now besieged by eager customers.

(www.economist.com, 30 September 2010;
The Economist, 2 October 2010, p. 71)

China produced 97 per cent of the world's rare earths last year [2009] ... During the 1980s global rare earths production shifted from the United States to China because of lower labour costs and also lower environmental standards – the mining and processing of these elements can be highly polluting ... China has 129 legally registered rare earths mines and many more that operate illegally, usually at great environmental cost ... For the industry as a whole ... there are signs that the Beijing government does not wish it to get too big. The consolidation of China's rare earths sector is part of a broader national effort to shift away from this type of low value-added, high environmental impact product. As a result, China has cut export quotas for rare earths and raised export taxes for the minerals. Export taxes for rare earths are currently around 15 to 25 per cent, and quotas for the mineral are so tight that they are traded around between the companies that receive quota allocations ... No country's manufacturers have more at stake than Japan's in the race to secure supplies of rare earths elements. The group of seventeen obscurely named minerals are crucial to much of what Japanese industry makes: from rechargeable batteries (lanthanum) and polished glass (cerium) to automobile exhaust systems (rhodium) and high-powered magnetic motors (dysprosium and neodymium). Japan consumes more rare earths than any other country, but has no deposits of its own ... There are two ways that Japanese manufacturers can wean themselves off Chinese rare earths: find new supplies elsewhere or use fewer of the minerals to begin with. Efforts are under way on both fronts. Several Japanese groups are now looking to revive rare earths mining outside China, where perhaps two-thirds of the world's deposits lie unexploited, according to geologists. Toyota Tsusho, the trading affiliate of Toyota Motor, is examining deposits in India, Vietnam and Canada. Sumitomo, the trading house, has teamed up with Kazatoprom of Kazakhstan to develop finds in Central Asia, and Mitsubishi, another trader, is evaluating deposits in a former tin mine in Brazil alongside Canadian company Neo Materials. Showa Denko opened a rare earth processing plant in northern Vietnam in May [2010], as part of its plan to 'establish a system for stable supply' ... Japan's government is also courting potential new suppliers. Prime minister Naoto Kan pledged to help fund exploration and development in Mongolia at a meeting with his Mongolian counterpart Sukhbaatar Batbold ... Manufacturers are meanwhile trying to do more with less.

(*FT*, 7 October 2010, p. 24)

A diplomatic showdown between Japan and China that began two weeks ago with the arrest of a Chinese trawler near disputed islands ended on Friday [24 September] when Tokyo seemed to blink by accepting Beijing's demands for his release. Japan freed the captain ... It appears to have resulted in a victory for China which prevailed by steadily ratcheting up the pressure on Japan with verbal threats and economic sanctions ... On Thursday [23 September] four Japanese construction company employees were detained ... On Friday prosecutors on Ishigaki Island, where the captain was held, cited diplomatic considerations in their decision to let him go ... The prosecutors said in a statement: 'Considering the effect on the people of our nation and on China–Japan relations, we decided that it was not appropriate to continue the investigation' ... [The United States said its] treaty obligations to defend Japan from foreign attack would include any moves against the islands where the Chinese captain was arrested. The islands, known as Senkaku in Japanese or Diaoyu in Chinese, are administered by Japan but claimed by China and also Taiwan.

(*IHT*, 25 September 2010, pp. 1, 7)

'Prosecutors in Japan ... said they did not perceive any premeditated intent to damage the patrol boats ... The [captain's] release came after four Japanese were detained in China on suspicion of illegally filming in a military area' (www.bbc.co.uk, 25 September 2010). 'The row began on 7 September when a Chinese trawler collided with two Japanese coastguard vessels off a series of disputed islands in the East China Sea' (www.iht.com, 21 September 2010).

> The release ... of the captain ... immediately exposed Japanese authorities to accusations that they had buckled in the face of pressure from Beijing ... Wen Jiabao, China's premier, this week said the Diaoyu Islands that are disputed by Japan and China were 'sacred territory', an indication of an increasingly bold attitude towards territorial claims.
>
> (*FT*, 25 September 2010, p. 5)

'The Senkakus, controlled by Japan, are surrounded by rich fishing grounds and near potentially huge undersea oil and gas deposits' (*Guardian*, 25 September 2010, p. 18).

> Tensions between China and Japan over the arrest of a Chinese trawler captain flared anew Saturday [25 September], a day after his release, with Beijing demanding an apology for the detention, and Tokyo refusing. Chinese authorities also continued to hold four Japanese nationals, whose detention two days ago was widely seen as a move by China to pressure Tokyo to release the captain ... The two-week standoff over the captain's detention near islands claimed by both nations had seemed to end Friday [24 September] when Japan gave in to Chinese pressure for his release. But no sooner had the plane carrying the captain landed in China than Beijing ratcheted up the pressure, this time by demanding an apology and compensation ... A Japanese foreign ministry spokesman: 'There is no territorial issue that needs to be resolved. The demand by the Chinese side for an apology and compensation is completely groundless and is utterly unacceptable.'
>
> (www.iht.com, 25 September 2010)

> After his [the captain's] release the Chinese foreign ministry issued a statement reiterating its 'strong protest' and what it called its 'indisputable' claim to the islands. The statement said: 'The Japanese side must make an apology and compensation for this incident.'
>
> (www.bbc.co.uk, 25 September 2010)

> Japan's prime minister has rejected China's demand for apology and compensation over the detention of a Chinese fishing boat captain, state media

said Sunday [26 September]. Japanese prime minister Naoto Kan: 'I have no intention of accepting [the demand] at all' ... Kan also said both countries should take a calm approach to the issue: 'It is important for both sides to act with a broader point of view' ... Kan's statement came after Japan's ministry of foreign affairs said Beijing's demand was 'completely groundless and is utterly unacceptable for Japan'. The foreign affairs ministry went on to assert Japanese jurisdiction over the islands where the captain was detained and declared that the dispute was handled in accordance with Japanese law ... [The captain] was detained earlier this month after his trawler collided with Japanese vessels near disputed islands in the East China Sea. He was freed on Friday [24 September]. Despite the call for an apology, China's foreign ministry said in a statement that the two sides should resolve the problems through dialogue and consultation, according to Chinese state media ... The arrest has increased tensions between the two countries, with Beijing accusing Japan of 'unlawful and invalid' arrest of the captain and his crew of fourteen, according to [China's state news agency] Xinhua. China considers the Daioyu Islands and most of the South China Sea its property, disputing neighbouring countries' claim. In Japan the islands are known as the Senkaku. The clash over territorial waters and islands – and the natural resources that go with them – is a flashpoint in the Asia-Pacific region.

(www.cnn.com, 26 September 2010)

Tensions between China and Japan over the arrest of a Chinese trawler captain took another turn for the worse on Sunday [26 September] as prime minister Naoto Kan of Japan rejected China's repeated demand that Tokyo apologize and offer compensation for the incident. The Chinese authorities also flexed their muscles on a wider front, becoming more assertive on trade policy, even as they continued to hold four Japanese nationals whose detention was widely seen as a move by China to put pressure on Tokyo to release the captain ... The unannounced halt on shipments of rare earth minerals to Japan continued over the weekend, while the Chinese commerce ministry imposed steep tariffs on poultry imports from the United States ... The Chinese commerce ministry's decision on poultry import tariffs concluded an investigation that the ministry had begun almost exactly a year ago, less than two days after President Barack Obama imposed steep tariffs on Chinese tyres ... The diplomatic standoff showed just how difficult it will be to overcome nationalistic sentiment stirred up by the trawler episode, which is affecting the deeply intertwined business ties between the two neighbours, which are the world's second and third largest economies, after that of the United States ... Beijing officials face intensifying political pressure to stand up for China's perceived national interests, as many Chinese have become increasingly outspoken and nationalistic in their postings on Chinese internet sites ... The two-week dispute over the captain's detention near islands claimed by both nations had seemed to end Friday [24 Septem-

Political developments

ber] when Japan gave in to Chinese pressure for his release. But no sooner had the plane carrying the captain landed in China than Beijing again ratcheted up the pressure, this time demanding an apology and compensation ... Mr Kan made the remarks after China reiterated its demand for an apology.

(www.iht.com, 26 September 2010; *IHT*, 27 September 2010, p. 16)

China–Japanese tensions over the arrest of a Chinese trawler captain re-escalated on Monday [27 September] when Japan said it would ask China to pay for repairs to two coastguard ships damaged by the trawler ... Japanese leaders had sought to minimize the episode, saying that the Chinese captain's release was a decision made by local prosecutors. Those assertions were met with broad scepticism, with many here [in Japan] holding the view that Japan capitulated to aggressive Chinese pressure.

(www.iht.com, 27 September 2010)

Japan will ask China to pay for damage to two patrol vessels caused by a collision with a Chinese trawler in disputed waters, Tokyo has said ... Japan said it believed the Chinese trawler had deliberately rammed the Japanese vessels ... Japanese prime minister Naoto Kan said the captain had been released without charge to promote 'mutually beneficial' ties with China. Beijing had cut off ministerial-level contacts between the two countries and thousands of Chinese tourists pulled out of trips to Japan. Concerts by Japan's top boy band SMAP due to take place in Shanghai were cancelled by the Chinese organizers.

(www.bbc.co.uk, 27 September 2010)

After weeks of escalating diplomatic tensions between Japan and China over the detention of a Chinese fishing captain, China appeared to ease up on the invective slightly on Tuesday [28 September] by calling on Tokyo to work together to resolve what has become a messy dispute over territorial sovereignty, compensation for damaged boats and such intangibles as wounded national pride. A Chinese foreign ministry spokeswoman: 'China highly values China–Japan relations. But safeguarding bilateral relations requires that the two sides meet halfway and requires Japan to take candid and practical actions' ... The comments were gentle in comparison to previous admonishments and threats by the Chinese, including a warning of 'full consequences' by the normally taciturn Chinese premier, Wen Jiabao, should Japan fail to acquiesce to its demands. The latest comments came a few hours after the Japanese prime minister insisted that there was nothing to discuss when it came to sovereignty over the string of islands in the East China Sea that both countries claim as their own. Foreign minister Seiji Maehara told parliament: 'No territorial issue exists' ... The imbroglio has been raging since 8 September when the Japanese arrested the Chinese trawler captain during a confrontation that may or may not have involved the captain intentionally ramming his ship into Japanese patrol vessels.

(www.iht.com, 28 September 2010; *IHT*, 29 September 2010, p. 5)

'The anniversary of Japan's invasion of China's north-eastern provinces in 1931 ... [was] on 18 September' (www.iht.com, 29 September 2010).

> An official at a trading house in Japan said early Wednesday [29 September] there were signs that Chinese authorities were issuing new export licences for rare earth shipments to Japan ... China's commerce ministry has steadfastly denied that China has imposed a ban on exports, which would violate WTO rules ... On Sunday [26 September] Chen Deming, China's commerce minister, said in an interview on Chinese television that the government had complied with WTO rules by not ordering a ban on rare earth exports to Japan. But he seemed to hint that a halt on exports might have occurred anyway when he said: 'I believe entrepreneurs, they will have their own feelings, and they will do their own thing' ... There are thirty-two companies with rare earth export licences in China, and ten of them are foreign companies. Mr Chen was not asked why foreign companies would have felt the need to stop shipments ... Rare earths are used to make many products ... Demand has risen in the last decade for their use in clean energy technology, like generators for large wind turbines and lightweight electric motors for cars ... The dispute comes at a politically difficult time for China, with the approach of National Day on 1 October, the anniversary of the creation of the People's Republic of China in 1949 after more than a half-century of Japanese incursions into the Asian mainland.
>
> (www.iht.com, 29 September 2010)

> China's customs agency has made minor procedural changes in its processing of applications for exports of rare earths to Japan, but still has not allowed regular shipments to resume, three rare earth industry officials said Wednesday [29 September] ... The latest procedural changes are not likely to allow more than a trickle of shipments, unless followed by further adjustments in Chinese policy to restore normal trade, the industry officials said. Extra Chinese customs agency controls on rare earth exports are separate from a broader decision by Chinese customs agents to step up their inspections of a wide range of shipments to and from Japan.
>
> (www.iht.com, 29 September 2010)

'[The islands in dispute are] roughly equidistant between Okinawa and Taiwan' (*FT*, 30 September 2010, p. 15).

'China needs to resolve the case of four Japanese citizens it is holding as the first step toward repairing ties that have been strained over a territorial dispute, the Japanese foreign minister, Seiji Maehara, said Wednesday [29 September]' (*IHT*, 30 September 2010, p. 6).

> China on Thursday [30 September] released three Japanese nationals after they admitted illegally entering a Chinese military zone and expressed regret, state-run media said. Another Japanese national, who worked with the three, remained under house arrest for illegally videotaping military targets and an investigation was continuing, the Xinhua news agency said

... All four Japanese nationals were arrested in Hebei province on 23 September ... By late afternoon Thursday China released no further details about the four Japanese nationals, or a Chinese co-worker who went missing at the same time as the arrests. The Chinese national was presumed arrested as well. All five worked for Fujita Corp., a mid-sized Japanese construction company. The four Japanese employees were sent to China for a Japanese government project to reclaim World War II weapons left by Japan's Imperial Army, Fujita said. Goldman Sachs Group acquired Fujita in April 2009. Beijing says the Diaoyu Islands and most of the South China Sea belong to China, disputing neighbouring countries' claims ... Japan has recently urged China to not unilaterally develop a gas field in the disputed area of the East China Sea, Japan's ministry of foreign affairs said Thursday.

(www.cnn.com, 30 September 2010)

The Japanese employer of the four men, a Tokyo-based construction company, said they had been preparing a bid to dispose of chemical weapons left in China by invading Japanese forces at the end of World War II. China arrested the men, accusing them of entering a closed military zone. According to state media, the three Japanese nationals released on Thursday [30 September] admitted violating Chinese law.

(www.bbc.co.uk, 30 September 2010)

In announcing the releases, the official news service, Xinhua, said the three men had admitted that they had violated Chinese law and 'showed regret for their mistake'. But it said one of the men ... would remain under 'house arrest' while the authorities continued their investigation. Xinhua described the accusations against him as 'illegally videotaping military targets' ... Officials at Fujita, the construction company that employed the men, said they were inspecting a potential construction site for a plant that would process abandoned chemical weapons. Fujita built a similar plant in Nanjing that disposes of munitions abandoned by the Japanese army during its occupation of China, the company said in a press release. The release of the three men comes amid signs that the diplomatic standoff between Japan and China may be easing. In recent days the official rhetoric from Beijing has dropped a notch while Chinese exports of rare earth metals to Japan ... have resumed.

(www.iht.com, 30 September 2010)

Japan's prime minister, Naoto Kan, has expressed concern over China's maritime activities and military build-up ... He called on China to act as a 'responsible member of the international community' ... Mr Kan told Japan's parliament (on 1 October): 'The rise of China has been remarkable in recent years. But we are concerned about its strengthening defence capabilities without transparency and accelerating maritime activities spanning from the Indian Ocean to the East China Sea ... The Senkaku Islands are an integral part of our country, historically and under international law' ... He said good relations with China – Japan's largest trading partner – were vital to both countries, but said China must act as a responsible member of the international community. Japan needed to adopt more active foreign and defence policies to deal with 'uncertainty and instability that exist in areas surrounding our country', Mr Kan said. His speech followed remarks from China's foreign ministry spokesman on Thursday [30 September] urging Japan to 'stop making irresponsible remarks and safeguard the larger interests of bilateral relations with concrete actions'. The spokesman said: 'We are willing to resolve our disputes through friendly negotiations but the Chinese government's and people's will and resolve are unswerving on issues involving China's territorial integrity and sovereignty.'

(www.bbc.co.uk, 1 October 2010)

Prime minister Naoto Kan of Japan in a policy speech on Friday [1 October]: '[Both sides should] proceed with calm ... We hope and expect that China will speak and act in a manner befitting its role as a responsible member of the international community ... [Japan has] concerns regarding the recent build-up of China's defensive capabilities, which lack transparency, as well as China's increasingly ambitious maritime activities in an area stretching from the Indian Ocean to the East China Sea.'

(*FT*, 2 October 2010, p. 8)

Anti-China protesters gathered Saturday [2 October] in Tokyo and six other major cities in Japan to rally against what it calls an invasion of disputed islands that both claim are part of their territories ... The rally was organized by Toshio Tamogami, a former Japanese Chief of Staff for the Self Defence Force.

(www.cnn.com, 2 October 2010)

The shipping ban was still in effect on Monday evening [4 October] in Japan, an industry official said, though a trickle of shipments seemed to be seeping out as a result of uneven enforcement of the ban by customs officers at various ports. China has allowed exports of Chinese-made rare earth magnets and other rare earth products to Japan, but not semi-processed rare earth ores that would enable Japanese companies to make products ... Heightened interest in alternative sources has been an impetus to plans to reopen or establish new rare earth mines in a handful of countries around the world, including South Africa, Australia and Canada, along with the United States, where Molycorp intends to expand a mine in Mountain Pass, California. The Japanese trading company Sojitz is negotiating the rights to a rare earth mine in Vietnam, while the industrial conglomerate Sumitomo plans to work with Kazakhstan's government to recover rare earth elements from uranium ore residues. Japan is also pushing for new manufacturing processes that do not require rare earths ... In Kosaka Dowa Holdings ... has built a recycling plant ... which started fully operating two years ago ... Recent problems with Chinese supplies of rare earths ... [have created] opportunities for Kosaka. The town's hopes for a mining comeback lie not underground but in what Japan refers to as urban mining – recycling the valuable metals and minerals from the country's huge stockpiles of used electronics and computers ... The salvaged parts come from around Japan and overseas, including the United States.

(www.iht.com, 4 October 2010)

The Chinese and Japanese prime ministers held an impromptu meeting in a hallway at a conference in Europe ... Chinese premier Wen Jiabao and Japanese prime minister Naoto Kan met briefly Monday [4 October] in Brussels, where both were attending the Asia–Europe Meeting and agreed to improve their ties. A statement issued by the Chinese foreign ministry: 'Both parties agreed to strengthen non-governmental exchanges and communications between the governments, and to hold high-level Chinese–Japanese talks at the appropriate time' ... Both sides remained firm on the territorial dispute. The statement said Mr Wen reiterated that the uninhabited islands – called Diaoyu by China and Senkaku by Japan – belong to China, while Japan's Kyodo news agency reported that Mr Kan said they were Japanese territory. In Tokyo Mr Kan's office confirmed that the two met for about twenty-five minutes ... The two met sitting on chairs in a hallway. The meeting was not on any public schedule ... In Tokyo on Tuesday [5 October] Japanese foreign minister Seiji Maehara reiterated Tokyo's claim of sovereignty over the islands and called on Beijing to meet and discuss ways the countries could avoid similar spats in the future. He said: 'There is no territorial dispute in the East China Sea. But I understand the importance of Japanese–Chinese relations, and if on both sides we can put our heads together we can find ways to prevent such unfortunate incidents from happening again in the future ... The Asia-Pacific Economic Co-operation forum summit ... which Chinese president Hu Jintao will attend ... [is to be held] in Yokohama on 13–14 November.

(www.iht.com, 5 October 2010)

'The leaders agreed that "deterioration in bilateral ties over maritime collisions is not desirable", Japan's Kyodo news agency said. They also agreed to "hold high-level talks on a regular basis" but no new meeting was set' (www.bbc.co.uk, 5 October 2010).

'Chinese state media quoted prime minister Wen Jiabao as saying the uninhabited islands ... had been "Chinese territory since ancient times". Prime minister Naoto Kan told reporters he stressed to Mr Wen the islets were an integral part of Japan's territory' (*FT*, 6 October 2010, p. 11).

Prime minister Wen Jiabao of China has told European political and business leaders that China has not imposed any bans of exports of rare earths for political purposes, and that it has no intention to stop exports in the future, according to a report on Friday [8 October] in *China Daily* ... an official English-language newspaper ... Mr Wen made his remarks in a speech on Wednesday [6 October] at a China–EU business summit in Brussels ... Prime minister Wen Jiabao: 'China is not using rare earths as a bargaining chip. We aim for the world's sustainable development' ... In his speech Wednesday Mr Wen defended the limits on exports by saying China's supply of rare earths must be carefully managed. He said: 'It is necessary to exercise management and control over the rare earth industry, but there won't be any embargo. What we pursue is to satisfy not only domestic demand but also the global demand for rare earth. We should not only stand from the present, but should also look forward to the future. If the rare earth minerals were used up, how would the world and China deal with the problem?' ... As of Monday night some rare earth shipments were still being blocked, an industry official said at the time ... The products being allowed through to Japan early this week were Chinese-made rare earth magnets and other rare earth products, but not semi-processed rare earth ores.

(www.iht.com, 8 October 2010)

[There was] front-page coverage on the rare earth comments [by prime minister Wen Jiabao] in *China Daily* ... Rare earth industry executives said that as of Thursday [7 October] Chinese customs officials were still refusing to let rare earth minerals be loaded aboard ships bound for Japan ... [Chinese] commerce minister Chen Deming suggested in a television interview on 26 September that Chinese entrepreneurs in the rare earth industry might have halted shipments because of their own feelings toward Japan. There are thirty-two companies in China with export licences for rare earths and ten of them are foreign. Mr Deming did not address why the ten foreign companies would have strong feelings toward Japan, or why all companies in the Chinese industry halted shipments on the same day, 21 September ... Throughout the halt on exports of rare earths minerals, China has allowed continued exports of manufactured products that use rare earths, like powerful magnets, and highly purified rare earth metals ... Even before questions arose over the exports to Japan in late September, China had been putting tighter caps on rare earth exports for the last five years. When the export halt was imposed, the quota for 2010 was within a month-and-a-half of being exhausted, but now shipments could continue into November if customs officials allow a resumption soon ... China has been laying the legal groundwork for defending its export quotas as an environmental measure if they are challenged at the WTO ... Rare earth is a misnomer: some of these seventeen minerals are rare, particularly those needed for clean energy applications, but others are not, and the biggest problems are that rare earth deposits are expensive and difficult to mine and almost always laced with radioactive thorium that is hard to separate and dispose of safely.

(www.iht.com, 9 October 2010)

[On Saturday 9 October] China released on bail the last of four Japanese men held on suspicion of intruding into a restricted military area in the northern province of Hebei ... He was instructed 'to write a statement of repentance' and had already 'left the place where he was residing under surveillance after going through legal procedures', Xinhua reported ... [He] had been detained 'for intruding [into] the Chinese military zone and illegal filming military targets', it added. The Japanese news agency, Kyodo, quoted the Japanese embassy in Beijing as saying he was in 'good condition' and might be back in Japan as early as Sunday [10 October] ... The other three were freed at the end of September after reportedly admitting they had violated Chinese law. A Japanese construction firm said they were preparing a bid to dispose of chemical weapons from World War II.

(www.bbc.co.uk, 9 October 2010)

Chinese officials continued to bar all exports of rare earth minerals to Japan over the weekend, industry officials said, but ... the last one of four employees of a Japanese construction company who had been detained near a Chinese military area returned to Japan on Sunday [10 October] ... Chinese officials have consistently taken the position that they have not imposed any regulations preventing rare earth exports; any such regulations could be easily challenged at the WTO ... Even before questions arose over the exports to Japan in late September, China had been putting tighter caps on rare earths exports for the last five years. When the export halt was imposed, the quota for 2010 was within a month-and-a-half of being exhausted. But shipments could continue into November if customs officials allow a resumption soon.

(www.iht.com, 10 October 2010)

Japan announced earlier this month [October] that it had developed the first high-performance motor, free of rare earths, for hybrid vehicles ... China could keep its dominant grip for years. It holds 35 per cent of global reserves, but supplies over 95 per cent of demand for rare earth oxides, of which 60 per cent is domestic, according to Industrial Minerals Company of Australia, a consultancy. Just as important, Chinese companies, many of them state controlled, have advanced in their quest to make China the world leader in processing rare earth metals into finished materials ... China recently cut its rare earth export quotas by 72 per cent for the second half of this year [2010] ... Chinese officials say that mass extraction of rare earths is causing extensive environmental damage in China and that is why the government has tightened controls over exploration, production and trade. Poisonous chemicals are used to mine rare earths, putting local water supplies and public health at risk ... Until around 1990 the United States was self-sufficient in rare earths and the world leader in processing and use. Yet within a decade the United States became more than 90 per cent reliant on rare earth imported either directly from China or from countries that received plant-feed materials from China. Environmental and regulatory problems made mining and processing unattractive at the rare earth site at Mountain Pass in California, which closed in 2002 ... Although tagged 'rare', rare earths are relatively common and widely dispersed around the world. However, in contrast to ordinary base and precious metals, they are seldom found concentrated in exploitable ore deposits.

(*IHT*, 11 October 2010, p. 8)

As a three-week-long Chinese suspension in exports of crucial minerals to Japan continues, American and Japanese trade officials have been considering whether to file cases against China at the WTO. Trade lawyers say an embargo case could be brought to the WTO, although they said it might be a hard case to win because China has not acknowledged the halt in exports through any documents or public statements ... China has been reducing its rare earth export quotas since 2006 and has imposed steep taxes on the exports ... The export restrictions have given a competitive advantage to manufacturers in China that use rare earths to make their products, while putting foreign rivals at a disadvantage, according to a little-noticed WTO study last June [2010] ... There are seventeen rare earth elements, and they are used to make things like hybrid cars, mobile phones and the special television screens recently unveiled by Japanese companies that provide a 3-D appearance without the need for special glasses ... Chen Deming, the commerce minister of China, said in a rare television interview on 26 September that his country fully complied with WTO rules ... Shortages could start to appear at some Japanese manufacturers at the end of this week, rare earth industry officials said. Japanese officials have hinted that they might pursue their own WTO case against China if shipments do not resume soon. But the way China has gone about the unannounced halt in exports – with Chinese customs officials blocking all shipments at ports but with no actual issuance of new regulations – makes the suspension hard to challenge at a WTO dispute resolution panel in Geneva, trade lawyers said ... Akihiro Ohata, the Japanese minister for trade and industry, told reporters on Tuesday [12 October] that if normal shipments did not resume by the end of the week he would consider dispatching his deputy to Beijing. He said: 'We will certainly take steps to address the situation, including possible direct negotiations with the Chinese' ... He did not refer to any steps to involve the WTO. Despite their name, most rare earths are not particularly rare, but so far most of the rest of the world has left it to China to do the dirty work of mining them. New mines elsewhere are likely to take three to five years to reach full production, according to industry executives. And despite their growing importance to technology manufacturers, rare earths have not been a particularly lucrative commodity. The world market for rare earths was only worth $1.5 billion last year [2009], before the recent halt in Chinese shipments sent prices soaring. Only a fraction of an ounce of rare earths is needed for some applications, like the power-steering motors in cars. China's longer-term restrictions on rare earth exports, involving quotas and taxes, came under criticism after the WTO secretariat in Geneva issued its review of China's trade policies in June. The WTO reviews each member country's policies once every two years. The report said: 'Whether intended or not, exports restraints for whatever reason tend to reduce export volumes of the targeted products and divert supplies to the domestic market' ... The timing of any WTO effort by the Obama administration could be driven by a statutory requirement to respond by 24 October [2010] to a petition by the United States Steelworkers union asking that the White House challenge China's clean energy policies at the WTO. The lead exhibits in the steelworkers' petition criticize the rare earth quotas as well as export taxes on rare earths for supposedly forcing manufacturers to move the production of clean energy technologies like wind turbine manufacturing to China. WTO rules bar exports and export taxes in most cases, and particularly prohibit exports restrictions to force other countries to buy more value-added products. But the rules have an exception for the conservation of scarce natural resources, and premier Wen Jiabao suggested in Europe last week that this was China's goal in restricting rare earth exports.

(www.iht.com, 14 October 2010)

Japanese prime minister Naoto Kan has said the release by China of the detained Nobel Peace Prize winner Liu Xiaobo is 'undesirable' ... China described Mr Liu as a criminal who had broken China's laws, and said the award was an insult to China's judicial system ... Liu Xiaobo was sentenced to eleven years in jail on subversion charges last December [2009], after co-writing Charter 08, a call for political reform ... Mr Kan said: 'From the viewpoint that universal human rights should be protected across national borders, it is desirable [that Mr Liu be released]' ... The comments from Japan's prime minister come soon after the two countries brought a tentative end to a damaging row over disputed territories in the sea between them.

(www.bbc.co.uk, 14 October 2010)

Demonstrations have been held in China and Japan about islands claimed by both countries in the East China Sea. In Tokyo demonstrators rallied against China's claim to the islands and delivered a note to China's embassy ... During Saturday's [16 October] demonstration in Tokyo hundreds of people carried banners reading 'Japan is in danger' and 'Don't forgive invader China' ... In China protesters chanted anti-Japanese slogans in three cities ... [namely] Changdu, Xian and Zhengzhou. Several thousand protesters carried banners with slogans such as 'Overthrow Japanese imperialism' and 'Protect the Diaoyu Islands'. Witnesses said at least one Japanese restaurant had its windows broken. In the past Chinese authorities have orchestrated large-scale demonstrations over the uninhabited islands, which are know as Senkaku in Japan and may have rich oil and gas deposits.

(www.bbc.co.uk, 16 October 2010)

Since 21 September Chinese customs officials have prevented the shipment of containers of rare earth minerals to Japan, and they have continued to block shipments through this weekend, although some smuggling has taken place, according to rare earth officials. A trickle of rare earths ... is still reaching Japan because of smuggling. The Japanese government has threatened to lodge a formal protest with China on Monday unless exports are allowed to resume. But even when exports resume, they may only last for another month or so, as the thirty-two exporters of rare earths in China had used three-quarters of their export quotas for this year [2010] by the end of August.

(www.iht.com, 17 October 2010)

The Chinese government plans a further reduction, of up to 30 per cent, next year [2011] in its quotas for exports of rare earth minerals, to try to conserve dwindling reserves of the materials, the official *China Daily* newspaper said on Tuesday [19 October]. Plans for smaller export quotas come just four days after American trade officials announced they would investigate whether China is violating international trade rules with a wide range of policies to help its clean energy industries. One of the policies under investigation involves China's steady reductions in rare earth export quotas since 2005 and its imposition of steep taxes on these exports ... A [Chinese] commerce ministry official told a conference in Beijing on Saturday [16 October] that China had sizeable reserves of the lighter elements among the seventeen rare earth elements, but only had fifteen or twenty years' worth of reserves left of medium and heavy rare earths and needed to conserve those. Light rare earths are used in lower-tech applications like oil refining and glass manufacturing, while medium and heavy earths are used more in clean energy and military applications ... The secretary-general of the Chinese Rare Earths Industry Association predicted at the conference on Tuesday that domestic demand for rare earths in China would soar to 130,000 tonnes in 2015, from 75,000 tonnes now ... Export quotas for this year [2010] total just 30,300 tonnes.

(www.iht.com, 19 October 2010)

'Deng Xiaoping ... the architect of China's economic transformation ... declared in 1992: "There is oil in the Middle East; there is rare earth in China"' (www.iht.com, 18 October 2010).

[On Monday 18 October] Japanese prime minister Naoto Kan expressed regret over anti-Japanese protest in China in the last few days. Mr Kan said he had requested protection for Japanese companies in China after reports said several company premises had been damaged ... Beijing authorities also expressed 'deep concern' over anti-Chinese protests held in Tokyo at the weekend ... Mr Kan's remarks follow reports that several Japanese business premises were damaged during demonstrations in some Chinese cities (Changdu, Xian, Zhengzhou and Mianyang) in support of China's claims to disputed islands in the East China Sea. The Japanese news agency, Kyodo, reported that protesters in Sichuan threw stones at a Japanese restaurant and broke the windows of Japanese-made cars.

(www.bbc.co.uk, 18 October 2010)

Thousands of Chinese joined in sometimes violent protests Saturday [16 October], hoisting signs protesting Japan's claim on what China calls the Diaoyu Islands. Japan calls them the Senkaku Islands. On Monday [18 October] dozens of young men scuffled with police who were trying to contain protesters in the central Chinese city of Wuhan ... Hundreds of youths – mostly young men – marched with flags and signs, some of which called for a boycott of Japanese goods, Japanese prime minister Naoto Kan said Monday that the protests were 'regrettable'. He said Japan asked China to ensure the safety and security of Japanese citizens and companies in China, and that the two countries must work 'calmly' to improve ties ... Tolerated by Chinese authorities, the demonstrations began peacefully but appeared to spin out of control with some marchers carrying crude, racist banners ... In Chengdu, a Chinese woman who was eating in a fast food restaurant along a demonstration route was forced to strip because marchers mistook her traditional dress for a kimono. She undressed in a bathroom and borrowed clothes from others ... Later the government warned the public to obey the law when expressing their nationalist feelings ... Japanese retailers Ito-Yokado and Isetan said protesters in the south-western city of Chengdu broke windows and showcases in their stores ... The website of the anti-Japanese China Federation for Defending Diaoyutai posted a photo that showed protesters in Chengdu holding a red and yellow canvas banner that called for Japan to be 'wiped off the face of the earth'. Others used English and Chinese profanities and urged violence against Japanese ... It was not clear whether the organizers of the protest in Chengdu had permission to demonstrate ... While allowing the demonstrations, the government also tried to quickly distance itself from the violence and offensive language of some protesters, posting a statement late Saturday that called for 'rational' patriotism ... China's state-run Xinhua news agency said more than 2,000 people protested in Chengdu and thousands of college students gathered in the northern city of Xian.

(www.iht.com, 18 October 2010)

Security forces patrolled the streets of many parts of China Tuesday [19 October] after three days of rowdy anti-Japanese protests. The protests began Saturday [16 October] and lasted through Monday [18 October]. Most of the demonstrations took place in central China, which is home to many Japanese factories. While reports on the size of the protests varied, Japanese news agency Kyodo placed the number at around 10,000 ... People in various locations chanted anti-Japanese slogans ... and called for a boycott of Japanese products. Chinese security forces protectively surrounded the Japanese embassy in Beijing.

(www.cnn.com, 19 October 2010)

'China recently surpassed Japan to become the world's second largest economy after the United States ... China is now Japan's biggest trading partner' (www.iht.com, 29 September 2010).

Political developments

> China has surpassed Japan in terms of nominal GDP, making the Chinese economy the world's second largest. Second quarter [of 2010] output in China came in at $1.337 trillion, to Japan's $1.288 trillion ... For comparison, America's second quarter nominal output was $3.522 trillion ... Japan's economy fell behind China's at market exchange rates in the second quarter. It has been number three in purchasing-power parity [PPP] terms for some time.
>
> (www.economist.com, 16 August 2010)

'[In purchasing-power parity] terms China overtook Japan almost a decade ago, and the exact moment when China's nominal US dollar GDP surpasses Japan's has a lot to do with exchange rates and technical statistical revisions' (*FT*, 17 August 2010, p. 5).

'For 2009 the IMF listed the United States as the world's largest economy at $14.26 trillion, followed by Japan at $5.07 trillion and China at $4.91 trillion' (www.cnn.com, 16 August 2010).

'[China's] annual output is expected to exceed $5.5 trillion this year [2010]' (IHT, 18 August 2010, p. 1).

> Just five years ago China's GDP was about $2.3 trillion, about half of Japan's ... [But China's] *per capita* income is more on a par with those of impoverished nations like Algeria, El Salvador and Albania – which, along with China, are close to $3,600 – than that of the United States, where it is about $46,000.
>
> (www.iht.com, 16 August 2010)

23 September 2010.

> A US-based rights group has urged Vietnam to investigate what it called widespread police brutality ... Human Rights Watch: 'Police brutality is being reported at an alarming rate in every region of Vietnam, raising serious concerns that these abuses are both systematic and widespread' ... In a statement Human Rights Watch said it had documented nineteen cases of police brutality in the past twelve months, resulting in the deaths of fifteen people ... The report comes in the wake of a high profile case in which a man arrested for riding a motorbike without a helmet died in police custody ... [He] was stopped by traffic police ... on 23 July and taken in for questioning ... Human Rights Watch said that in many cases those who died in custody had been arrested for minor offences, like traffic violations or petty thievery. The group also accused police of using excessive force in public areas. In May a forty-five-year-old man and a twelve-year-old boy were shot and killed ... when police tried to disperse crowds protesting against a government industrial project.
>
> (www.iht.com, 23 September 2010)

6 October 2010.

> Vietnam has demanded the unconditional release of nine fishermen detained by China last month [September], Vietnamese media reported today [6

October], as tension rose in the latest dispute in the South China Sea. The demand came a week before a meeting in Hanoi that will bring together defence ministers of the region as well the US Defence Secretary, Robert Gates. China has accused the fishermen, who were taken near the disputed Paracel Islands, of breaking the law by fishing with explosives and said they would be released after a fine is paid. Vietnam has responded by describing the arrest as 'irrational'. A Vietnamese official: 'Fishing boat QNg 66478TS was carrying out its ordinary operations in Vietnam's Haong Sa [Paracel] archipelago sovereign waters. There were no explosives on the boat. On 15 September Vietnam's embassy in China received a note from China which did not mention that the boat was carrying explosives' ... Vietnam says the fishermen were on a routine fishing trip in Vietnamese waters, using fishing nets and lamps. Its foreign ministry has sent a diplomatic note to the Chinese embassy in Hanoi, stressing that the arrest had seriously violated Vietnam's sovereignty.

(www.guardian.co.uk, 6 October 2010)

China is reported to be building an anti-ship ballistic base in the southern province of Guangdong, with missiles capable of reaching the Philippines and Vietnam. The base is regarded as an effort to enforce China's territorial claims to vast areas of the South China Sea claimed by other nations – and to threaten US aircraft carriers that now patrol the area unchallenged ... Chinese military leaders, who earlier this year [2010] snubbed a proposal by Defence Secretary Robert Gates to visit Beijing, signalled last week that the visit would be scheduled soon. And Wednesday [6 October] Xinhua, the state-run press agency, said defence minister Liang Guanglie would meet with Mr Gates next week at a security conference in Hanoi.

(*IHT*, 8 October 2010, p. 6)

Last week Vietnam demanded the release of a fishing boat and nine crew members arrested a month ago near disputed islands. China has said that the crew must pay a fine, and Vietnam has asserted that the crew members have been mistreated.

(www.iht.com, 10 October 2010)

An explosion at the scene of a planned fireworks display in Vietnam's capital has killed at least four people and injured three others, officials say. The blast occurred just before noon at the My Dinh stadium, where Hanoi's 1,000th anniversary celebrations were to culminate on Sunday [10 October 2010], witnesses said. The stadium was filled with people rehearsing for the ceremony. It has now been sealed by military police. Unconfirmed reports said foreign technicians could be among the dead ... The authorities have spent $63 million preparing Hanoi for its ten days of millennium celebrations. The fireworks display was to be the grand finale.

(www.bbc.co.uk, 6 October 2010)

78 *Political developments*

> A fireworks explosion in Hanoi killed four people and injured three others Wednesday [6 October], state media reported. The blast occurred ... when a shipment of fireworks blew up near My Dinh National Stadium, one of the twenty-nine sites in the capital city where pyrotechnics were planned for Hanoi's 1,000th anniversary, the official Vietnam News reported. The explosion was blamed on 'carelessness' during the transport of two containers of fireworks, the news agency said.
>
> (www.cnn.com, 7 October 2010)

> 'One Singaporean and two Vietnamese were among the dead, while another body was burned beyond recognition and would require DNA testing for positive identification, police said. The injured included technicians from Singapore and Germany' (*The Independent*, 7 October 2010, p. 30).

10 October 2010. The 1,000th anniversary of Hanoi.

> [Hanoi's] population is more than 6 million, with some of the most expensive and most densely populated real estate in the world ... As an urban landscape ... Hanoi seems mostly to be succeeding, where other Asian cities have failed, in integrating development with preservation. Zoning laws have maintained the low-rise heart of the city with its shade trees and broad sidewalks. Most development has been shifted to the western suburbs. Many of the elegant villas of the old French quarter have been preserved, and the bustling Ancient Quarter, choked with tourists and commerce, survives. The area around Hoan Kiem Lake has so far resisted development ... Everyone in Hanoi ... [complains] about the traffic ... It is a rule of thumb [it is said] ... that for a city this size roads should cover 15 per cent of land space. In Hanoi the figure is just 5 per cent.
>
> (www.iht.com, 8 October 2010)

> The 1,000th anniversary of the founding of Hanoi [is being celebrated] ... Over that millennium, China and Vietnam have a long history of bloody competition. One that was buried for the years that Vietnam was aided by China in pushing back American involvement ... China was an ally of North Vietnam in its war against the United States in the 1960s and 1970s.
>
> (www.iht,com, 10 October 2010)

> Celebrations [are] being held from 1 to 10 October, when the capital officially turns 1,000 years old. There are no more international tourists than usual though ... According to government estimates, Vietnam sees 3.3 million tourist arrivals each year. This number might be inflated by the sort of old-fashioned processing methods that can count even a foreign resident's visa as a tourist arrival ... Vietnam has a return rate of just 5 per cent compared to Thailand's 50 per cent ... [But Vietnam] only reopened to the world in 1986 – long after Thailand was a vastly popular destination. But poor marketing of services and overall problems with infrastructure, 'same-

Political developments 79

same' package trips and various tourist-targeting scams have kept Vietnam as a one-off destination, when it could be much more.

(www.economist.com, 9 October 2010)

US Defence Secretary Robert Gates landed on Sunday [10 October] in Vietnam ... Mr Gates has scheduled private talks with his Vietnamese counterpart [General Phung Quang Thanh] during a conference of defence ministers from across the region, where a key issue will be how to manage Beijing's expanded claims of maritime rights in the South China Sea ... Vietnam's worries over Chinese encroachment can be seen in its recent choices for weapons purchases. Last year [2009] Vietnam signed deals with Russia to buy six Kilo-class diesel-powered hunter-killer submarines for $1.8 billion and eight Sukhoi jet fighters for another $500 million ... Both weapons are designed for protecting territorial and air space, and the arms deals illustrate Russia's desire to support nations trying to curb China's power. The United States ... has offered little in the way of weapons, mostly focusing its assistance on military training and officer education ... China is expected to offer an invitation to visit Beijing ... China froze military relations with the United States earlier this year [2010] when the Obama administration announced $6.4 billion in arms sales to Taiwan.

(www.iht.com, 10 October 2010)

Vietnam has been at pains to reassure China ... that it would have no alliances, military bases or military coalitions that threaten it ... Trade relations [between Vietnam and the United States] were normalized in 2006. Ports calls by American Navy ships have become more frequent since the first one in 2003.

(www.iht.com, 10 October 2010)

Washington has continuing human rights concerns with Vietnam ... [there are] American concerns over human rights abuses in Vietnam ... The Vietnamese often use the phrases 'peaceful evolution' and the 'colour revolutions', expressions that refer to its view that the collapses of the Soviet Union and other European communist governments were brought about at least partly by outside support for democracy and human rights.

(www.iht.com, 10 October 2010; *IHT*, 11 October 2010, p. 2)

11-12 October 2010.

The defence ministers of South-east Asian nations, China, Japan and the United States have met in Vietnam for the first time ... US Defence Secretary Robert Gates met his Chinese counterpart Liang Guanglie ... On the sidelines of the meeting in Hanoi, Mr Liang and the Japanese defence minister Toshimi Kitazawa held their first direct talks since a heated maritime dispute last month [September] ... Mr Liang later said the talks were 'very good' and were positive for bilateral ties. Meanwhile, China is mounting a large military exercise involving more than 30,000 soldiers and the deployment of transport planes, fighter jets and attack helicopters.

(www.bbc.co.uk, 11 October 2010)

US Defence Secretary Robert Gates met here [in Hanoi] on Monday [11 October] with his Chinese counterpart to make a case for restoring military-to-military relations frozen by Beijing because of American arms sales to Taiwan. On the eve of a conference for Asian defence ministers, Mr Gates spent half an hour with General Liang Guanglie of China ... The defence secretary said the Chinese official had invited him to Beijing. Mr Gates is expected to make the visit next year [2011] ... Chinese behaviour across the region has figured heavily in the run-up to Tuesday's session of defence ministers of the Association of South-east Asian Nations, in particular feuds over sovereignty claims regarding islands, fishing rights and mineral wealth in regional seas. Mr Gates said (noting that the topic was expected to be discussed during Tuesday's session [on 12 October]): 'We have a shared interest in freedom of navigation and access to maritime domain' ... Mr Gates has sought to balance, on the one hand, his desire to restore military relations with China and, on the other, American support for international law and the right of passage through common air space and sea lanes in the face of Chinese assertions of expanded sovereignty ... Mr Gates's day was spent in a sequence of private sessions with counterparts not only from China but also from Japan, Vietnam and the Philippines that were consciously low key if still high-level.

(www.iht.com, 11 October 2010)

US and Chinese defence chiefs locked horns over US arms sales on Taiwan on Monday [11 October] as they met for the first time since Beijing lifted a freeze on US military ties. US Defence Secretary Robert Gates called the meeting with his counterpart, Liang Guanglie, constructive and accepted an invitation to visit China next year [2011]. But China said both acknowledged 'problems and obstacles' in military relations. Top among them, in China's view, are US arms sales to Taiwan ... The United States switched diplomatic recognition from Taipei to Beijing in 1979, recognizing 'One China'. But the United States remains Taiwan's biggest arms supplier and is obliged by the 1979 Taiwan Relations Act to help in the island's defence ... [A spokesman for] China's defence ministry told reporters after the meeting: 'Minister Liang pointed out that arms sales to Taiwan were an impediment to wider and deeper bilateral defence relations' ... Gates also raised eyebrows with a public speech he made on Monday in which he indirectly challenged China's insistence on a bilateral approach to territorial disputes. Gates and Liang will attend Asia-Pacific defence talks on Tuesday [12 October]. Gates told an audience at Vietnam National University: 'Relying on the bilateral relationships is not enough – we need multilateral institutions' ... China has in the past insisted its territorial disputes be handled bilaterally, not in a multilateral forum. Brunei, Malaysia, the Philippines, Taiwan and Vietnam all claim parts of the potentially oil and gas rich South China Sea as well as areas like the Spratly and Paracel Islands. Beijing effectively claims ownership over the whole maritime region. Gates and

Liang did not discuss maritime territorial disputes in the South China Sea and it was unclear to what extent they would be discussed on Tuesday at the meeting of defence chiefs from the ten-member Association of South-east Asian Nations (Asean) plus the United States, China, Japan, South Korea, Russia, India, Australia and New Zealand.

(www.iht.com, 11 October 2010)

US Defence Secretary Robert Gates has accepted an invitation to visit China and Australian officials said military ties with Vietnam have improved. The progress in regional defence links is taking place as part of a major Asian security meeting under way in Hanoi ... Vietnamese prime minister Nguyen Tan Dung: 'This meeting is a new and important step forward in Asean's defence co-operation' ... [Vietnam] holds the current chairmanship of the grouping.

(www.bbc.co.uk, 12 October 2010)

The United States and China sought to defuse tensions over disputed territorial seas on Tuesday [12 October], with US Defence Secretary Robert Gates urging nations to honour specific rights of free transit through international waters and his Chinese counterpart saying the region has nothing to fear from Beijing's armed forces. The statement by Mr Gates to a forum of Asian defence ministers was emphatic in calling on all countries that share the South China Sea to renounce threats or coercion in resolving their competing claims of sovereignty. But he was equally diplomatic in not specifically naming China as the perceived aggressor in disputes over transit lanes, fishing rights, territory and undersea resources that have roiled relations with several neighbours, in particular Japan and Vietnam. In one recent round of the continuing disagreements, China for the past three weeks has cut off shipments to Japan of rare earth minerals, crucial to that country's auto, electronics and clean energy industries. Beijing's delegation also spoke in measured terms, emphasizing that China's military growth was not a threat. China's message, while delivered in broad, non-specific terms, was interpreted as representing an effort to calm concerns over Beijing's maritime intentions. Even so, no fewer that seven nations in attendance raised the issue of how to guarantee maritime security for all nations sharing the South China Sea. Robert Gates told Asean, which was meeting in an expanded forum that also included China and Russia: 'We have a national interest in freedom of navigation, in unimpeded economic development and commerce, and in respect for international law' ... Although Mr Gates warned that disputes over the oceans and their resources are 'a growing challenge to regional stability and prosperity', he noted that 'the United States does not take sides on competing territorial claims, such as those in the South China Sea'. The central theme of his comments was that 'competing claims should be settled peacefully, without force or coercion, through collaborative diplomatic processes and in keeping with customary international law'. In a balanced tone he has sustained during his three-day visit to

Vietnam, Mr Gates reassured regional partners of US support for international law even as he defused tensions with China. On Monday [11 October] officials from China invited Mr Gates to visit Beijing ... Chinese defence minister General Liang Guanglie: 'China's defence development is not aimed to challenge or threaten anyone, but to ensure its security and promote international and regional peace and stability. China pursues a defence policy that is defensive in nature' ... US officials who track Chinese public statements noted that the defence minister did not describe the South China Sea as a region of its 'core interests', as China has in the past ... China has sought through words and actions to extend its territorial claims beyond the 12-nautical-mile limit accepted through customary international law and codified by the United Nations Convention on the Law of the Sea. While the US Defence Department and, in particular the Department of the Navy, support ratification of the UN Law of the Sea Treaty, it remains frozen in Congress, although it has been signed and ratified by about 160 other nations. Pentagon officials are never anxious for a comparison of the United States to the few other nations that also have not ratified the sea pact – a group that includes North Korea and Iran.

(www.iht.com, 12 October 2010; *IHT*, 13 October 2010, p. 4)

On 12 October defence ministers from the ten members of the Association of South-east Asian Nations (Asean), along with America, Australia, China, India, Japan, New Zealand, Russia and South Korea convened in Hanoi ... It has provided a forum for the two biggest armies in the region – America's and China's – to resume contacts. These were suspended by China in anger at America's continued sales of arms to Taiwan. China, understandably, sees these as in breach of America's 1982 promise gradually to reduce weapons sales. In Hanoi, however, Robert Gates, America's Defence Secretary, met his Chinese counterpart, General Liang Guanglie, and agreed to visit Beijing early next year [2011] to resume high-level military dialogue ... In the South China Sea China (and Taiwan, whose claims mirror China's) have various disputes: over the Paracel Islands, which it occupies, but Vietnam claims; over other reefs and atolls; and over the Spratly chain, claimed in whole or in part by Brunei, Malaysia, the Philippines and, again, Vietnam. China has published a map which shows virtually the whole sea as its own, giving rise to a potential further maritime dispute with Indonesia. China has so far refused to discuss any of this in multilateral forums, preferring to pick off rival claimants one by one. Fears about its intensions are one factor behind a big boost in military spending in the region ... The defence ministers meeting in Hanoi were unable to do more than air differences, at best. General Liang repeated China's view that 'practical co-operation within multilateral frameworks does not mean settling all security issues' ... If, as seems likely, the forum becomes a regular event, it offers one of the more hopeful bases for security co-operation. Its membership is at present confined to the countries admitted to the East Asia Summit [EAS], to be held later this month [October], also in Hanoi (though America and Russia will not formally join until next year [2011]). This gives it a tighter focus than the Asean Regional Forum (ARF). It also helps explain why the EU is so keen on membership of the summit.

(Banyan's notebook, www.economist.com, 12 October 2010)

The Vietnam War: the human toll

'The first deployment of American combat forces in Vietnam was made here [Danang] on the beach on 8 March 1965' (*IHT*, 30 April 2005, p. 6).

'[In 1968] US forces became embroiled in a vicious guerrilla war with the Vietcong, the South Vietnamese communist militia' (*The Independent*, 14 November 2006, p. 25).

'At the peak of US involvement in 1969 there were half a million American troops in Vietnam' (*Guardian*, 30 April 2005, p. 3).

'American ground troops reached a high of more than 500,000. At the beginning of 1964 there were 15,000 American military advisers in South Vietnam' (*IHT*, 20 July 2005, p. 4).

> The Paris Peace Accords of 27 January 1973 formally recognized the sovereignty of both sides. All US combat troops were withdrawn by 29 March 1973. The North again invaded and overpowered the South in 1975 and on 2 July 1976 South Vietnam was officially reunified with the North as the Socialist Republic of Vietnam.
>
> (*The Independent*, 14 November 2006, p. 25)

'[The number of] US servicemen and women [who] lost their lives during [the Vietnam War] ... [is] 58,249' (*IHT*, 28 May 2007, p. 4). 'Names etched in black granite at the Vietnam memorial in Washington ... [number] 58,256' (www.iht.com, 7 September 2007).

'The Vietnam War ran from 1959 to 1975 ... An estimated 4 million Vietnamese civilians were killed; 1.1 million communist fighters were killed; 200,000 to 250,000 South Vietnamese troops were killed; 58,200 US troops were killed or missing in action' (www.bbc.co.uk, 22 August 2007).

'There are still 78,000 Americans missing from World War II, far more than from any later conflict. By contrast, there are 8,100 people missing from the Korean War and 1,757 from Vietnam, according to figures provided by the Pentagon' (www.iht.com, 14 July 2008).

'The Vietnam War claimed the lives of 3 million Vietnamese and some 60,000 US soldiers' (www.bbc.co.uk, 30 April 2010).

> Since the war ended an estimated 10,000 Vietnamese have been killed or maimed by landmines ... Children continue to be born with terrible deformities, the legacy of Agent Orange and other chemical defoliants that were sprayed from the air to destroy the jungle hideouts of Vietcong guerrillas. The Vietnamese government estimates that half a million children have been

born with congenital defects, and that 2 million have suffered cancers and other ill effects ... Unlike American war veterans, the victims of Agent Orange have never received compensation. US servicemen who came into contact with the chemical, which contains dioxin, received a multimillion dollar settlement after suing the manufacturer in 1984. A report published earlier this year [2006] found that much of the environmental damage caused by the defoliant has not been repaired. An estimated 20 million gallons of chemicals were dumped on Vietnam's forests by the Americans between 1961 and 1971 ... more than half of Vietnam.

(*The Independent*, 14 November 2006, p. 25)

Vietnamese victims of Agent Orange are still seeking compensation. But the *Washington Post* this week quoted officials as saying the two countries had struck a deal in which America will pay towards removing residues of the chemical from Vietnamese soil. This month [November] the two countries agreed to start the second phase of a joint programme to remove the huge amounts of wartime bombs and landmines that litter Vietnam, causing casualties even now.

(*The Economist*, 18 November 2006, p. 65)

Whether conditions ... [such as] limb deformities and deafness [in Vietnam] are the result of dioxin remains unproved, though the Institute of Medicine at the National Academy of Sciences [in the United States] has linked Agent Orange exposure in US veterans to an increased risk of some health problems, including lung cancer and diabetes.

(www.iht.com, 18 September 2007)

The US government has doubled its funding for dealing with the environmental and heath consequences of its wartime use in Vietnam of the toxic herbicide Agent Orange, the embassy said Friday [29 May 2009]. President Barack Obama recently signed a bill increasing from $3 million to $6 million ... Most of the money is being used in Danang, where US troops mixed and stored Agent Orange at an air force base before loading it onto planes ... Agent Orange and other herbicides [were sprayed] across the country to strip Vietnamese guerrillas of ground cover and kill their crops.

(*IHT*, 30 May 2009, p. 4)

Vietnam is staging 'Orange Day' to raise funds for people it says suffered because of the spraying of Agent Orange by US troops during the Vietnam War. The organizers hope to raise more than $3 million to help the victims of the dioxin-laced herbicides. They say Agent Orange was first used by the United States forty-eight years ago. In March [2009] America's top court let stand the dismissal of lawsuits by Vietnamese nationals and US war veterans seeking damages from the chemical makers. Hanoi says Agent Orange, named after its orange-striped containers, caused some 400,000 deaths and millions of cases of cancer and other illnesses. Washington has argued that there is no internationally accepted scientific evidence linking Agent Orange to birth defects and other illnesses. The United States is currently involved in a project to help clean up dioxin 'hot spots' in Vietnam's central city of Danang and is helping fund services to the disabled communities in the country.

(www.bbc.co.uk, 10 August 2009)

More than a third of the land in six central Vietnamese provinces remains contaminated with land mines and unexploded bombs from the Vietnam War, according to a study released Friday [31 July 2009] ... Vietnamese citizens are still routinely killed and maimed by leftover mines and other explosives. Vietnam estimates that more than 42,000 people have been killed in such accidents since 1975. The study, by the Vietnam Veterans of America Foundation and the Vietnamese National Defence Ministry, provides the most detailed information to date about the amount and location of unexploded ordnance in a region that suffered some of the heaviest fighting and bombardment during the war.

(*IHT*, 1 August 2009, p. 4)

Communist Party membership

In 1996 Communist Party membership was 2.2 million (*FT*, 29 June 1996, p. 3).

'In a nation of 76 million the party accounts for 2.4 million members. Less than 12 per cent are below the age of thirty; more than 41 per cent are over fifty ... Over half of Vietnam's population [is] below twenty-five' (*FEER*, 24 August 2000, p. 26).

'The party claims almost 3.2 million members' (*The Economist*, Survey, 26 April 2008, p. 16).

The boat people

In recent years many of the estimated 2.7 million Viet Kieu (overseas Vietnamese) have begun trickling back, encouraged by the government. Vietnam does not have a super-rich diaspora like China's. Last year [2007] the Vietnamese government recorded business investment by Viet Kieu of only $89 million, though they are probably spending much more on personal consumption, from cars to property. A much more important contribution are the remittances – officially $5.5 billion last year, but probably more – that Vietnamese emigrants send home to their families.

(*The Economist*, Survey, 26 April 2008, p. 9)

Religion

'The United States dropped Vietnam on Monday [13 November 2006] from its list of nations that severely violate religious freedom, citing improvement in its tolerance for religious expression' (www.iht.com, 14 November 2006).

The United States has removed Vietnam from a list of countries which it says severely violate religious freedom. The list is published annually by the State Department and includes China, North Korea, Iran and Sudan. Vietnam was removed just days before President George W. Bush travels to Hanoi for a meeting of the Asia-Pacific Economic Co-operation (Apec) forum ... The US State Department said there had been 'significant improvements toward advancing religious freedom' in the country ... While Vietnam has been taken off the US list of Countries of Particular Concern (CPC) regarding religious freedoms, Uzbekistan has been added ... The State Department said Burma, China, North Korea, Eritrea, Iran, Saudi Arabia and Sudan would remain on the list.

(www.bbc.co.uk, 14 November 2006)

In April [2006] America praised the country's advances in several areas, such as releasing some political dissidents and signing an agreement on religious freedom. As a result, on 13 November, it removed Vietnam from a blacklist of countries that suppress religion. The same day Vietnam sent back to America a Vietnamese-American democracy activist it had detained for fourteen months for 'terrorist activities'.

(*The Economist*, 18 November 2006, p. 65)

Today [25 January 2007] Nguyen Tan Dung becomes the first Vietnamese prime minister to pay an official visit to the Holy See ... Hanoi approves new seminaries and the enrolment of seminarians, the organization of religious classes and conferences, the construction and renovation of religious facilities, the ordination of priests and the promotion of clergy ... Catholicism is Vietnam's second largest religion, with an estimated 6 million to 8 million adherents, or up to 10 per cent of Vietnam's 84 million people. Jesuit missionaries introduced it in the seventeenth century, and one, Alexandre de Rhodes, is credited with developing the Vietnamese alphabet ... After the Vietnam War and national reunification under communist rule in 1975, Hanoi nationalized most church property, as it had done in northern Vietnam after 1954 ... Vietnam by religion: Buddhist, 50 per cent; Catholic, 8 per cent to 10 per cent; Hoa Hao, 1.5 per cent to 4 per cent; Cao Dai, 1.5 per cent to 3 per cent; Protestant, 0.5 per cent to 2 per cent; Moslem, less than 0.1 per cent; no religion, 31 per cent to 38 per cent.

(*FT*, 25 January 2007, p. 10)

Pope Benedict XVI's meeting Thursday [25 January 2007] with the prime minister of Vietnam marked an important step toward establishing diplomatic relations, the Vatican said. It was the highest-level meeting between the Holy See and the communist government, and followed decades of tension ... Vietnam has 6 million Catholics, South-east Asia's second largest Catholic population after the Philippines. For decades there have been tensions between the Vietnamese government and the church, particularly over Hanoi's insistence on having the final say in most church appointments.

(*IHT*, 26 January 2007, p. 3)

For several weeks church leaders and their followers in Hanoi have been gathering daily to pray in front of the old Vatican embassy, one of the many church properties taken over by the government after 1954. The church wants the government to hand back the one-hectare (2.5-acre) lot in central Hanoi ... Hanoi officials maintain that a former priest voluntarily turned the property over to the government in 1960 ... The Vietnamese Catholic Church, which counts 6 million members, was established by missionaries and grew during French colonial rule in Vietnam. It is the second largest faith in Vietnam, which is predominantly Buddhist.

(www.iht.com, 25 January 2008)

The Communist Party has all but given up religious persecution, though Buddhist monks, Catholic priests and Cao Dai followers are still arrested for political activities. Indeed, senior officials now praise the positive contribution of religion to society, though they still insist on vetting senior clerical appointments.

(*The Economist*, Survey, 26 April 2008, p. 15)

'Cao Dai, Vietnam's syncretistic home-grown religion, mixes Buddhism, Taoism, Christianity, Islam and other religions, teaching that all faiths are manifestations of "one same truth". The religion was founded in 1926 by Ngo Van Chieu, a government official' (p. 5).

The [US] State Department's annual report on religious freedom around the world [was published in September 2008] ... The lengthy report has individual sections dealing with each country separately and covers the period from July 2007 to July 2008 ... The report is used to compile a blacklist of 'countries of particular concern', which the State Department announces towards the end of each year. China, Saudi Arabia, Iran, Eritrea and Burma are among those who appear on the blacklist for 2007 ... The report noted some improvements in Saudi Arabia and Vietnam.

(www.bbc.co.uk, 20 September 2008)

A court convicted eight Roman Catholics on Monday [8 December] on charges of disturbing public order and damaging property during a series of prayer vigils to get back confiscated church land, but gave them light sentences. One defendant received a warning while the others were given suspended sentences ranging from twelve to fifteen months. They received up to two years of probation and were sent home ... The defendants could have received up to seven years in prison ... The defendants were arrested several months ago during a series of prayer vigils held to demand the return of land near the Thai Ha church. Hundreds of Catholics gathered at the site for several weeks ... The Hanoi authorities say the Thai Ha church and its surrounding land belong to the city. They say a former parish priest signed papers turning the property over to Hanoi in 1962. Church members insist that they have documents verifying their claim on property ... Earlier this year [2008] Catholics also held vigils at a second valuable parcel of land in Hanoi, the site of the former Vatican embassy in Vietnam, which closed after the communists took power in North Vietnam in 1954. In each case the Catholics began their demonstrations after hearing rumours that the government planned to sell the properties to developers. As the conflicts escalated the government announced that it would convert each site into a public park and open a library at the former Vatican site. With more than 6 million followers, Roman Catholicism is the second largest religion after Buddhism in the country of 86 million.

(www.iht.com, 8 December 2008)

Followers of a Buddhist teacher were seeking refuge in a temple yesterday [2 October 2009] as police stepped up efforts to evict them. About 380 monks and nuns loyal to Thich Nhat Hanh have been holed up inside the temple after being forced out of their monastery by riot police and an angry mob last Sunday [27 September]. They claim they are being targeted because Nhat Hanh, who was forced into exile in the 1960s because of his opposition to the Vietnam War, has called for an end to religious persecution. Police say the standoff is part of a dispute between Nhat Hanh's followers and a rival Buddhist faction.

(*Guardian*, 3 October 2009, p. 30)

A Zen master famed for spreading Buddhism in the West ... has accused Vietnam's government of dispatching violent mobs to attack his followers and force them from their monasteries. Thich Nhat Hanh fled into exile in France four decades ago ... The Buddhist leader spoke out after hundreds of his followers were forced to flee when gangs including members of the police assaulted terrified nuns and monks. Following the first attack in September [2009] they took shelter in another monastery, only to be targeted again last month [December 2009]. The government ... denies any involvement in the attacks and dismisses them as a dispute between separate Buddhist groups. But supporters of Thich Nhat Hanh say they have been targeted ever since he made a highly publicized appeal to the government to broaden religious freedom ... Yesterday [11 January 2010] Vietnamese officials, who have long pressured Buddhists to join the 'official' church and have outlawed 'dissident' sects, denied the claims made by the influential religious leader ... Last month [December 2009] a report by Human Rights Watch confirmed the attacks on the Buddhist leader's supporters and claimed undercover police and Communist Party officials were involved.

(*The Independent*, 12 January 2010, p. 27)

Vietnam on Monday [15 March] released one of its leading human rights activists, the Reverend Nguyen Van Ly, from a prison near Hanoi after he spent three years, and suffered two strokes, in solitary confinement ... Father Ly ... a Catholic priest ... was sentenced to eight years in prison in 2007 for disseminating anti-government propaganda. Father Ly accused Vietnamese officials of practising 'the law of the jungle'.

(www.iht.com, 16 March 2010)

'The Reverend Thadeus Nguyen Van Ly was released for a one-year medical parole ... It was unclear whether he would have to return to prison if his health improved' (*IHT*, 17 March 2010, p. 7).

The internet

An estimated 11 million to 12 million Vietnamese – about 13 per cent of the population – regularly use the internet, up from just under 100,000 six years ago. Although Vietnam has just under 2.5 million computers in use, that number is expected to rise to about 3.5 million by the end of the year [2006 ... Vietnamese authorities have already imprisoned a number of so-called 'cyber-dissidents', including Pham Hong Son, a doctor jailed for translating an essay entitled 'What is democracy?' – taken from the US embassy website – and distributing it electronically.

(*IHT*, 24 May 2006, p. 12)

'[Vietnam's] press is strictly controlled, as in China, but the growing number of internet surfers have free access to most foreign news websites: there is no Vietnamese equivalent of the Great Firewall of China' (*The Economist*, Survey, 26 April 2008, p. 6).

This year [2009] the government tightened restrictions on blogging, banning political discussion and restricting postings to personal matters. The police have arrested several bloggers for writing about sensitive subjects ... The growing legions of Facebook users fear that the government might be blocking the popular networking website, which has been difficult to access over the past few weeks. Facebook has more than 1 million users in Vietnam, and the number has been growing quickly since the company added a Vietnamese language version of the site. During the last week access to Facebook has been intermittent.

(*IHT*, 18 November 2009, p. 19)

Populist anger erupted this year [2009] over a contract that the Vietnamese government gave to Aluminium Corp. of China to mine bauxite, one of Vietnam's most valuable natural resources, using Chinese workers. Dissidents, intellectuals and environmental advocates protested. General Vo Nguyen Giap, the revered ninety-eight-year-old military leader, wrote three open letters criticizing the Chinese presence to Vietnamese party leaders ... Over the summer the central government shut down critical blogs, detained dissidents and ordered Vietnamese newspapers to cease reporting on Chinese labour and the bauxite issue. But in a nod to public pressure, the government also tightened visa and work permit requirements for Chinese and deported 182 Chinese labourers from a cement plant in June, saying they were working illegally. Hanoi generally bans the import of skilled workers from abroad and requires foreign contractors to hire Vietnamese for civil works projects, though that rule is sometimes violated by Chinese companies – well-placed bribes can persuade officials to look the other way, Chinese executives say.

(*IHT*, 21 December 2009, p. 16)

Google ... says it has identified cyber-attacks aimed at silencing critics of a controversial, Chinese-backed bauxite mining project in Vietnam ... Google said malicious software was used to infect 'potentially tens of thousands of computers', broadly targeting Vietnamese-speaking computer users around the world ... Google said the attack may have infected the computers of tens of thousands of people who downloaded Vietnamese keyboard language software ... Infected machines had been used to spy on their owners and to attack blogs containing messages of political dissent, wrote Neel Mehta of the company's security team in a post late Tuesday [30 March] ... McFee, the computer security firm, said: 'The perpetrators may have political motivations and may have some allegiance to the government of the Socialist Republic of Vietnam ... These attacks have tried to squelch the opposition to bauxite mining efforts in Vietnam, an important and emotionally charged issue in the country.'

(www.iht.com, 31 March 2010)

'Computer security firm McFee ... which has been working with Google to uncover the hacking ... suggested the perpetrators could be connected to Vietnam's government' (www.bbc.co.uk, 31 March 2010).

Vietnamese activists opposed to a Chinese mining investment in their country have been targeted in a cyber-attack, Google revealed on Wednesday [31 March]. The internet company said a virus had been used to attack dissident websites ... The virus created a so-called 'botnet', a network of computers that could be controlled by the writers of the software ... Google said the software was used both to spy on users and to launch strikes against dissident Vietnamese websites ... The bauxite plan has gone ahead on a limited scale.

(www.ft.com, 1 April 2010)

Demography

'More than half of Vietnam's population is under thirty' (*The Independent*, 14 November 2006, p. 25).

For the first time since record keeping began in 1960, the number of deaths of young children around the world has fallen below 10 million a year according to figures from the United Nations Children's Fund [Unicef]

Political developments 91

being released Thursday [13 September 2007] ... [The estimated figure was] 9.7 million deaths of children under five ... In 1960 about 20 million children died annually, but the drop since then has been steeper than 50 per cent because the world population has grown. If babies were still dying at 1960 rates, 25 million would die this year [2007] ... Among countries that made particularly rapid progress since 2000 are the Dominican Republic, Vietnam and Morocco, which all cut child deaths by more than one-third.

(www.iht.com, 13 September 2007)

Vietnam is now positioned where China was a decade ago, logging about 110 boys born to every 100 girls ... the sex ratio at birth generally should equal about 105 boys to 100 girls, according to the report ... by the UN Population Fund ... In China the 2005 estimate was more than 120 boys born to 100 girls ... China has a one-child policy, while Vietnam encourages only two children per family after relaxing an earlier ban restricting couples from having more.

(www.iht.com, 31 October 2007)

Faced with a baby boom, Vietnam is planning a crackdown to stop couples having more than two children. The government in the country of 86 million – two-thirds of whom are under thirty-five – fears a new population explosion will knock its economic growth off track and strain health and education services. A two-child policy introduced in 2003 was scrapped, though the state's rulers continued to encourage couples to have small families ... But a spike in births this year [2008] to couples who already have two children caused alarm. In the first nine months 93,000 babies were born to these couples, a 10 per cent rise on last year [2007]. This week the cabinet agreed a draft order for the two-child rule that will be voted on in the national assembly.

(*Guardian*, 22 November 2008, p. 35)

AIDS

'[Internationally] the HIV virus [was] first noticed in 1981' (*IHT*, 29 July 2005, p. 6).

Vietnam is a country teetering on the brink of a serious epidemic, with more than 250,000 people infected with HIV and only 10 per cent of those who fall ill receiving the treatment they need. The disease is spreading fast from its core population of intravenous drug users.

(*IHT*, 24 May 2006, p. 2)

'An estimated 40 million people worldwide are infected with HIV, the vast majority in the developing world' (*IHT*, 2 June 2007, p. 8).

HIV, the virus that causes AIDS, [is] a disease that has killed some 25 million people in the past quarter century ... There is still some uncertainty about its origin ... [There is the suggestion] that the virus jumped to humans from a Cameroonian population of chimps early in the last century. The virus probably made the leap twice more since ... [the second involving] a separate group of chimps in Cameroon ... Wild gorillas ... are probably responsible for a third form of the virus.

(www.economist.com, 24 June 2007)

The United Nations AIDS-fighting agency ... Unaids ... plans to issue a report Tuesday [20 November] acknowledging that it overestimated the size of the epidemic and that new infections ... have been dropping each year since they peaked in the late 1990s ... Unaids will lower the number of people it believes are infected worldwide to 33.2 million from the 39.5 million it estimated late last year [2006] ... Although new infections have dropped, the number of people with the disease is growing because more AIDS victims are living longer, thanks to antiretroviral drugs ... Better surveys, particularly a household survey in India, have driven the figures down.

(www.iht.com, 20 November 2007)

The total of 33.2 million by major regions was as follows: Sub-Saharan Africa, 22.5 million; Asia, 4.9 million; North America/West and Central Europe, 2.1 million; Eastern Europe/Central Asia, 1.6 million; Latin America, 2.1 million. '[Critics say that] because the vast majority of people who are infected with HIV do not know it, there is actually no way to know if this new WHO figure is any more reliable than the previous estimation' (www.bbc.co.uk, 20 November 2007).

'Unaids said on Tuesday [20 November] that many fewer people have HIV than it thought before ... This drop is a result of better counting' (www.economist.com, 20 November 2007).

The AIDS virus has been circulating among people for about 100 years, decades longer than scientists thought, a new study suggests. Genetic analysis pushes the estimated origin of HIV back to between 1884 and 1924, with a more focused estimate at 1908. Previously scientists had estimated the origin at around 1930. AIDS was not recognized formally until 1981, when it got the attention of public health officials in the United States ... Scientists say HIV descended from a chimpanzee virus that jumped to humans in Africa, probably when people butchered chimps. Many individuals were probably infected that way, but so few other people caught the virus that it failed to get a lasting foothold, researchers say. But the growth of African cities may have changed that by putting many people close together and promoting prostitution.

(www.iht.com, 2 October 2008)

Infection with the AIDS virus in China is spreading beyond the country's original high risk groups – heroin addicts in the south and blood sellers in rural central counties. A new study finds that the virus has spread to all provinces, and cases are rising quickly among gay men and female prostitutes. Heterosexual transmission is increasing ... Although the number of estimated cases – 700,000 – is low for a population of 1.3 billion, it has risen 8 per cent since 2005 ... Scientists believe AIDS entered in the 1980s with drug traffickers in Yunnan, which borders South-east Asia's opium 'Golden Triangle'. It grew in Henan, where illegal banks pooled blood from indigent farmers, spun it to remove clotting factors and returned mixed red cells to all sellers. Tracking HIV subtypes suggests the virus has moved along drug trafficking routes, creating an outbreak in western Xinjiang.

(www.iht.com, 7 October 2008)

In recent years Vietnam's prevention and treatment programmes have been improving ... although so far only 30 per cent of people who need life-saving antiretroviral drugs receive them. About 290,000 people in Vietnam, a country of 86 million, carry HIV today ... Although the rate of increase was slowing, the infection was spreading outside the high risk groups such as intravenous drug users.

(www.iht.com, 13 October 2009; *IHT*, 14 October 2009, p. 3)

Although the [Chinese] government pays for HIV medication, AIDS is so widely feared that many hospitals refuse to admit people with the disease. In Beijing, for example, only a handful of surgeons will operate on those who are positive ... Compared to other developing countries, the prevalence of HIV in China is relatively low, with fewer than a million people thought to be carrying the virus, according to government figures issued last week.

(*IHT*, 1 December 2009, p. 2)

Days before travellers worldwide are to begin arriving for Shanghai's world exposition, China has lifted a two-decade ban on travel to the country by people who carry the virus that causes AIDS or who have other sexually transmitted diseases. The action also removed a long-standing ban on travel to China by people with leprosy. The government approved amendments to a 1986 law governing quarantines and a 1989 law regulating entry by foreigners, removing prohibitions related to people with HIV, which causes AIDS, China's State Council reported Tuesday [27 April 2010] ... With the changes, the ban on travel is officially limited only to people with infectious tuberculosis, serious mental disorders and 'infectious diseases which could possibly greatly harm the public health'. China has temporarily lifted the ban on HIV-positive travellers for major events in the past, but the revision of long-standing laws indicates the latest change will be permanent ... A spokesman for the health ministry ... [said] the ministry had been working to permanently remove the prohibition since the 2008 Beijing Olympics ... Between 450,000 and one million Chinese are infected with the HIV virus, according to ... the United Nations health organization. Roughly 75,000 of those have developed AIDS. The proportion of HIV-infected people in China is far below that of neighbouring countries – Vietnam, for example, records about 20,000 AIDS deaths a year – but health exports have worried that China's HIV population may be poised to expand. The infection is most common among sex workers, migrant workers and residents of some border areas, like Yunnan province in south-west China, where drugs are smuggled into the country. In January the United States dropped its own ban on visitors who are HIV positive. The ban had been in effect for twenty-two years.

(www.iht.com, 28 April 2010)

Xinhua reported Tuesday [27 April] that China's State Council decided to repeal the ban after realizing it did little to prevent the spread of disease and caused problems when the country was hosting international events. The revision came days before the opening of the six-month Shanghai World Expo, which organizers expect will draw 70 million people. The government had previously lifted the ban temporarily for other large-scale events, including the 2008 Olympics in Beijing. Xinhua said the health ministry estimates the number of people living with HIV in China had reached 740,000 by October 2009, with deaths caused by AIDS totalling 49,845 since the first case was reported in 1985 ... Until January the United States was one of seven countries with laws barring entry of people with HIV.

(www.cnn.com, 28 April 2010)

Wan Yanhai, the founder of a prominent AIDS activist group in Beijing, has left China for the United States with his family because of increasing pressure from the government, Mr Wan and his supporters said Monday [10 May] ... In recent months the group that Mr Wan led, the Aizhixing Institute, had come under increasing scrutiny from tax officials and even the fire department, he said ... Mr Wan is arguably the most outspoken AIDS campaigner in China. He founded Aizhixing in 1994 to support the cause of AIDS awareness and prevention. At the time the Chinese government was reluctant to speak publicly about AIDS. Mr Wan helped turn an international spotlight on villages in Henan province where residents had become infected with HIV in the 1990s because of poor government oversight of blood transfusions. He was detained for four weeks in 2002 because of that advocacy. Although Mr Wan and his group had come under pressure before, the latest scrutiny coincides with a wider crackdown on civil society groups and organizations that operate independently of the government. The authorities have been especially wary of groups that receive any financing from abroad and have imposed news restrictions on such financing.

(www.iht.com, 10 May 2010)

Wan Yanhai's departure comes less than a year after another AIDS campaigner moved to America ... Wan said he expects to stay in the United States for two to three years ... Wan had been detained and questioned several times, but said he felt increasing pressure in recent months, following checks by tax, education and propaganda officials, and the state administration for industry and commerce. Tightened regulations on foreign donations have also caused funding problems, he said ... Gao Yaojie, who blew the whistle on Henan province's HIV epidemic, moved to the United States last year [2009]. Hu Jia, another HIV/AIDS activist, is serving a three-and-a-year prison sentence for inciting subversion.

(*Guardian*, 11 May 2010, p. 24)

SARS

SARS (Severe Acute Respiratory Syndrome) is a highly infectious strain of pneumonia.

'The earliest cases of SARS appeared in Guangdong [province in China] in November [2002], but the WTO [World Health Organization] first heard about the disease in February [2003]' (*The Economist*, 5 April 2003, p. 13).

> The World Health Organization on Monday [28 April 2003] declared Vietnam the first SARS infected country cleared of the virus ... Outbreaks of the disease had peaked in Canada, Singapore and Hong Kong, but not in China ... [Vietnam] was one of four countries in which local transmission of the disease took place ... Although sixty-three people became infected with the disease in Vietnam, including five medical workers who died, there have been no new cases since 8 April.
>
> (*IHT*, 29 April 2003, p. 5)

'SARS cost east Asia an estimated 2 per cent of GDP in the second quarter of 2004' (*FT*, Survey on the World in 2006, 25 January 2006, p. 6).

> Officials in southern China are cracking down on illegal trade in civet cats to prevent an outbreak of SARS in the coming months, state news media said Monday [19 February 2007]. About 7,000 health inspectors have been mobilized in Guangdong province, where severe acute respiratory syndrome first emerged in 2002, and have checked 10,000 restaurants for civet cats ... Civet cats, mongoose-like animals, are considered a delicacy in southern China and are suspected of spreading SARS to humans, although the original source of the virus has not been determined. In January 2004 Guangdong banned the raising, selling, killing and eating of civet cats. But health departments have been receiving increasing reports of illegal trade in the animals since November [2006] ... During recent inspections a live civet cat and several frozen ones were confiscated and eighteen restaurants were fined ... The disease that was eventually identified as SARS was first reported in Guangdong in November 2002. It was spread by travellers to dozens of countries and killed 774 people worldwide before subsiding in June 2003. There were 349 deaths reported on the Chinese mainland. China was heavily criticized for being slow to release information on its outbreak and has since been trying to co-operate in investigating emerging diseases like SARS and bird flu.
>
> (www.iht.com, 19 February 2007)

As Typhoon Krosa barrelled toward eastern China over the weekend every level of the Chinese government was whipped into action, evacuating 1.4 million people from the two coastal provinces on which Krosa set its sights ... Analysts and observers said China's ability to move hundreds of thousands of people out of harm's way speaks to the country's exceptional ability to mobilize resources and people to deal with disasters ... The efficiency cannot be entirely attributed to a central communist regime and obedient populace, said ... the American Red Cross ... [which argues that] the situation really dramatically changed after the SARS scare ... in 2003 and 2004 ... [which] really highlighted the gaps.

(www.cnn.com, 9 October 2007)

A fast-spreading viral outbreak in eastern China has killed twenty-one children, sickened nearly 3,000 others and caused panic among parents in an impoverished corner of Anhui province, state news media reported Friday [2 May 2008]. The intestinal virus, commonly known as hand, foot and mouth disease, has been spreading in the city of Fuyang since early March, but local officials only announced the outbreak last week, raising questions of whether they were trying to conceal word of the growing problem ... In recent days the Chinese media have heavily criticized the government response, offering comparisons to the SARS epidemic of 2003, which drew widespread attention to China's shaky public health system and official attempts to cover up the outbreak. On Thursday [1 May 2008] the WHO warned that the disease, which thrives in warm weather, could spread in the coming months ... The virus, which has no relation to the foot-and-mouth disease that infects livestock, is easily passed between children. The illness begins with a fever and often leads to mouth ulcers and blisters on the hands, feet and buttocks. There is no vaccine or cure ... Health officials in Fuyang say that 700 children remain hospitalized, thirty-six of them in serious condition. All of the fatalities have been in children younger than six, the majority of them under two ... Fuyang is perhaps best known as the epicentre of a powdered milk scandal four years ago that sickened infants, killing thirteen of them ... In recent days the Chinese media have not been shy about lambasting health officials for waiting a month to sound the alarm bells. In mid-April [2008], they noted, local officials who were confronted by reporters denied there was a problem. Two weeks later, after more than a dozen children had died, they were forced to acknowledge that an outbreak was well under way ... During the SARS outbreak Chinese officials withheld information from the WHO, restricted media reporting and undercounted the cases of those stricken. After the disease spread beyond China's borders and provoked worldwide panic, the government apologized and pledged to confront future health emergencies with greater openness.

(www.iht.com, 2 May 2008)

China has issued a nationwide health alert in an effort to control the outbreak of a virus which has killed twenty-two children in the east of the

Political developments 97

country. A statement from the health ministry said it was taking urgent measures to prevent the spread of the infection, known as Enterovirus 71 (EV71). The highly contagious intestinal virus can cause fever, blisters in the mouth and a rash on the hands and feet. Official fear the virus has spread from eastern provinces to the south. Health authorities across the country have been told to report all cases of the virus within twenty-four hours ... The outbreak emerged in Fuyang city in March, but was only reported last week. The delay has led to accusations of a cover-up by local authorities. The Chinese health ministry has rejected charges that it has failed to handle the situation properly, arguing that medical teams had been trying to work out what the illness was. The number of children infected with EV71 has risen sharply since the outbreak was disclosed. Public health experts think cases will keep rising before peaking around June or July [2008], the WHO said ... Almost 1,000 children are currently receiving hospital treatment, fifty-eight of whom are in a critical or serious condition, the health ministry said.

(www.bbc.co.uk, 3 May 2008)

China's health ministry strengthened surveillance and dispatched specialists to eastern China's Anhui province as the death toll from a virulent disease climbed to twenty-two, the country's Xinhua news agency reported. As of Friday [3 May] there were 3,321 reported cases of the virus in children. The illness – known as Enterovirus 71 – can cause hand, foot and mouth disease (HFMD). A total of 978 children are hospitalized, an Anhui province official told Xinhua, Forty-eight of them are in critical condition ... [The health ministry issued] a nationwide order ... The order said preventing infectious diseases was needed 'to guarantee the smooth staging of the Beijing Olympics and Paralympics and to practically preserve social stability'. As well as hand, foot and mouth disease, the order targeted other infectious diseases including hepatitis A and measles.

(www.cnn.com, 3 May 2008)

'The death toll from a common illness that typically causes little more than a fever has risen to twenty-four children and health officials fear the worst may be yet to come as outbreaks occur in neighbouring countries' (*IHT*, 5 May 2008, p. 4).

Cases of a virus that has killed twenty-four children ... may continue despite efforts to contain it, the WHO warned yesterday [Sunday 4 May]. Enterovirus 71 (EV71), which causes a severe strain of hand, foot and mouth disease, normally peaks in June and July. Experts fear that infections could increase as the weather becomes warmer ... In Fuyang, eastern Anhui province, twenty-two deaths have occurred ... WHO China representative Hans Troedsson: 'I do not see it at all as a threat to the Olympics or any upcoming events' ... There is no vaccine or cure for hand, foot and mouth disease ... It is a common illness among infants and children and it is not usually fatal. However, the virus EV71 can result in a more serious form of the illness and complications including meningitis and heart problems can prove fatal ... Two more children were reported dead this weekend, in Guangdong province, 1,000 miles south of Anhui. But Troedsson said the virus had probably come from different sources rather than spread, as had small outbreaks reported in Shaanxi and Hubei ... This weekend's order from the health ministry warned than anyone covering up or delaying disclosure of outbreaks faced punishment. The virus EV71 was first identified in the 1960s. But the past decade has witnessed several large outbreaks across Asia.

(*Guardian*, 5 May 2008, p. 14)

The toll from an intestinal virus ... is continuing to rise ... A child died in Zhejiang province bringing the number of deaths from Enterovirus 71 to twenty-six. According to state media, more than 8,500 cases have now been reported, with 5,151 of these in Anhui province. EV71 is highly contagious, causing fever, blisters in the mouth and a rash on the hands and feet. The outbreak emerged in Fuyang city in March, but was only reported in mid-April ... Twenty-two have died in the province [Anhui] and three deaths have also been reported in Guangdong province. The delay in reporting the outbreak has led to accusations of a cover-up by local authorities ... But on Sunday [4 May] the WHO's representative in Beijing, Hans Troedsson, defended the authorities. He said: 'The reason why there was a delay in the reporting at the provincial level was that they did not know what the causes for these different cases were.'

(www.bbc.co.uk, 5 May 2008)

China on Monday [5 May] reported a sharp increase in the number of children affected by hand, foot and mouth disease, saying that more than 9,700 cases had been reported. At least twenty-four deaths in Anhui and Guangdong provinces have been attributed to EV71, one of several viruses that cause the disease ... Two other children, one in Guangdong province and one in Zhejiang province, also died from the disease, but it was not clear by which strain.

(*IHT*, 6 May 2008, p. 4)

Hand and mouth disease [HFMD] has struck 11,905 people and has proved fatal in twenty-six cases, all of them children, China's state-run news agency Xinhua reported Monday [5 May]. The official count has increased dramatically in recent days, the result of an order issued Friday by the ministry of health mandating that all cases be reported ... The worst hit province [is] Anhui in rural eastern China, where twenty-two of the fatalities have occurred, all of them blamed on EV71, one of the most common causes of HFMD ... HFMD can be caused by a number of intestinal viruses, of which EV71 and Coxsackie A16 are among the most common ... All the deaths in Anhui occurred in Fuyang city and 1,314 of the 4,496 children infected in

Political developments 99

> the city were hospitalized ... Of the total 5,840 child infections in the province, 689 were registered Sunday [4 May] ... Fuyang officials have been accused of sitting on information of the outbreak last month [March] even as children were dying. But a WHO official said weeks passed between the outbreak in mid-March and the first reports because they did not know what they were dealing with. Local officials say they are doing all they can. Though the case fatality rate has dropped from 11 per cent during March to 0.2 per cent during April, according to the WHO, the number of people infected shows no signs of decreasing. Zhejiang province in east China has reported 1,198 infections among children this year [2008]; a five-year-old boy died last month [April]. It reported 101 cases in 2005, 793 cases in 2006 and 1,607 cases last year [2007] ... Guangdong province reported 1,692 cases ... Cases have been identified in ... Chongqing municipality ... Beijing ... Hebei province ... [and] in the provinces of Jiangsu, Hunan, Shaanxi, Jiangxi and Henan ... A large outbreak of HFMD occurred in Taiwan in 1998 with seventy-eight deaths, and smaller outbreaks recurred there in 2000 and 2001.
>
> (www.cnn.com, 6 May 2008)

> The death toll from China's outbreak of HFMD has climbed to twenty-eight – all of them children, Xinhua reported Wednesday [7 May]. The latest deaths were reported by the health bureaus in central China's Hunan province and the Guangxi Zhuang Autonomous Region in the south-west ... Authorities reported 15,799 cases of the disease on Tuesday [[6 May].
>
> (www.cnn.com, 7 May 2008)

'China last year [2007] saw a total of 80,000 cases and seventeen deaths' (*The Economist*, 10 May 2008, p. 80).

> Beijing ... recorded its first death from hand, foot and mouth disease on Wednesday [14 May] ... The illness has sickened tens of thousands of children across the country and killed at least forty-two people. A child died Sunday [11 May] on the way to hospital ... Another child died of the illness in Beijing, but the death was counted in the victim's home province of Hebei, which neighbours Beijing. A twenty-one-month boy also died of the virus Monday [12 May] in Hubei province ... The three newly reported deaths raise the countrywide death toll to forty-two since late March. Hand, foot and mouth disease has sickened more than 24,934 children in seven Chinese provinces plus Beijing ... Xinhua said 3,606 infections had been reported in Beijing as of Monday [12 May] ... Cases have been reported from Guangdong province in the south to Jilin province in the north-east, and in major cities like Beijing and Shanghai ... The death rate has gone down drastically since early May [according to the WHO] ... Most cases in China this year [2008] have been blamed on EV71.
>
> (www.iht.com, 14 May 2008)

Bird flu

'Humans infected with bird flu [number] 186 in all since 1997 ... Of the world's confirmed human cases ninety-three are from Vietnam' (*IHT*, 28 March 2006, p. 4).

'Two young girls have been infected with bird flu, raising to eight the number of human cases of the virus in Egypt, the health minister said Sunday [2 April]' (*IHT*, 3 April 2006, p. 10).

> The bird flu found in domestic fowl in the eastern Germany state of Saxony was the deadly H5N1 strain [it was announced on 5 April] ... The confirmation of bird flu at a large poultry farm was the second instance of H5N1 in domestic fowl in the EU after an outbreak in France in late February.
>
> (*IHT*, 6 April 2006, p. 4)

> Germany's first case of the deadly H5N1 bird flu strain has been confirmed on a poultry farm east of Leipzig. The cull of the farm's flock of 10,000 geese, turkeys and chickens had begun after about twenty birds were found dead earlier this week ... The H5N1 strain has killed at least 107 people worldwide.
>
> (*The Independent*, 6 April 2006, p. 23)

'An Egyptian girl died from bird flu on Thursday [6 April], taking to three the country's human death toll from the [H5N1 strain of the] virus ... The government put the number of people who have caught the virus at eleven' (www.iht.com, 6 April 2006).

> The Scottish swan is the first confirmed wild case in Britain of infection with the H5N1 virus that has killed an estimated 200 million birds in forty-five countries, either directly or through preventative culling ... The mute swan was found on 29 March ... Bird flu has killed 109 people.
>
> (*FT*, 7 April 2006, p. 2)

> A swan found dead in eastern Scotland [Fife] has tested positive for the deadly strain of bird flu, making it the first recorded case of the disease in a wild bird in Britain. The bird [is] believed to be a native mute swan ... Bird flu has been gradually making its way across Europe, striking countries like Germany, France, Denmark, Italy, Poland, Switzerland and Greece.
>
> (*IHT*, 7 April 2006, p. 3)

'DNA tests confirmed a swan found dead of H5N1 in Scotland had been a migrating species ... [It] probably came from Germany' (*FT*, 12 April 2006, p. 9).

'This week Vietnamese health officials said chickens smuggled over the border from China had reintroduced bird flu into their nation, which had reported no cases for four months' (*IHT*, 14 April 2006, p. 1).

'A twenty-one-year-old migrant worker in Hubei province has died of bird flu ... It is China's twelfth known human death from bird flu' (*IHT*, 21 April 2006, p. 8).

'The [H5N1] virus has infected 196 people ... and killed 110 of them, according to the WHO. At least thirty-three countries have reported initial outbreaks in animals since February' (*IHT*, 24 April 2006, p. 15).

A dozen human H5N1 cases, four of them fatal, have been confirmed in Egypt, according to the WHO. Since late 2003 204 cases have been reported worldwide, the WHO said. Outbreaks of bird flu in poultry and fowl in Africa have been found in Burkina Faso, Cameroon, Egypt, Niger, Nigeria and Sudan, according to the World Organization for Animal Health.

(*IHT*, 26 April 2006, p. 13)

The flocks of migratory birds that winged their way south to Africa last autumn [2005] and then back over Europe in recent weeks did not carry the H5N1 flu virus or spread it during their annual journey, scientists have concluded, defying officials' dire predictions ... It is quiet now in terms of cases, which is contrary to what many people had expected ... In thousands of samples collected in Africa this winter, H5N1 was not detected in a single wild bird, officials and scientists said. In Europe there have been only a handful of cases detected in wild birds since 1 April, at the height of the northward migration. The number of cases in Europe has decreased so dramatically compared to February, when dozens of new cases were found daily, that experts believe the northward spring migration played no role. There was one grebe in Denmark on 28 April – the last case – as well as a falcon in Germany and a few swans in France, according to the World Organization for Animal Health ... The February cases in Europe were attributed to infected wild swans that travelled west to avoid severe cold in Russia and Central Asia but apparently never carried the virus to Africa ... Worldwide ... the H5N1 bird virus ... has killed about 200 humans, almost all people who were in extremely close contact with sick birds ... While avian influenza has become a huge problem in domestic poultry on farms in a few African countries, like Egypt, Nigeria and Sudan, experts increasingly suspect that it was introduced there through imported infected poultry and poultry products ... Farm-based outbreaks of avian influenza are still occurring constantly in a number of countries, although not in Europe. The Ivory Coast had first outbreak of bird flu, on a farm, last week.

(www.iht.com, 10 May 2006; *IHT*, 11 May 2006, pp. 1, 7)

Even as it crops up in the far corners of Europe and Africa, the virulent bird flu that raised fears of a human pandemic has been largely snuffed out in the parts of South-east Asia where it claimed its first and most numerous victims. ... 'In Thailand and Vietnam, we have had the most fabulous success,' said David Nabarro, chief pandemic flu co-ordinator for the United Nations. Vietnam, which has had almost half of the human cases of A(H5N1) flu in the world, has not seen a single case in humans or a single outbreak in poultry this year [2006]. Thailand, the second hardest hit nation until Indonesia recently passed it, has not had a human case for five months [correction in *IHT*, 17 May 2006,

p. 3] or one in poultry in six months. Encouraging signs have also come from China, though they are harder to interpret ... Confounding expectations, birds making the spring migration north from Africa have not carried the virus into Europe. David Nabarro and other officials warn that it would be highly premature to declare any sort of victory. The virus has moved rapidly across continents and is still rampaging in Myanmar and other countries nearby. It could still hitchhike back in the illegal trade in chicks, fighting cocks or tropical pets, or in migrating birds ... Very different tactics led to success in ... Thailand and Vietnam ... While Vietnam began vaccinating all its 220 million chickens last summer [2005], Thailand did not because it has a large poultry export industry, and other nations would have banned its birds indefinitely. (Vaccines can mask the virus instead of killing it.) Instead, Thailand culled wide areas around infected flocks, compensated farmers generously and deputized a volunteer in every village to report sick chickens. It vaccinates fighting cocks, which can be worth thousands of dollars, and even issues them passports with their vaccination records so they can travel ... Thailand and Vietnam also delivered the antiviral drug Tamiflu to even the smallest regional hospitals and told doctors to treat all flu patients even before laboratory diagnoses could be made ... Hints suggest that the disease is being beaten back in China, the country where it is assumed to have begun. International officials tend to greet official public health reports from China sceptically, in part because it concealed the outbreak of the SARS virus there for months. It did not officially report any bird cases for years, even though many scientists contend the virus incubated there between its first appearance in humans in Hong Kong in 1997 and the current outbreak, which began in Vietnam in 2003 ... China's reported human cases have remained low: eight last year [2005] and ten this year [2006]. Perhaps more important, its poultry cases ... seem to be dropping ... China said it had outbreaks in sixteen provinces in 2004. In 2005 it reported outbreaks in only twelve provinces, but one in November [2005] was so large that 2.5 million birds were culled to contain it. After that the agriculture minister announced that it would vaccinate every domestic bird in China ... In Cambodia and Laos, which separate Thailand and Vietnam, the situation is vague. Laos has reported no human cases and last reported outbreaks two years ago. Cambodia's reported human cases dropped to two this year [2006], from four last year [2005]. No poultry outbreaks were reported, but surveillance is so spotty that some must have occurred and gone unnoticed ... because the country's six human victims were infected by poultry ... Where the South-east Asian governments have taken action, however, the risk of the virus returning is ever present, David Nabarro said. For example, he said, it probably exists in Vietnam in Muscovy ducks, which can harbour the virus but do not get sick, and it has turned up in isolated birds in open-air markets near the Chinese border. (Single birds do not constitute an outbreak.) Since Chinese farmers can get three times as much for a chicken in Vietnam as they can at home, the temptation to smuggle persists.

(Donald McNeil, *IHT*, 15 May 2006, p. 4)

Political developments 103

The number of confirmed human deaths from bird flu for 2003, 2004, 2005 and 2006 (as of 12 May), respectively, are as follows: Thailand: 0, 12, 2 and 0; Cambodia: 0, 0, 4 and 2; Vietnam: 3, 20, 19 and 0 (p. 4).

'A fifth member of an Indonesian family has died of bird flu, according to local tests – it was announced on 14 May] ... Samples from the patients have been sent to the WHO' (*Guardian*, 15 May 2006, p. 22).

> WHO officials said Thursday [18 May] that the five avian flu deaths confirmed this week on Sumatra were probably not a result of human-to-human infection and did not suggest that the virus had mutated into a more deadly form. Five family members were confirmed dead from the H5N1 strain of avian influenza by the WHO on Wednesday, the largest such cluster yet recorded. A sixth family member died of flu-like symptoms but was not tested for the virus ... [The WHO said] the number of deaths raised eyebrows but that so far ... the recent cluster ... is similar to other outbreaks in Indonesia, which were caused by close contacts with infected poultry ... Indonesia's toll has now reached thirty, second only to Vietnam, which has recorded forty-two. Indonesia, however, has been recording bird flu deaths at a much higher rate than any other country in recent months ... A woman died of bird flu in Egypt on Thursday, the sixth death from the disease in that country.
>
> (www.iht.com, 18 May 2006; *IHT*, 19 May 2006, p. 5)

> Reacting to the death Monday [22 May] of an Indonesian man, the WHO said that the case appeared to be the first example of the avian flu jumping from human to human to human. But the health agency quickly cautioned Tuesday that this did not necessarily mean that the virus had mutated into a strain that could start a pandemic by jumping rapidly between people as ordinary flu does. It is a 'definite possibility' that the virus jumped more than once inside a family, said ... a spokeswoman for [the WHO] ... In the past there have been at least three cases of suspected human-to-human transmission of the H5N1 strain of bird flu; all were between family members who spent hours in close contact and would have inhaled large amounts of virus-contaminated droplets. The virus is known to attach itself to receptors deep in the lungs, not in the nose and throat as seasonal flu does ... The man who died was thirty-two and became sick on 15 May. He is believed to have caught the flu while caring for his ten-year-old son, who died of the disease on 13 May.
>
> (www.iht.com, 24 May 2006)

> The WHO says it is extremely worried about a cluster of recent human deaths from the virulent H5N1 strain of bird flu. Seven people from the same family in northern Sumatra [Indonesia] died from the disease this month [May] ... [The WHO] said there was no sign of diseased poultry in the immediate area. Investigators are looking into the possibility that the virus spread from human to human ... [but it was] emphasized that there

was no indication the virus had mutated ... The Sumatran cases ... [are] the largest cluster of human cases to date ... All seven who died were members of the same family. An eighth family member is also thought to have the disease ... The initial victim was a woman, who became ill at the end of April. She died in early May and was buried before laboratory tests could be carried out. The subsequent six victims – all of whom were positively identified as having the virus – had close and prolonged exposure to either her or other family members with the disease ... The H5N1 virus has already killed more than 120 people worldwide since 2003.

(www.bbc.co.uk, 24 May 2006)

'To date there have been 218 infections and 124 human deaths from the virus' (*FT*, 25 May 2006, p. 9).

Preliminary tests have found that bird flu killed two more siblings in Indonesia, officials said Friday [26 May], as the country grappled with a separate outbreak involving the largest cluster ever reported within one family ... International health officials so far have confirmed thirty-three human deaths from bird flu in Indonesia, out of 124 worldwide ... The newest cases came as Indonesia investigated a separate family cluster in northern Sumatra in which six of seven family members died of bird flu, the most recent Monday. An eighth family member who died was buried before tests could be done, but she was also considered to be among those infected ... Similar isolated cases of transmission among humans are believed to have occurred in four or five other family clusters.

(*IHT*, 27 May 2006, p. 2)

'[The brother] has died from bird flu, the thirty-sixth death in Indonesia, according to the WHO' (*The Times*, 30 May 2006, p. 35).

Wild birds carry only part of the blame for spreading the deadly strain of bird flu and experts said Tuesday [30 May] that they should not be killed but rather studied to understand how the virus spreads ... Scientists [were] at an international conference ... organized by the Animal Health Service at the United Nations Food and Agriculture Organization ... and the World Organization for Animal Health ... Migratory birds brought the disease into Russia and Eastern Europe, but in the case of the recent outbreaks in Africa there is little evidence pointing to wild birds ... The H5N1 virus has killed at least 127 people worldwide.

(*IHT*, 31 May 2006, p. 3)

The 300 experts in attendance made little new headway ... concluding that far more basic research was needed to understand basic questions, like which species of wild bird are vulnerable to the virus ... Wild migrating birds could introduce bird flu into a new country, but it was probably human commerce in poultry that moved it from village to village and from farm to farm. While wild birds have been implicated in spreading the disease to many European nations, their role in Africa has not been established. ... A number of countries in the throes of serious bird flu outbreaks are underreporting the extent of the problem, generally because they do not have the money, veterinary expertise or health systems to track the disease adequately, international health experts said ... Countries might be underreporting, but they do not do it deliberately ... African nations give inadequate reports, as well as China and Indonesia ... Forty-eight people in Indonesia have now been diagnosed with the disease and thirty-six have died, nearly half of them in the past month – a sign that bird flu is widespread in the country.

(*IHT*, 1 June 2006, p. 8)

In the wake of a cluster of avian flu cases that killed seven members of a rural Indonesian family, it appears likely that there have been many more human-to-human infections than the authorities have previously acknowledged. The numbers are still relatively small and they do not mean that the virus has mutated to pass easily between people – a change that could touch off a worldwide epidemic. All the clusters of cases have been among relatives or in nurses who were in long, close contact with patients. But the clusters – in Indonesia, Thailand, Turkey, Azerbaijan, Iraq and Vietnam – paint a grimmer picture of the virus's potential to pass from human to human than is normally described by public health officials, who usually say such cases are 'rare'. Until recently WHO representatives have said there were only two or three such cases ... [For example] on 30 May Maria Cheng, a spokeswoman for the UN health agency, said there were 'probably about half a dozen'. She added: 'I don't think anybody's got a solid number' ... Most clusters are hard to investigate because they may not even be noticed until a victim is hospitalized and are often in remote villages where people fear talking about it ... The WHO is generally conservative in its announcements and, as a UN agency, is sometimes limited by member states in what it is permitted to say about them. Still, several scientists have noted that there are many clusters in which human-to-human infection may be a more logical explanation than the idea that relatives who fell sick days apart got the virus from the same dying bird ... Henry Niman, a biochemist in Pittsburgh ... has argued for weeks that there have been twenty to thirty human-to-human infections ... Niman also said that clusters were becoming more frequent, especially in Indonesia. On 2 June two more emerged there, one including a nurse whose infection has not yet been confirmed. With thirty-six deaths Indonesia is expected to eclipse Vietnam soon as the world's worst-hit country.

(www.iht.com, 4 June 2006)

Avian influenza was first identified over 100 years ago; since then the disease has been reported at irregular intervals in all regions of the world. In addition to the current outbreak in Asia, recent epidemics have occurred in Hong Kong in 1997–8 and 2003, in the Netherlands in 2003 and in the

Republic of Korea in 2003. Once domestic birds are infected avian influenza outbreaks can be difficult to control and may cause major economic damage to poultry farmers in affected countries, since mortality rates are high and infected fowl generally must be destroyed – the technical term is 'culled' – in order to prevent the spread of the disease. The outbreak is caused by the highly pathogenic H5N1 strain of the virus ... East and South-east Asia has suffered significant human and economic losses owing to the present outbreak. Small and medium-sized farmers, whose stocks are often not insured and who have no alternative sources of income, have been the hardest hit. Overall, 140 million birds have been destroyed so far. Poultry meat imports from affected areas were prohibited in many countries. As the size of the poultry industry ranges from 0.6 per cent of GDP in Thailand and Vietnam to over 2 per cent of GDP in the Philippines, a fall in poultry output by 15 per cent, as has already been the case in Vietnam, can imply a reduction in GDP by up to 0.3 per cent. Across the region the total losses from the damaged poultry sector amounted to about $10 billion by the end of 2005. The estimates of deaths from a possible global pandemic of highly pathogenic avian influenza depend on several factors ... The economic losses associated with an avian influenza pandemic could well amount to $200 billion in just one quarter, with the Economic and Social Commission for Asia and the Pacific region bearing most of the brunt. This corresponds to 2 per cent of world GDP. The impact on some specific sectors, however, could be catastrophic. Tourism, one of the industries to be potentially affected by an outbreak, accounts for over 9 per cent of GDP in East Asia and about 11 per cent in South-east Asia.

(United Nations 2006: 113)

Bird flu was found in a north-eastern Ukrainian village ... bordering Russia ... officials said Monday [12 June], the first confirmation of the virus's spread beyond the nation's Black Sea regions ... The news media reported it was the H5N1 strain ... ... An outbreak of the H5N1 strain hit Ukraine in December [2005], but the cases were confined to Crimea and other Black Sea regions. No human cases have been recorded in Ukraine.

(*IHT*, 13 June 2006, p. 10)

Confirmation of the thirty-eighth death from avian flu in Indonesia has indicated that the situation in the country is continuing to worsen. Indonesia is now in second place after Vietnam, which has forty-two deaths, but none this year [2006], while Indonesia's caseload is climbing rapidly and includes many family clusters ... [Indonesia] said Thursday [15 June] that the 1 June death of a seven-year-old girl ... was the country's thirty-eighth from avian flu. The girl's ten-year-old brother died on 29 May, but he was buried before specimens were taken, so he was not included in the count. Chickens in the family's household had died earlier ... The outbreak in Indonesia has a very high death rate: of the fifty known cases thirty-eight have died ... [Indonesia] said Friday [16 June] that a fourteen-year-old had died Wednesday ...

Local tests indicated he was infected with the H5N1 strain of the virus but that an international laboratory would confirm the diagnosis. If the case is confirmed it would raise Indonesia's death toll to thirty-nine ... The World Bank said Monday that the country was mounting a disorganized and under-financed response to the flu.

(www.iht.com, 16 June 2006)

[On 20 June it was announced that WHO] tests confirmed that a fourteen-year-old boy had died from the disease, bringing the death toll [in Indonesia] from the disease to at least thirty-nine people ... An Asian Development Bank report in April said that Indonesia's 2006 budget allocated just $14 million to combat the disease, despite the government's own estimate that at least thirty times that amount is needed ... At least 120 people have died worldwide since the virus began ravaging Asian poultry in late 2003.

(www.iht.com, 20 June 2006)

An Indonesian man who died after catching the H5N1 bird flu virus from his ten-year-old son represents the first laboratory-confirmed case of human-to-human transmission of the disease, a WHO investigation of an unusual family cluster has concluded, the agency said Friday [23 June]. The WHO investigators also discovered that the virus had mutated slightly when the son had the disease, although not in any way that would allow it to pass more readily among people ... In previous cases where human-to-human transmission was suspected, researchers could not test from the patients, or the virus in the patients was the same as that in poultry in the area ... International health officials have been in Indonesia for much of the past month, investigating a family outbreak that affected seven relatives ... Six of the seven died ... The family had no known direct contact with sick birds, although the first death was a woman who sold vegetables in a market that also sold birds.

(www.iht.com, 23 June 2006; *IHT*, 24 June 2006, p. 3)

A Chinese man who died of pneumonia in November 2003 and was at first classified as a SARS victim might have died of avian influenza – two years before Beijing reported any human bird flu infections on the mainland to the WHO, Chinese researchers reported. The case of the death in Beijing raises the possibility that others attributed to SARS may have actually been caused by the deadly H5N1 flu. But in a confusing development at least one of the researchers asked Wednesday [21 June] that the letter reporting the case be withdrawn from publication.

(www.iht.com, 22 June 2006)

Did China have a death from avian flu two years before it admitted having any human cases? The mystery has deepened and the possibility has been raised that someone had tried to block the publication of that event from a prestigious American medical journal. The *New England Journal of Medicine* on Friday [23 June] reversed an announcement it had made two days before, saying that, in fact, the eight Chinese authors of a letter describing a man's death in 2003 from avian flu had insisted that they really did want it printed. The timing of the death is important because scientists believe that the H5N1 virus had circulated among China's chickens for many years, but it was not until last November [2005] that the government admitted to having a human case. To date it has officially reported nineteen cases and twelve deaths. In 2003 China covered up dozens of cases of SARS deaths for months after the epidemic began there. The journal had gone to press Wednesday [21 June] when the editors received several email messages asking that the letter describing the 2003 death not be printed ... The letter said that doctors initially thought the twenty-four-year-old man had SARS, but tests on his lung tissue proved negative.

(www.iht.com, 25 June 2006)

Four people have died after catching avian flu from infected swans, in the first confirmed cases of the disease being passed from wild birds ... The victims, from a village in Azerbaijan, are believed to have caught the lethal H5N1 virus earlier this year when they plucked the feathers from dead birds to sell for pillows. Three other people were infected by the swans but survived ... Almost all of the 220 other confirmed human cases of bird flu, including 130 deaths, have been linked to domestic poultry. A handful are believed to have caught the disease directly from humans.

(*Guardian*, 26 June 2006, p. 15)

Spain yesterday [7 July] detected its first case of bird flu after carrying out an autopsy on a dead great crested grebe ... The dead bird was found in northern Spain ... The government said ... there are no poultry farms in the area ... Spain lies on a main migration route for birds flying between Europe and Africa.

(*FT*, 8 July 2006, p. 7)

Only a fraction of nearly $1.9 billion pledged by international donors in January to help the developing world prepare for a bird flu pandemic has been paid out so far, the United Nations said Monday [10 July]. In a joint report with the World Bank, the UN bird flu co-ordinator, David Nabarro, said donor countries had allocated $1.5 billion for bird flu aid in their budgets by the end of April, but had transferred just $331 million to recipients ... The donor funds were designated for improving veterinary systems, vaccination drives and education about animal hygiene, Nabarro said more money was needed to ensure that poorer countries in Africa, Latin America and elsewhere were ready for a resurgence of the bird flu threat later this year.

(*IHT*, 11 July 2006, p. 3)

Vietnam has not recorded any new human deaths this year [2006], thanks in part to an aggressive campaign to slaughter all birds in infected areas. Indonesia has been criticized by some for not carrying out widespread culling ...

[Indonesia] has an estimated 2 billion chickens and the virus is endemic in twenty-seven of its thirty-three provinces. Culling all the birds would require a huge amount of compensation to farmers and backyard chicken owners ... [Indonesia has] 230 million people spread across 17,000 islands ... [On 17 July Indonesia said] a WHO laboratory had confirmed the bird flu death of a three-year-old girl, bringing the country's total from the virus to at least forty-two, tying it with Vietnam for the most deaths worldwide. The WHO, however, does not recognize one of Indonesia's bird flu deaths because of the testing method used. The agency, which is co-ordinating the world's fight against the virus, still lists forty-one bird flu deaths in Indonesia. Bird flu has killed at least 132 people worldwide since it started ravaging Asian poultry stocks in late 2003, according to the WHO.

(www.iht.com, 17 July 2006)

Indonesia is poised to surpass Vietnam as the country hardest hit by avian flu. And while Vietnam has not had a single human case or poultry outbreak this year [2006], public health officials and experts say the situation in Indonesia is likely to get worse. Indonesia received word from a Hong Kong laboratory that a forty-four-year-old man who died last week near Jakarta had tested positive for the H5N1 virus, the Indonesian health ministry said Thursday [20 July]. That brought the number of confirmed bird flu cases in Indonesia to forty-two since the first human case was confirmed a year ago, equal to the toll in Vietnam. The flu is ubiquitous in thousands of Indonesian backyard flocks, and appears to be killing more birds every month, increasing the likelihood of human cases ... Although the H5N1 flu came relatively late to Indonesia, it soon spiralled out of control and deaths have mounted quickly. Unlike Thailand, which quenched outbreaks by killing millions of chickens, or Vietnam, which used mandatory vaccination, Indonesia has tried a mix of limited culling and vaccination in rings around the cull – so far with little success ... The biggest obstacle to beating the disease, international flu experts say, is the decentralized Indonesian government ... The country is not only slow to report human cases, but it no longer even reports poultry outbreaks to the World Organization for Animal Health in Paris ... Shortages of trained veterinarians and slow compensation of farmers have also been major obstacles to crushing the outbreak ... Given the huge population ... 245 million Indonesians, living on about 6,000 populated islands [Vietnam has 84 million people] ... avian flu remains a relatively rare disease ... But Indonesian cases have clustered.

(www.iht.com, 20 July 2006)

Thailand on Wednesday [26 July] confirmed that a sixteen-year-old boy who died this week [on 24 July] was infected with bird flu ... The boy became Thailand's fifteenth bird flu fatality and the country's first confirmed case in humans this year ... Agriculture officials on Tuesday had confirmed the H5N1 bird flu virus in chickens [in a northern province] ... The new cases were the first to be found in Thai poultry in more than eight months ...

The Thai authorities culled millions of chickens and ducks when a wave of bird flu struck Asia in 2004. Thailand, one of the world's biggest chicken exporting countries, has since conducted regular surveys to check for bird flu among poultry. The last bird flu fatality was a five-year-old boy in December [2005].

(www.iht.com, 26 July 2006)

Last week Indonesia announced its forty-third human death from bird flu. It has now recorded more fatalities than any other nation and, in stark contrast to all other countries, its death toll is climbing regularly ... [Among the reasons is the fact that] farmers are being compensated ... well below the market price ... per bird ... thereby discouraging farmers from reporting outbreaks ... Pledges to vaccinate hundreds of millions of birds have not been met ... SARS [was a] threat in 2003 that never materialized.

(*The Economist*, 29 July 2006, p. 60)

A bird flu vaccine for humans that uses only a very low dose of its active ingredient has proved effective in clinical tests and could be mass produced in 2007, the drugmaker GlaxoSmithKline said Wednesday [26 July] ... While Glaxo's vaccine offers protection against the H5N1 virus now circulating, its impact on any mutated strain of the virus is not certain.

(www.iht.com, 26 July 2006; *IHT*, 27 July 2006, p. 3)

Vietnam ... is an example of how determined, comprehensive efforts can check the potentially lethal virus. After culling 51 million birds, or more than 17 per cent of the domestic poultry population, and conducting a comprehensive vaccination campaign, Vietnam has not registered any avian influenza cases since mid-November [2005], nor any outbreaks in birds since mid-December ... [Vietnam has used a] combination of aggressive culling, vaccination and intensive surveillance ... Bird flu spread widely in Vietnam before authorities recognized the threat in early 2004 and moved into battle mode ... When outbreaks persisted through mid-2005 Hanoi raised the compensation for dead and culled birds to 50 per cent of the market value, up from 10 per cent, encouraging more co-operation from farmers. Then in October Vietnam launched an expensive, logistically complicated campaign to vaccinate domestic poultry. The measures appear to have checked the virus ... [But] Vietnam's battle against bird flu is far from over ... Hanoi is worried about bird flu in China and the uncontrolled cross-border poultry trade ... Public complacency poses another risk ... Agricultural experts caution that the lethal H5N1 virus is almost certainly present in migratory birds, waterfowl and ducks ... Small disease outbreaks could be passing unnoticed ... Hanoi has asked the international community for $266 million in aid to boost veterinary services and disease control, restructure its poultry industry and improve health services.

(*FT*, 2 August 2006, p. 7)

'A dead swan at a zoo in eastern Germany has tested positive for H5N1 ... The bird was found in a pond at the Dresden zoo on Monday [31 July]' (*The Independent*, 5 August 2006, p. 26).

Beijing confirmed on Tuesday [8 August] that the country's first human case of the H5N1 bird flu virus in 2003 was two years earlier than originally reported ... The case has spurred questions about whether there might have been other human H5N1 infections in mainland China before what had been its first reported human case, near the end of 2005 ... A spokesman [for China]: 'Although this human infection confirmed in the mainland was two years earlier than previous figures, it has no indication that China had an outbreak of bird flu in 2003' ... Eight Chinese researchers published a letter in the *New England Journal of Medicine* in June saying a twenty-four-year-old soldier, who was admitted to a hospital in November 2003 for respiratory distress and pneumonia, had been infected with H5N1 ... China's health ministry confirmed the case on Tuesday by 'parallel laboratory tests' carried out in co-operation with the WHO ... [The WHO] said the health ministry had told the WHO that military scientists first tested the man and found he was infected with the H5N1 virus but did not tell the health ministry until much later ... Experts in Hong Kong have long suspected that the virus has always been present in mainland China, but the Chinese authorities have denied that. Even after several members of a Hong Kong family contracted the virus in Fujian province in southern China, the incident was swept under the carpet.

(www.iht.com, 8 August 2006; *IHT*, 9 August 2006, p. 4)

A new technique for making human vaccines against H5N1 avian influenza produces inoculations that are effective at very low doses, potentially solving the vexing problem of how the world will make adequate numbers of shots in the event of a flu pandemic. In research being published by the journal *The Lancet*, a team of Chinese researchers at the Sinovac Biotech Company in Beijing described how they had made a vaccine using a slightly altered whole bird flu virus, and then enhanced its effect with another chemical, called an adjuvant. The researchers inoculated 120 volunteers and found that nearly 80 per cent given two shots at the optimal dose developed immunity to avian influenza ... The study was small, but the results are more encouraging than with previous attempts to create a vaccine.

(*IHT*, 7 September 2006, p. 4)

In an emergency enough could be produced for 675 million people. The Chinese vaccine consists of the H5N1 avian flu virus inactivated so that it cannot cause disease, combined with an additive (adjuvant) that enhances the immune response ... The manufacturer is Sinovac Biotech, a Beijing-based pharmaceutical company, which jointly developed it with the Chinese Science and Technology Ministry and the country's Centre for Disease Control and Prevention.

(*The Times*, 7 September 2006, p. 25)

Avian flu kills in much the same way the 1918 flu did, by drowning victims in fluid produced in their own lungs, a new study has found. The study also suggest that immediate treatment with antiviral drugs is crucial ... Because the body's own immune response does part of the damage, doctors should consider giving anti-inflammatory drugs along with antivirals like Tamiflu. Although the results of the relatively small study ... eighteen people with the H5N1 avian flu in 2004 and 2005 ... are precisely what flu experts had predicted from laboratory work ... [one expert] called it a major advance because so little clinical information had previously been gleaned from the 241 known cases of the disease.

(*IHT*, 11 September 2006, p. 2)

A fifty-nine-year-old man who bred and raised fighting cocks in northeastern Thailand contracted the H5N1 bird flu virus and has died, bringing the country's death toll from the disease to seventeen, health official said yesterday [26 September] ... He died on 10 August.

(*FT*, 27 September 2006, p. 8)

'An eleven-year-old Indonesian boy has died of bird flu, an official ... said yesterday [15 October] ... "so confirmed cases [in Indonesia] are now seventy-one, fifty-three of whom died" [he said] The boy, from south Jakarta, died on Saturday [14 October]' (*FT*, 16 October 2006, p. 6).

'Vietnam has the highest number of bird flu cases recorded by the WHO since 2003 and the highest number of fatalities after Indonesia' (www.iht.com, 26 October 2006).

The WHO's new plan for ramping up the production of flu vaccine is a measure of how unprepared the world is to cope with an onslaught of pandemic influenza. The plan, conceived by a group of more than 120 experts, lays out a sensible path toward vaccine sufficient – but it will take years to complete and cost up to $10 billion ... So far only 256 people in ten countries – mostly people in close contact with chickens in Asia – but the highly lethal pathogen has killed some 60 per cent of those.

(Editorial, *The New York Times*, in *IHT*, 30 October 2006, p. 8)

Margaret Chan, a bird flu expert, won the nomination Wednesday [8 November to become the world's top health official, a position that would make her the first Chinese national to hold a top United Nations post ... The executive board of the WHO chose Chan to be its next director-general over four other candidates in a tight race to fill the post vacated by the death in May [2006] of Lee Jong Wook ... Anders Nordstrom has been acting director-general ... The board set Chan's term to start on 4 January [2007] and to last until the end of June 2012 ... Chan's nomination must be approved by a two-thirds majority at a special session of the agency's governing World Health Assembly, comprised of all 193 member countries. The World Health Assembly has never rejected a recommendation from the executive board.

(www.iht.com, 8 November 2006)

Margaret Chan of China [is the WHO's] top official on bird flu ... She is a former director of the department of health in Hong Kong whose career has been focused on public health ... She had been the frontrunner to replace Lee Jong Wook of South Korea, who died unexpectedly in May from a blood clot in the brain, three years into his five-year term as director-general ... Chan stepped aside from her job as the WHO's assistant director-general for communicable diseases to run for the top job in global health ... China has recently been criticized for dragging its feet in reporting outbreaks of bird flu to the WHO and supplying virus samples to the global health community for analysis.

(*IHT*, 9 November 2006, p. 5)

China agreed Friday [10 November] to share its sample of the bird flu virus ... from 2004 and 2005 ... with international health authorities, after rejecting scientists' findings that a new, vaccine-resistant strain was circulating in the country ... The decision came after China rejected findings in a paper published ... in *The Proceedings of the National Academy of Scientists* ... last week by Hong Kong and US scientists that reported they had detected a new strain of H5N1 in the southern Chinese province of Fujian last year [2005] ... [China said that when it] had co-operated in the past, the samples had been misused and had encroached upon intellectual property rights ... H5N1 has caused twenty-one human infections in China since late 2003, killing fourteen people.

(www.iht.com, 10 November 2006)

Studies published Thursday [23 November] ... [by] a mix of experts from Indonesia, the WHO and the Centers for Disease Control and Prevention in Atlanta ... were of family clusters of flu cases in Turkey and Indonesia ... The studies followed clusters in three separate families in Indonesia in 2005 and in what appears to have been one extended family near Dogubayazit, in eastern Turkey, in January [2006]. Case clusters particularly worry public health officials because they raise the possibility that the flu is mutating to spread faster between people. In the Indonesian cases the authors ... concluded that human-to-human transmission had probably taken place in two of the three family clusters. In one case a thirty-eight-year-old government auditor appeared to have caught the flu from his eight-year-old daughter or her one-year-old sister. All three died; his wife and two sons did not become ill. No one in the family had any known contact with poultry, wild birds, animals or sick people, so the source was a mystery ... 'But you cannot tell what a young child has done,' said [one of the authors] ... The Dogubayazit cluster was a cause célèbre for some internet flu-watchers following Turkish media reports in January. They argued that widespread human-to-human transmission seemed to be taking place, and that it may have begun at a banquet in late December [2005] attended by members of two related families ... The Turkish government and the WHO did not link the cases or families and tentatively blamed all transmission on birds ... Only eight were confirmed by a WHO laboratory. All were children; four died and four survived ... The lead author ... said he believed there had been no human-to-human transmission because all the children had been in close contact with poultry within seven or fewer days before they fell ill and because none of their parents or the hospital staff that treated them had become sick.

(www.iht.com, 24 November 2006; *IHT*, 25 November 2006, p. 8)

South Korean quarantine officials on Sunday [26 November] began slaughtering ... poultry after an outbreak of the virulent H5N1 form of bird flu at a chicken farm ... The outbreak occurred last week ... South Korea killed 5.3 million birds during the last known outbreak of bird flu in 2003. The H5N1 virus began ravaging Asian poultry stocks in late 2003 and has killed at least 153 people worldwide. So far the disease remains hard for people to catch and most human cases have been traced to contact with birds.

(www.iht.com, 27 November 2006)

Having killed millions of chickens and geese, the bird flu epidemic is now claiming the lives of pet dogs and cats in South Korea ... Confirmed cases of bird flu in humans [number] 258 ... At least 153 people have died of the H5N1 virus in ten countries since [2003] ... Most of those who have died from H5N1 have been in South-east Asia, especially in Indonesia and Vietnam. Nearly all the infections have occurred in people who lived on farms or villages in close daily proximity to chickens or ducks ... A mutation of a virus is believed to have created the Spanish flu, which killed between 20 million and 100 million people across the world in 1918 and 1919. Human-to-human infections may have occurred during outbreaks of bird flu in Hong Kong and Europe in 1997, which remained under control.

(*The Times*, 28 November 2006, p. 38)

South Korea will cull more than half a million fowl ... having already killed 150,000 chickens ... Last week South Korea confirmed it had its first outbreak of the deadly strain in about three years ... Between December 2003 and March 2004 about 400,000 poultry on South Korean farms were infected. In that outbreak 5.3 million birds were destroyed.

(*FT*, 1 December 2006, p. 8)

Several cases of avian flu have spread from poultry to humans in the Nile Delta, the Egyptian health authorities said this week as they worked to halt the outbreak among chickens and ducks. A fifteen-year-old girl died Monday [25 December], a day after the death of a woman in her thirties whose family members showed symptoms of infection. Egypt has reported nine confirmed human deaths from H5N1 avian flu since it was first found in birds in February and in a person in March.

(*IHT*, 28 December 2006, p. 3)

An outbreak of the lethal H5N1 strain was found on a poultry farm [in Vietnam] in December [2006], the first in almost a year. New WHO chief

Margaret Chan has warned that bird flu remains a global threat ... [She] said reports of bird flu had started to surface in recent weeks after a lull and that the danger was particularly severe in poor countries.

(www.bbc.co.uk, 5 January 2007)

Indonesia has the world's highest human death toll from the H5N1 virus and registered more bird flu deaths in 2006 than any other nation ... Two women in Indonesia have died after contracting bird flu ... raising the country's total number of human deaths to sixty-one ... The latest deaths are the third and fourth fatalities of 2007 in Indonesia ... Criticism over the country's handling of the disease has led to fresh attempts over the past year to raise awareness.

(www.bbc.co.uk, 13 January 2007)

The deadly H5N1 strain of avian influenza is making a seasonal resurgence in Asia and could easily spread to Europe again this year [2007], the WHO warned yesterday [14 January 2007]. The alarm follows four human deaths in Indonesia in the last five days, the first human case in China for six months (though the infected man has since recovered) and new poultry outbreaks in Vietnam – despite a huge campaign against it – and northern Nigeria ... [The WHO said it was] convinced that we are in a repeat of last year and the year before when the virus began to get very active again [in the northern hemisphere winter] and spread from Asia into the Middle East and beyond. Indonesia, where sixty-one people have died, remained the 'biggest flashpoint' ... The strain detected in Asia is a mutation of last year's, but it is not showing any sign of moving to a strain that would be more dangerous to humans or have a great likelihood of human-to-human transmission ... All four human fatalities in Indonesia contracted the virus from infected birds ... The latest outbreak in Vietnam, in six southern provinces despite a widespread poultry cull and tight controls on birds that had resulted in no human cases since 2005.

(*FT*, 15 January 2007, p. 7)

Thailand has suffered an outbreak of the deadly H5N1 strain of bird flu, its first for six months ... Vietnam says bird flu has reached a seventh province in the Mekong Delta region ... Health officials across Asia are on alert as a growing number of countries have reported cases in both birds and humans in recent weeks ... Japan is culling 12,000 birds after an outbreak at a farm south-west of Tokyo at the weekend. It is not clear if the virus is the deadly H5N1 strain ... Bird flu has claimed more than 150 lives since it began ravaging Asian poultry farms in late 2003.

(www.bbc.co.uk, 15 January 2007)

Officials in Japan have confirmed that a recent outbreak of bird flu at a poultry [chicken] farm was the deadly H5N1 strain of the virus ... There were a number of H5N1 outbreaks in Japan in early 2004, but there have been no human deaths from the virus.

(www.bbc.co.uk, 16 January 2007)

116 *Political developments*

History's most virulent influenza strain, the 1918 Spanish flu, killed millions of previously healthy young adults by sending their immune system into fatal overdrive, a study of monkeys infected with the virus shows ... The 1918 virus was reconstructed by genetic engineering from human victims of the great epidemic. All the animals were dead within a week, their lungs overwhelmed by an excessive immune response ... The experiment ... helps explain why so many of the 50 million killed by Spanish flu were healthy men and women in the prime of life ... Many of the 161 human deaths from H5N1 infection since 2003 showed symptoms of an excessive immune reaction similar to that in the monkeys killed by the 1918 virus.

(*FT*, 18 January 2007, p. 9)

Hungary yesterday [24 January] confirmed that the ... H5 virus killed domestic fowl that died over the weekend, raising the prospect of a new outbreak of bird flu in Europe ... Preliminary laboratory results suggested it was the N1 strain, in what would be the first outbreak of H5N1 since August last year [2006].

(*FT*, 25 January 2007, p. 9)

The EU has confirmed that the deadly H5N1 strain of bird flu has been found on a farm in Hungary ... A flock of 3,000 geese on the infected farm has been destroyed. It is the EU's first case of bird flu for about six months ... The virus first appeared in the country in February last year [2006] in wild geese, swans and domestic poultry.

(www.bbc.co.uk. 29 January 2007)

So far only 163 people worldwide have died from the virus – mostly in Indonesia, Vietnam, Thailand and China ... In 2006 the virus became deadlier, killing 70 per cent of the people who caught it ... The UN's Food and Agriculture Organization (FAO) reckons H5N1 has cost South-east Asia's poultry farmers $10 billion since 2003.

(*The Economist*, 27 January 2007, p. 57)

'The number of cases among humans is also rising – by the end of 2006 the number of human deaths from the disease had more than doubled in a year, with a noticeably higher mortality rate of almost 60 per cent' (www.bbc.co.uk, 26 January 2007).

The World Health Organization (WHO) has provided information on the number of human cases (total 269) and deaths (total 163) as of 22 January 2007. The respective figures for countries (in alphabetical order) are as follows: Azerbaijan, 8 and 5; Cambodia, 6 and 6; China, 22 and 14; Djibouti, 1 and 0; Egypt, 19 and 11; Indonesia, 80 and 62; Iraq, 3 and 2; Thailand, 25 and 17; Turkey, 12 and 4; Vietnam, 93 and 42 (www.bbc.co.uk, 27 January 2007).

Officials in Japan have confirmed that a recent outbreak of bird flu at a poultry farm was the deadly H5N1 strain of the virus ... The earlier out-

Political developments 117

break occurred in mid-January at a farm in the same region ... There have been a number of H5N1 outbreaks in Japan since early 2004.

(www.bbc.co.uk, 27 January 2007)

'Japan has confirmed only one human H5N1 infection and no human deaths' (www.iht.com, 26 January 2007).

Nigeria's first human fatality from bird flu has been confirmed by the WHO. Tests in London confirmed that a twenty-two-year-old woman [from Lagos] who died on 17 January was infected with the deadly H5N1 strain. Nigeria reported several human cases last Wednesday [31 January] ... Nigeria reported Africa's first cases of H5N1 about a year ago. Other cases have been reported in Egypt and Djibouti, which have suffered human deaths, and also in Cameroon, Djibouti, Niger, Ivory Coast, Sudan and Burkina Faso.

(www.bbc.co.uk, 3 February 2007)

'It is understood that the dead woman bought the infected chickens from a local farmer' (www.bbc.co.uk, 31 January 2007).

The British authorities confirmed on Saturday [3 February] that bird flu among turkeys at a poultry farm in the east of the country has been caused by the potentially deadly H5N1 strain that has killed humans in other parts of the world. It was the biggest outbreak of that strain reported in Britain ... The virus had been found in only one of the farm's twenty-two turkey sheds ... The outbreak near Lowestoft has killed 2,500 turkeys ... and a further 160,000 birds will now be culled ... It is the first time the H5N1 strain had been found on a British farm. The virus was identified as the highly pathogenic Asian strain, similar to that found in Hungary in January ... The outbreak is the first known instance of H5N1 in Britain since an infected wild swan was found ... washed up ... in Scotland [in April 2006] ... Government scientists said it had probably carried the infection from Germany ... Turkeys and chickens are more susceptible to H5N1 than wild birds, which can carry the virus over long distances without showing symptoms ... Since 2003 164 people, most of them in Asia, have died of the disease.

(www.iht.com, 3 February 2007; *IHT*, 5 February 2007, p. 3)

The avian flu virus which killed 2,600 turkeys at a Bernard Matthews farm in Suffolk has been confirmed as the Asian strain of the H5N1 virus ... A spokeswoman for the [UK] Department for the Environment, Food and Rural Affairs [Defra] ... said the flu was the 'highly pathogenic' Asian strain, similar to the virus that was found in Hungary in January. In that incident, the first time bird flu had re-occurred in the EU since August 2006, a flock of 3,000 geese were killed ... It is the first case on a UK commercial farm of an H5N1 infection ... The strain has killed 164 people – mainly in South-east Asia – since 2003 ... Britain's deputy chief veterinary officer said an investigation was under way but the most likely source of the outbreak was wild birds ... Professor John Oxford, a virologist, said: 'The most likely explanation is that a small bird has come in through a ventilation shaft. One good thing about this virus is that it's easily destroyed. You can kill it with a bit of detergent' ... In [April] 2006 a wild swan found dead in Fife [Scotland] was found to have the H5N1 strain of the virus.

(www.bbc.co.uk, 3 February 2007)

'Officials [in the UK] were uncertain how the virus entered the turkey shed at the Bernard Matthews farm, but there were suspicions that faeces or other matter from waterfowl were carried in by a contaminated worker, feed or equipment' (*FT*, 5 February 2007, p. 1).

'To date there have been 270 human cases and 164 deaths, but only a few reports of human-to-human transmission ... [The H5N1 virus has] got a huge mortality rate, around 61 per cent, but it is very hard to catch' (www.bbc.co.uk, 5 February 2007).

The H5N1 virus remains primarily a disease of birds ... Turkeys are particularly vulnerable because stocks are so inbred, meaning they are all genetically similar ... It has killed or forced the slaughter of more than 200 million birds. But it does occasionally infect people. There have been 271 confirmed bird flu cases in humans worldwide and 165 deaths since 2003, according to the WHO ... The latest death, that of a twenty-two-year-old Nigerian woman, was the first known human fatality from the H5N1 virus in sub-Saharan Africa.

(www.iht.com, 5 February 2007)

The bird flu outbreak at a Bernard Matthews farm in Suffolk may be linked to imports from the firm's plant in Hungary, a government vet has said. The pathogenic H5N1 strain was found on a Hungarian geese farm in January ... [The deputy chief vet] said imported 'poultry product' was a possible route of infection. Meanwhile, tests on culled turkeys from three sheds on the Suffolk farm, near the shed in which the virus was first found, also showed strains of H5N1 ... Defra said preliminary tests showed the Hungary and UK viruses 'may well be identical' ... Defra confirmed 'partly processed' turkey had been transported by lorry from Hungary to the Suffolk farm each week up to the time of the Suffolk outbreak. The turkeys were taken to a processing plant next to the premises which became infected ... [The vet] said the 'working hypothesis' was that the infection came into the farm through such an import. He said the latest tests 'seem to indicate that this is an infection that has been passed from poultry to poultry', rather than from wild birds ... [A spokesman for Bernard Matthews said that] 'we don't move live birds between Hungary and the UK'.

(www.bbc.co.uk, 8 February 2007)

The poultry company at the centre of the avian flu outbreak admitted yesterday [5 February] that lorries from Hungary had made regular visits to its Holton [Suffolk, UK] plant ... Government vets are investigating urgently possible links between the Bernard Matthews firm and the outbreak of the H5N1 virus on a goose farm in Hungary ten days ago ... A possible link through the movement of human beings from Hungary is being investigated.

(*The Times*, 6 February 2007, p. 6)

'Experts discounted suggestions that the virus might have been brought to Suffolk on a lorry or the boots of a worker from Hungary ... Bernard Matthews owns Saga poultry, the largest poultry producer in Hungary' (*The Independent*, 6 February 2007, p. 4).

Turkish officials have confirmed that there has been an outbreak of avian influenza [among chickens] in the country's south-east ... Turkey saw the first human deaths from H5N1 outside Asia, in January 2006, when twelve people were infected, four of whom later died.

(www.bbc.co.uk, 8 February 2007)

The deadly H5N1 strain of bird flu has been found close to the Pakistani capital, Islamabad. All the chickens in the infected flock died from the flu or were slaughtered ... Last March [2006] H5N1 was found in north-west Pakistan, India and Afghanistan.

(www.bbc.co.uk, 6 February 2007)

Indonesia has signed a preliminary deal with a US drug manufacturer to jointly develop a human bird flu vaccine in a move that has stirred controversy. Under the memorandum of understanding Indonesia will provide samples of the bird flu virus to Baxter International. In return, Baxter will offer Indonesia technical help to produce a vaccine ... [The WHO] said Indonesia had not shared samples since the start of the year [2007] ... [Indonesia] says it wants to maintain intellectual property rights over the strains of the H5N1 virus that are discovered in the country ... [and that it] cannot share (virus) samples for free.

(www.bbc.co.uk, 7 February 2007)

Indonesia decided to act after a foreign company announced work on a vaccine that would be based on its samples. Indonesia stopped co-operating with the WHO and started negotiations to send future samples to another vaccine maker in return for technology that would allow Indonesia to make its own vaccine.

(www.iht.com, 16 February 2007)

('Indonesia agreed yesterday [16 February] to resume sharing samples of the deadly bird flu virus with the WHO, but only after steps were taken to ensure developing countries get fair and equitable access to vaccines ... Indonesia [said it] would wait until the new mechanisms were in place ... Indonesia stopped sharing in mid-January after learning that the Australian pharmaceutical group CSL had developed a vaccine using the Indonesian H5N1 human strain without permission. It blamed the WHO for providing drug companies with free access to the samples ... Last week Jakarta signed a deal with Baxter International that gave the American company commercial rights to the Indonesian bird flu strain in return for supplying Indonesia with cheap vaccines ... Indonesia wants intellectual property rights over its bird flu strain': *FT*, 17 February 2007, p. 7. 'Indonesia will resume sending avian flu samples to the WHO as soon as it is guaranteed access to affordable vaccines against the disease ... A meeting of Asian nations to work out the guarantee, announced late Friday [16 February], was scheduled for next month [March] ... Indonesia stopped sending virus samples to the health organization early last month [January], complaining that it and many other poor countries did not want their flu strains made into patented vaccines that only rich countries could afford ... [The WHO] said that a fund to buy vaccines for poor countries could be discussed at the March meeeting and that the agency would help Indonesia eventually develop its own vaccine factories ... Baxter Healthcare said it had not asked Indonesia to stop co-operating with the health organization': www.iht.com, 18 February 2007; *IHT*, 19 February 2007, p. 7. '[Indonesia said the Baxter] deal would go ahead despite Friday's agreement with the WHO': www.bbc.co.uk, 16 February 2007.)

> [UK] government inspectors are investigating whether an outbreak of avian flu at a turkey farm in Suffolk owned by Bernard Matthews last week was caused by the importation of infected meat from Hungary. After previously discounting a Hungarian connection, officials have discovered that the H5N1 virus identified in Suffolk is the same strain as one found on a goose in Hungary in January. Officials are looking into movements of lorries of partly processed infected carcasses to and from a Bernard Matthews-owned processing plant near to the Suffolk farm. They do not know from where in Hungary the infected meat might have originated ... Bernard Matthews has fifteen farms in Hungary and owns Saga Food, the country's largest poultry exporter ... Bernard Matthews said it had voluntarily agreed to suspend the movement of poultry products temporarily to and from Hungary until the investigation was complete 'as a precautionary measure'.
>
> (*FT*, 9 February 2007, p. 3)

'[On 8 February] Turkey said it was culling birds after new infections were discovered in the south-east of the country' (*FT*, 9 February 2007, p. 6).

> [UK] governments scientists ... now believe ... the infection ... was most likely imported into the [Suffolk] factory from infected meat it acquired in Hungary ... The nearby meat processing plant has continued to operate and only last Thursday [8 February] stopped using meat from Hungary. Officials believe infected meat carcasses from the Suffolk processing plant may have been dumped in skips left open to the air, which may have allowed rats or seagulls to contact the virus and then spread by gaining access to sheds where turkeys were being raised nearby ... Defra ... said it was continuing to investigate the lorry transport of 'partly processed meat' ... The British

Food Standards Agency is considering the withdrawal of processed turkeys from shops across the UK.

(*FT*, 10 February 2007, p. 2)

Health workers in South Korea have begun to cull thousands of chickens after a new bird flu outbreak was discovered near Seoul. Chickens began dying on Tuesday [6 February] The outbreak is the country's sixth since bird flu reappeared there three months ago, after a three-year absence. It is not yet known whether it is the H5N1 strain of the virus.

(www.bbc.co.uk, 10 February 2007)

The outbreak [in South Korea] ... was caused by the H5 strain of the virus, but further tests are needed to determine whether it has been caused by the N1 type ... In January South Korean officials said that the deadly H5N1 strain of the virus had been transmitted to a human being during a recent outbreak among poultry, but the person showed no symptoms of the disease as the poultry farm worker developed natural immunity to the disease.

(www.iht.com, 9 February 2007)

A twenty-year-old woman from West Java who had tested positive for bird flu died Sunday [11 February] ... Her death raised Indonesia's overall avian flu to sixty-four fatalities, the highest of any country in the world. After a lull last year [2006] concern has grown since the virus flared in Asia in recent months, spreading through poultry flocks in South Korea, Japan, Thailand and Vietnam. Also over the weekend the deadly H5N1 flu strain was confirmed in chickens at a home in Islamabad, the third case in Pakistan in a week, an official said Saturday.

(*IHT*, 12 February 2007, p. 4)

Hungary said Bernard Matthews exported turkey meat last week to the country, where the UK outbreak may have begun ... [Hungary said] that meat had left the Holton plant and arrived at Bernard Matthews' Hungarian site on either Wednesday [7 February] or Thursday [8 February] ... [The] farm at Holton, where bird flu was detected, was shut down after the outbreak was first suspected – but a processing unit on the same site continued to operate ... Reports on Sunday [11 February] said Bernard Matthews imported turkey from Hungary in the days after the outbreak ... [Defra] said exporting cooked poultry from an exclusion zone was allowed under European rules.

(www.bbc.co.uk, 12 February 2007)

The Suffolk farm ... is resuming the slaughtering and processing of turkey ... The government has now given the go-ahead to restart operations ... The first consignment arrived on Tuesday [13 February] ... A spokeswoman for the [Bernard Matthews] company said turkeys were arriving from more than fifty Bernard Matthews farms around Britain not affected by the exclusion zone in Suffolk.

(www.bbc.co.uk, 13 February 2007)

The strains of H5N1 bird flu found in the UK and Hungary are 'essentially identical', [UK government] scientists said. They found the virus that killed turkeys at the Bernard Matthews plant at Holton, Suffolk, was 99.96 per cent similar to one that infected geese in Hungary. The deputy chief vet [in the UK] ... said the most likely transmission route for the outbreak was from poultry to poultry but investigations were continuing. No evidence of 'illegal' movements of poultry products has been found ... [Hungary] denied reports claiming that geese in Hungary infected with bird flu had been culled at the same plant in the city of Kecwskemet that had processed turkeys exported to England.

(www.bbc.co.uk, 13 February 2007)

Most of the scattered bird flu outbreaks so far this year [2007] can be traced to illegal or improper trade in poultry, scientists believe. This probably includes recent outbreaks in Nigeria and Egypt as well as the large outbreak on a turkey farm in England. Last winter wild migrating birds were deemed the primary culprit in the bird flu infestations that hopscotched across Europe and Africa. Dead swans and ducks were found in many countries, including Austria, France and Italy ... No outbreaks have been attributed to wild birds so far this season and not a single infected wild bird has been detected in Europe or Africa, despite a heightened surveillance system developed in the wake of the crisis last year. In most of the world there have been fewer outbreaks compared to a similar period in 2006 ... Partially processed meat was routinely shipped from the [Bernard Matthews] company's Hungarian farm to the one in Suffolk for final processing. Although the avian influenza virus is killed by cooking, it survives well in raw meat and such shipments may have been brought into England and onto the property. It could have been transported from the processing plant into the animal pens on workers' shoes or farm equipment ... Scientists are unsure why wild birds have not been implicated in spreading bird flu this year, although they speculate it might have to do with warmer weather. Last year extremely cold weather in areas in central Asia where bird flu is endemic might have forced birds like swans that normally do not migrate very far to travel longer distances across Europe ... Globally 272 people are know to have contracted bird flu.

(*IHT*, 13 February 2007, pp. 1, 8)

The bird flu virus ... killed more people in 2006 than it did in 2005 or 2004, and its fatality rate is rising – 61 per cent now, up from 43 per cent in 2005... The disease is out of control in birds in more locations than ever, including places like the Nile Delta and Nigeria ... the 1918 virus had a 2 per cent fatality and yet still killed 50 million to 100 million because it was so transmissible ... The virus is out of control in poultry in three countries – Indonesia, Nigeria and Egypt – with combined populations of 447 million people. A year ago it was out of control only in Indonesia, and Thailand and Vietnam had stifled outbreaks, though the virus returned. China remains a

Political developments 123

mystery; despite official denials there is evidence that it is circulating there, too ... Eighty per cent of all Indonesian households keep poultry ... For unknown reasons, possibly weather patterns and better poultry vaccination in northern China, not as many migrating swans and geese carried the virus up to Siberia, across Western Europe and down into Africa this winter as did last winter. The main culprit now in spreading the virus seems to be illegal or improper trade in poultry, health officials say.

(*IHT*, 15 February 2007, p. 2)

A thirty-year-old Egyptian woman has died of bird flu, bringing the number of confirmed deaths from the virus in Egypt to thirteen ... Egypt has the largest known number of human cases of bird flu outside Asia. Most of those who have contracted the disease have died.

(www.bbc.co.uk, 16 February 2007)

Bernard Matthews was warned about hygiene lapses at its Suffolk turkey farm before the bird flu outbreak. Defra says gulls were seen taking meat waste from open bins ... The report says poultry imported to the UK from Hungary is the 'most plausible' cause of the bird flu outbreak ... There were holes in the houses that could have allowed birds or rodents in.

(www.bbc.co.uk, 16 February 2007)

'[The Defra report also said that] water was leaking from roofs into shed, meaning infection could spread' (*Guardian*, 17 February 2007, p. 6).

The UK's chief scientist ... [says that] bird flu does not appear to have infected the UK's wild bird population ... He confirmed that it was likely that the virus had spread to poultry at the Bernard Matthews factory through infected meat or on the boots of a worker.

(*FT*, 24 February 2007, p. 4)

('No definitive source has been found for a bird flu outbreak on a British farm earlier this year, but it was probably caused by poultry meat imported from Hungary, a [UK] government report said Thursday [19 April]. Defra said the H5N1 bird flu strain ... was essentially identical to the strain that had earlier infected geese in southern Hungary': *IHT*, 20 April 2007, p. 8.)

'[On 16 February Russia reported that] the H5N1 strain of bird flu has killed poultry in the Moscow region for the first time' (*FT*, 17 February 2007, p. 7).

Tests have confirmed the presence of the H5N1 bird flu strain in poultry found dead in two suburban Moscow districts ... west and south of Moscow ... It was the first such outbreak to be recorded so close to the Russian capital ... No human cases of bird flu have been reported in Russia. Bird flu cases were registered in ninety-three towns or settlements in Siberia and southern Russia last year [2006] ... The country's first outbreak this year was registered last month [January] in the Krasnodar territory, an agricultural region near the Black Sea.

(www.iht.com, 18 February 2007)

Russian officials traced dead domestic poultry in several suburban Moscow districts to a single market just outside the city limits Sunday [18 February] as experts reported new outbreaks and tightened quarantines following confirmation of the presence of the H5N1 avian flu strain. The presence of the deadly strain, confirmed by tests Saturday [17 February], was the first such outbreak to be recorded so close to the Russian capital.

(*IHT*, 19 February 2007, p. 7)

The outbreaks of avian flu that shut down farms and markets in the suburbs of Moscow over the weekend are a sign that the virus is moving westward along migratory bird routes, as it did last winter. The Russian authorities confirmed Sunday [18 February] that the H5N1 avian influenza virus had been found on at least six farms within 50 kilometres, or 30 miles, of the capital ... Since December [2006] related deaths have been reported in domestic and wild birds in other countries bordering the Black Sea, including Turkey, Azerbaijan and Georgia, the same countries to which migrating birds brought the flu in the winter of 2005–6. Although it is too early to be certain, the pattern of the Moscow outbreak indicates that it could have been caused by poultry trucked north, rather than by migrating birds.

(*IHT*, 21 February 2007, p. 5)

China's southern Guangdong province is the source of the dangerous H5N1 avian flu virus, according to a genetic analysis of the virus published on Monday [5 March]. And Guangdong appears to be the source of renewed waves of the H5N1 strain ... the team at the University of California Irvine reported ... The researchers' maps show China's north-west Qinghai province to be another source of bird flu's spread ... In contrast to China the researchers found that Indochina – Thailand, Cambodia and Vietnam – appeared to absorb strains of the virus. They said H5N1 spreads there but does not spread from there to anywhere else ... Since 2003 H5N1 has spread to more than fifty countries as far away from China as Nigeria and Britain ... So far it has infected 277 people and killed 167 of them, according to the WHO.

(www.cnn.com, 6 March 2007)

Officials in southern China are cracking down on illegal trade in civet cats to prevent an outbreak of SARS in the coming months, sate news media said Monday [19 February 2007]. About 7,000 health inspectors have been mobilized in Guangdong province, where severe acute respiratory syndrome first emerged in 2002, and have checked 10,000 restaurants for civet cats ... Civet cats, mongoose-like animals, are considered a delicacy in southern China and are suspected of spreading SARS to humans, although the original source of the virus has not been determined. In January 2004 Guangdong banned the raising, selling, killing and eating of civet cats. But health departments have been receiving increasing reports of illegal trade in the animals since November [2006] ... During recent inspections a live civet cat

Political developments 125

and several frozen ones were confiscated and eighteen restaurants were fined ... The disease that was eventually identified as SARS was first reported in Guangdong in November 2002. It was spread by travellers to dozens of countries and killed 774 people worldwide before subsiding in June 2003. There were 349 deaths reported on the Chinese mainland. China was heavily criticized for being slow to release information on its outbreak and has since been trying to co-operate in investigating emerging diseases like SARS and bird flu.

(www.iht.com, 19 February 2007)

A forty-two-year-old woman has become the first person to die from avian influenza in Laos, officials have said. Authorities said they were awaiting further tests to see if the woman was infected with the H5N1 strain ... On Thursday [1 March] the country confirmed a fifteen-year-old girl ... had been infected with H5N1. She is being treated in Thailand.

(www.bbc.co.uk, 4 March 2007)

A thirty-two-year-old Indonesian man has died of bird flu, officials said yesterday [16 March], raising the death toll in the country worst hit by the virus to sixty-five. The victim died on Thursday [15 March] ... In Laos health authorities confirmed that a woman who died this month had contracted the H5N1 virus.

(*FT*, 17 March 2007, p. 7)

Bird flu virus has been found among dead crows in Islamabad, the Pakistani capital, a government official said [on 22 March] ... At least two have tested positive for the H5N1 virus among six to eight samples of more than fifty that died.

(*FT*, 23 March 2007, p. 9)

[It was announced on 22 March that] the deadly H5N1 strain has been found ... in a poultry farm ... 25 kilometres from Dhaka ... Many experts will be worried by the news that Bangladesh has its first case. Many residents live in close proximity to farmed birds and the country has one of the highest human population densities in the world ... Bangladesh is also situated in major migratory routes for wild birds and this particular outbreak is close to a wild bird sanctuary ... The virus has been found in Pakistan, India and Afghanistan in the last year.

(www.bbc.co.uk, 23 March 2007)

Indonesian health officials continued to project a defiant tone Monday [26 March] at the start of a three-day meeting with the WHO over Indonesia's refusal to share its H5N1 bird flu samples with the organization's researchers unless it is guaranteed affordable access to vaccines. Indonesia's announcement in February was criticized by researchers as a major departure from a fifty-year-old worldwide system of free virus sharing, one that would severely limit the ability of the WTO to monitor the ever-changing

126 *Political developments*

> virus. But the country has stood firm on the need to change a system that it says keeps life-saving pharmaceuticals out of the reach of poor countries ... Indonesia has had the most human cases of the H5N1 strain of bird flu. Of 281 cases worldwide, eighty-one were recorded there and sixty-three were fatal ... Countries now send samples of the virus to research centres accredited by the WHO in the United States, Britain, Japan and Australia. Those centres develop potential vaccines that are freely shared with pharmaceutical companies, which then manufacture vaccines that are often too expensive for most developing nations.
>
> (www.iht.com, 26 March 2007)

> [Indonesia] reached agreement with the WHO on Tuesday [27 March] to resume sharing samples of the bird flu virus for research ... After two days of talks WHO officials said they had 'struck a balance' between the need to continue sharing virus samples and addressing the concerns of poorer nations. Under the deal drug companies will require the consent of countries to access their virus samples.
>
> (www.bbc.co.uk, 28 March 2007)

> At the close of an emergency meeting ... [in Jakarta] on Tuesday [27 March] ... the Indonesian health minister announced that she had reached an agreement on vaccines and would begin sharing samples of bird flu viruses again immediately ... The agreement stipulates that until a new system of sharing is developed the WHO will not hand over potential vaccines developed from samples taken from Indonesia to pharmaceutical companies without the consent of the Indonesian government ... [The WHO] said a complete revision of the virus sharing system would not be finalised for at least three months.
>
> (www.iht.com, 27 March 2007)

'[On 26 March] Indonesia recorded two more deaths from the H5N1 strain of bird flu, bringing the total number of deaths to sixty-eight' (www.iht.com, 27 March 2007).

'Three people in Indonesia have died from bird flu, taking the country's death toll to sixty-nine ... [One died] on Saturday [24 March] ... [one] on Sunday [25 March] ... [and one] on Wednesday [28 March]' (www.bbc.co.uk, 28 March 2007).

> Indonesia announced two more deaths from H5N1 bird flu yesterday [29 March] ... bringing the country's confirmed human death toll from the H5N1 virus to seventy-one ... China said a teenage boy had died from the virus. The virus has spread to more than fifty countries.
>
> (*FT*, 30 March 2007, p. 5)

'The deadly H5N1 strain of bird flu has spread to Ghana, the WHO has confirmed ... This is the first time it has been confirmed in Ghana' (*The Independent*, 3 May 2007, p. 27).

'President Chen Shui-bian has named Chang Chun-hsiung from his ruling Democratic Progressive Party as the island's new prime minister ... Mr Chang is Taiwan's former top negotiator with mainland China' (www.bbc.co.uk, 14 May 2007).

'A twenty-six-year-old pregnant woman has become the nineteenth person to die from bird flu in Indonesia this year [2007]' (*The Times*, 15 May 2007, p. 35).

Indonesia said yesterday [15 May] it had resumed sharing samples of the H5N1 bird flu virus from infected humans with the WHO. But it warned it would not allow pharmaceutical companies to use the samples for vaccines unless they were swiftly and affordably made available to the developing world ... The country's health minister told delegates at the annual World Health Assembly in Geneva that ... any vaccine producers must pledge preferential pricing, technology transfer and distribution to countries based on need, not wealth ... Indonesia introduced a resolution on sharing viruses that would require 'the transparent, fair and equitable sharing of benefits' from vaccines developed from virus samples. It said vaccines must be 'affordable and readily available in developing countries' ... Indonesia is the country worst affected by bird flu with seventy-six deaths.

(*FT*, 16 May 2007, p. 8)

China has confirmed a new outbreak of the deadly H5N1 strain of the bird flu virus in the central province of Hunan ... [where] poultry died ... China's last reported case was in March, when chickens died at a poultry market near the Tibetan capital, Lhasa ... A total of fifteen people have died in China from the H5N1 virus ... Officials are working to vaccinate billions of domestic poultry by the end of May in preparation for the northward migration of wild birds in the summer.

(www.bbc.co.uk, 19 May 2007)

The H5N1 strain of bird flu – which appeared in Asia in 2003 and has led to the death of 185 people – is infecting fewer wild birds, indicating it may be dying out in the wild, The World Organization of Animal Health said yesterday [21 May]. But a form of the bird flu virus which can be transmitted between domestic flocks remained unchanged, the OIE said.

(*FT*, 22 May 2007, p. 8)

'On Tuesday [22 May] Ghana reported that it had found a second confirmed case of the H5N2 virus in the centre of the country, some distance from the first case, discovered at the beginning of May' (www.bbc.co.uk, 23 May 2007).

Vietnam confirmed its first human bird flu case in a year and a half on Wednesday [23 May] as the virus continued to spread through its poultry stocks ... Relatives said he [the man concerned] had helped prepare chickens for a wedding reception before falling ill. It is the country's first human infection of H5N1 since November 2005 and comes as bird flu outbreaks have been reported across Vietnam ... No poultry outbreaks were reported in 2006, but cases of the virus emerged again early this year ... The H5N1 virus has killed forty-two people in Vietnam and 185 worldwide, according to the WHO. Meanwhile a five-year-old Indonesian girl has died of bird flu, according to the country's health ministry. Her death brings the number of confirmed human fatalities in Indonesia to seventy-seven, the highest in the world.

(www.iht.com, 23 May 2007)

'The WHO says it has reached a framework agreement to ensure all countries share samples of the deadly H5N1 strain of the virus' (www.bbc.co.uk, 23 May 2007).

Bird flu [striking on Friday 25 May] has spread to two more provinces in Vietnam, as the country's first human case in eighteen months began to improve in health, officials said Monday [28 May] ... [The cases bring] the number of provinces and cities hit by the virus to ten over the past month ... At least forty-two people have died of bird flu in Vietnam, but none since November 2005.

(www.iht.com, 28 May 2007)

'An Indonesian girl has died of bird flu ... bringing the national death toll from the H5N1 virus to seventy-nine, a health ministry spokeswoman said Sunday [3 June] ... Bird flu has killed at least 187 people worldwide since 2003' (www.iht.com, 3 June 2007).

A man has died of bird flu in Vietnam, in the first confirmed human death from the virus there since 2005, health officials said ... [He] died of the H5N1 strain of the virus on 10 June ... Bird flu has killed forty-three people in Vietnam and officials have warned of more human cases as the virus spreads rapidly in poultry in many provinces. None of the country's five recent human bird flu cases has been confirmed by the WHO ... In May Vietnam announced its first human case of the deadly H5N1 virus after containing a previous outbreak since November 2005. The H5N1 strain has killed more than 190 people [worldwide] since 2003, according to WHO figures. Indonesia has been the hardest hit, with eighty deaths.

(www.bbc.co.uk, 16 June 2007)

'Two swans and a duck have died of the H5N1 strain of bird flu ... at a lake in Nuremberg in southern Germany' (*The Times*, 25 June 2007, p. 33).

'Czech authorities have culled thousands of birds at a poultry farm in the east of the country following the discovery of the H5N1 avian influenza virus, A similar outbreak was discovered last week at a nearby turkey farm' (*FT*, 29 June 2007, p. 1).

Tests have confirmed that three swans found dead in eastern France died from the H5N1 bird flu virus, France's first cases of the disease in more than a year, the agriculture ministry said Thursday [5 July] ... Germany said it was raising its assessment of the risk of bird flu following the French announcement and after officials Wednesday [4 July] discovered more birds that had died of the H5N1 virus in the eastern state of Thuringia ... This year's outbreaks probably spread through the migration of infected water birds. Last year [2006] thirteen EU states confirmed bird flu cases – Germany, Austria, Denmark, Italy, Greece, Britain, the Czech Republic, Poland, Slovakia, Slovenia, Sweden, France and Hungary. In France the virus was found in more than sixty wild birds and at a farm with 11,000 turkeys. It has not been detected in the country since April 2006 ... The large flu epidemic that appeared after World War I, also known as Spanish flu, was of avian origin ... Since 2003 the [H5N1] virus has sickened 317 people in a dozen countries, killing 191 of them, according to the WHO.

(*IHT*, 6 July 2007, p. 3)

The German authorities have discovered the H5N1 bird flu virus in domestic poultry for the first time this year [2007]. A goose ... in the state of Thuringia was found to be infected with the virus ... The infected bird lived on a small farm in a remote area.

(*IHT*, 7 July 2007, p. 6)

'Bird flu has killed its first human victim on the Indonesian island of Bali ... The twenty-nine-year-old woman died on Sunday [22 August] ... Indonesia has now confirmed eighty-two human deaths from bird flu' (www.bbc.co.uk, 13 August 2007).

'Only 308 people have succumbed to bird flu worldwide' (*IHT*, 24 August 2007, p. 4).

'An outbreak of bird flu on a poultry farm in Bavaria was identified yesterday [26 August] as the pathogenic strain of the H5N1 virus ... Officials described [it] as the largest culling action in recent German history' (*FT*, 27 August 2007, p. 5).

'Officials confirmed the first H5N1 bird flu outbreak [in China] since May [2007] ... [The] outbreak [was] in Guangzhou' (*FT*, 19 September 2007, p. 14).

A woman has died from ... the deadly H5N1 strain of ... bird flu ... on the Indonesian island of Sumatra ... bringing the country's toll from the disease to eighty-seven ... [Indonesia] has confirmed 108 human cases of the virus, eighty-seven of whom have died.

(www.bbc.co.uk, 8 October 2007)

The type of bird flu found in turkeys on a Suffolk [free-range] farm is the virulent strain, according to [UK] government vets. The virus was discovered on Sunday [11 November] ... All 6,500 birds ... at the affected premises – including approximately 5,000 turkeys, 1,000 ducks and 500 geese – will be slaughtered.

(www.bbc.co.uk, 13 November 2007)

'[This] is the fourth case of avian influenza in the UK this year [2007] and the H5N1 virus has been found in the UK, the Czech Republic, Hungary, France and Germany this year' (www.guardian.co.uk, 13 November 2007).

[The] free-range turkeys ... [were] reared outdoors ... Wild swans and ducks regularly gather at the [Suffolk] farm. There is also a lake within a mile from the family farm that is another favourite gathering place for birds ... Tests on wild birds are being stepped up ... To date, however, there has not been one positive test for avian flu on birds in the UK.

(www.thetimes.co.uk, 13 November 2007)

An outbreak of bird flu in a poultry farm in Bavaria, southern Germany, was identified Sunday [11 November] as the pathogenic strain of the H5N1 virus ... The culling [of] 160,000 ducks and other birds on the farm ... [was] described as the largest such culling action in recent German history.

(www.ft.com, 13 November 2007)

Around 24,000 birds on four [more] premises are being culled as a precaution ... The five premises shared the same farming staff ... Acting chief vet Fred Landeg ... said his department [Defra] was keeping an 'open mind' about how the virus reached the farm, but added that early indications were that it was related to outbreaks in the Czech Republic and Germany – which suggested a wild bird source. The affected birds were free-range – meaning they had access to the outdoors and were located near a lake used by a number of wildfowl ... There was an H5N1 outbreak at a turkey farm ... in Suffolk in February.

(www.bbc.co.uk, 14 November 2007)

A cull of poultry suspected of having bird flu is under way at a second Suffolk farm [one of the four] ... Defra says 5,500 turkeys are ... being 'slaughtered on suspicion' of having the disease ... Precautionary culls are also under way at three additional farms ... Defra ordered the culling of a total of 22,000 free-range turkeys at these three farms.

(www.bbc.co.uk, 15 November 2007)

'[The second] farm where turkeys were being slaughtered on suspicion ... has been given the all-clear, the owners say' (www.bbc.co.uk, 16 November 2007).

The 200th death [worldwide] occurred in September 2007. The first human deaths from H5N1 outside Asia ... in Turkey ... [occurred] in January 2006 ... In June 2007 Indonesia became the first country to have 100 confirmed cases of H5N1 among humans ... The first outbreaks in the EU were recorded in January 2006 when cases were confirmed in wild swans in Italy, Greece, Germany and Austria.

(www.bbc.co.uk, 14 November 2007)

As of 12 November 2007, according to the World Health Organization, there were 335 human cases of H5N1 and 206 deaths. The number of deaths by country was as follows: Indonesia (91); Vietnam (46); Thailand (17); China (16); Egypt (15); Cambodia (7); Azerbaijan (5); Turkey (4); Iraq (2); Laos (2); Nigeria (1) (www.bbc.co.uk, 14 November 2007).

Political developments 131

'A second case of the deadly H5N1 strain has been found in turkeys ... The farm was one of the four where culls were taking place because of fears of "dangerous contact" with the initial case' (www.independent.co.uk, 20 November 2007).

> Indonesia's health minister reiterated Sunday [25 November] that she would not send bird flu specimens to the WHO, saying poor nations needed assurances that any pandemic vaccines developed from the virus would be affordable. Siti Fadilah Supari made the comments on her return from Geneva, where the WHO held an intergovernmental conference aimed at rebuilding a global system for sharing flu viruses following a months-long standoff with Indonesia ... Siti Fadilah Supari: 'The meeting failed to come up with a material of transfer agreement. So we have no obligation to send bird flu virus samples to the WHO' ... Indonesia has been harder hit by the H5N1 bird flu virus than any other country in the world, accounting for ninety-one of the 206 known human deaths from the virus. Vietnam ranks second with forty-six deaths and Thailand third with seventeen. Though Indonesia has been reluctant to share bird flu samples with the WHO, saying it was worried the virus would be used to make vaccines that would be affordable only to the rich, it made exceptions following several human deaths on the Indonesian island of Bali. That appeared, however, to be an attempt to lure tourists back to the resort island, which has been hit by a string of terrorist attacks in recent years. Supari wants to change its fifty-year-old virus-sharing system so that developing countries that hand over samples retain the rights over their biological resources, saying this was not the time for 'safety'.
>
> (www.iht.com, 25 November 2007)

> [On 27 November] a man in China's eastern province of Jiangsu died from the deadly H5N1 strain of bird flu ... [It was] said he had no known contact with dead poultry and no outbreaks of bird flu were reported nearby. A total of seventeen people have died in China from the H5N1 virus and millions of birds have been killed.
>
> (www.bbc.co.uk, 3 December 2007)

> The father of a Chinese man who died of bird flu has also been infected with the virus ... The WHO said it could not rule out the possibility that the H5N1 virus had spread from the son ... [who died] on 2 December ... to the father ... Of the twenty-six cases confirmed to date in China, seventeen have been fatal. Suspected human-to-human transmission of H5N1 has been reported in Hong Kong, Vietnam and Indonesia, but none of the cases have been proven.
>
> (www.bbc.co.uk, 7 December 2007)

> A second woman from Egypt's Nile Delta region died of bird flu on Monday [31 December], the health ministry said, bringing the week's toll from the virus to four. The deaths are thought to have resulted from exposure to

poultry infected with the H5N1 strain ... Nineteen people have now died of bird flu in Egypt in the past two years. The government says the large number of people who keep poultry at home makes it difficult to eradicate the disease. Egypt has the largest known number of human cases of bird flu outside Asia and most of those who have contracted the virus have died. Most of the Egyptians who have died have been women. Women and girls are often responsible for looking after poultry in Egypt. The WHO announced earlier this year [2007] that some of those who had died in Egypt had been infected with a strain of the virus that showed moderate resistance to the antiviral drug Tamiflu. More than 213 people have died of H5N1 bird flu since the disease's resurgence in December 2003 – most of them in South-east Asia. Experts point out that cross-infection to humans is still relatively rare and usually occurs where people have been in close contact with infected birds. But they say if the H5N1 strain mutates so it can be passed between humans, it could become a global pandemic.

(www.bbc.co.uk, 31 December 2007)

Three mute swans in Dorset [a county on the south coast of England] have been found dead with the virulent H5N1 strain of bird flu. Other birds are being tested at Abbotsbury Swannery, near Weymouth ... The swans' carcasses were found following routine surveillance ... Culling of wild birds has been ruled out because experts fear this may disperse birds further ... Defra has set up two restricted areas – a wild bird control area and a larger wild bird monitoring area.

(www.bbc.co.uk, 10 January 2008)

[The] Abbotsbury Swannery holds 600 swans ... Ornithologists say mute swans rarely migrate so it is most likely the virus got into the colony from a passing wild bird. This is not a major migration season, but wintry weather could have prompted some birds to fly to Britain from Europe in search of food ... Dorset is not an area of extensive poultry production.

(www.bbc.co.uk, 11 January 2008)

A fourth swan has tested positive for the virulent H5N1 strain of bird flu ... The fourth swan was one of four found dead at the swannery on Friday [11 January]. Test on the other three proved negative ... Defra said there was currently no evidence to suggest the disease was widespread among wild birds in the area.

(www.bbc.co.uk, 16 January 2008)

As of January 2008 the WHO had confirmed 348 cases of H5N1 in humans in Azerbaijan, Cambodia. China, Djibouti, Egypt, Indonesia, Iraq, Lao People's Democratic Republic, Myanmar, Nigeria, Pakistan, Thailand, Turkey and Vietnam, leading to 216 deaths ... Scientists studying a case in Vietnam found the virus can affect all parts of the body, not just the lungs ... After bird flu claimed its first human victim – a three-year-old boy in Hong Kong in May 1997 – the disease was not detected again until Febru-

Political developments 133

ary 2003, when a father and son were diagnosed with H5N1, again in Hong Kong. Since then it has spread westwards through Asia, the Middle East, Europe and Africa ... The mortality rate presently stands at around 50 per cent of confirmed cases.

(www.bbc.co.uk, 11 January 2008)

Health and veterinary workers are culling thousands of chickens in the Indian state of West Bengal after an outbreak of bird flu was confirmed ... Nearly 10,000 chickens were found dead in the area in the past week ... The birds were found to be carrying the deadly H5N1 virus ... Several outbreaks of bird flu in India in recent years have all been brought under control ... India faced a major outbreak of bird flu [in 2007].

(www.bbc.co.uk, 16 January 2008)

Last year [2007] for the first time since avian flu emerged as a global threat, the number of human cases was down from the year before ... There were eighty-six confirmed human cases compared with 115 in 2006, according to the WHO, and fifty-nine deaths compared with seventy-nine. Experts assume that the real numbers are several times larger, because many cases are missed ... David Nabarro, the senior United Nations co-ordinator for human and avian flu, recently conceded that he worried somewhat less than he did three years ago: 'Not because I think the threat has changed, but because the response to it has gotten so much better' ... The world is clearly more prepared. Vaccines have been developed. Stockpiles of Tamiflu and masks have grown. Many countries, cities, companies and schools have written pandemic plans ... In the worst-hit countries – all poor – laboratories have become faster at flu tests. Government veterinarians now move more quickly to cull chickens. [There are] hospital wards for suspect patients, and epidemiologists trace contracts and treat all with Tamiflu – a tactic meant to encircle and snuff outbreaks before the virus can adapt itself to humans ... The most worrisome aspect of H5N1, virtually all scientists agree, is that it persists in birds without becoming less lethal to them ... David Nabarro: 'This is the most serious bird flu that has ever been known. By 2007 it was in sixty countries. It must be dealt with' ... Despite the culling of hundreds of millions of birds and the injection of billions of doses of poultry vaccine, the virus is out of control in some of the most populous countries – though exactly which ones are in dispute, because some are touchy about conceding that they cannot rid their flocks of it. Bernard Vallat, director-general of the World Organization for Animal Health, has named three countries where it [H5N1] is now endemic in local birds: Egypt, Indonesia and Nigeria. Nabarro added Bangladesh, Vietnam and parts of China. Reports of recurrent outbreaks also persist in parts of India, Myanmar and Pakistan. Last week villagers in India were reported to be killing and eating their flocks before government cullers, who paid less than a third of market value, could seize them ... In December [2007] dying birds were found in Poland and Russia, in Saudi Arabia and even a kindergarten petting zoo in Israel. On 8 January [2008] it reached one of England's most famous swan breeding grounds, the Abbotsbury Swannery, which has been around since the eleventh century ... Pakistan had its first human cases last year [2007], as did Laos, Myanmar and Nigeria.

(www.iht.com, 22 January 2008; *IHT*, 23 January 2008, p. 2)

Three people died of bird flu this week, pushing the number of deaths in Indonesia to 101 – nearly half of all the bird flu deaths in the world. The other countries with the highest reported death tolls are Vietnam (with forty-eight), Egypt (with nineteen) and China and Thailand (each with seventeen). The mortality rate in Indonesia is also the highest in the world. Only twenty-four of the 125 people reported to have been infected have survived. The virus is known to have infected 358 people around the world in fourteen countries, killing 224 of them, according to the WHO. Experts say that because of poor reporting of infections and deaths, the true number could be much higher.

(*IHT*, 1 February 2008, p. 5)

Aviaries at a popular Hong Kong theme park were closed to the public for three weeks beginning Thursday [31 January] after tests indicated that a wild heron found dead in the park may have been killed by bird flu, agriculture officials said ... Last year [2007] Hong Kong discovered twenty-one wild birds infected with H5N1, but it has not suffered a major outbreak of the disease since 1997, when the virus killed six people, prompting the government to slaughter the territory's entire poultry population of about 1.5 million birds.

(www.iht.com, 31 January 2008)

An Indonesian woman died of bird flu [on 2 February] ... bringing the country's death toll from the disease to 103, the health ministry said ... A spokesman said: 'Her death raised the Indonesian death toll to 103 out of 126 cases.'

(www.iht.com, 4 February 2008)

The bird flu epidemic has spread to over half of Bangladesh's sixty-four districts ... Officials in the Indian state of West Bengal – which neighbours Bangladesh – said the virus has been detected in thirteen of the state's nineteen districts ... But so far no cases of human infection have been reported either in India or Bangladesh. Bird flu has also been reported recently in Pakistan ... Last month [January] the UN's Food and Agriculture Organization said that the virus 'appeared to be endemic' in [Bangladesh].

(www.bbc.co.uk, 4 February 2008)

'A forty-year-old man died of bird flu and another man was infected after coming into contact with infected chickens. The latest death was the second in Vietnam this year [2008] and brings the toll to forty-nine' (*The Times*, 15 February 2008, p. 43).

Health authorities [in Hong Kong] tightened surveillance measures against avian influenza Monday [25 February] following the fourth death in mainland China suspected to have been caused by the virus since late last year [2007] ... Her death follows several confirmed cases of bird flu infection since 2 December [2007] ... The WHO has reported 232 deaths worldwide in the past four years, twenty-nine of them in China. Almost all the reported cases have been as a result of close contact between humans and infected birds.

(www.iht.com, 25 February 2008)

'Two more people have died of bird flu in Indonesia, bringing the death toll in the country worst hit by the virus to 107, the health ministry said Monday [31 March] ... Both died last week' (www.iht.com, Monday 31 March 2008).

Beijing has given the go-ahead to a Chinese drug maker to begin large-scale production of a human bird flu vaccine, after a second clinical trial [in November 2007] showed the vaccine was safe and effective, the company said Thursday [3 April]. The vaccine uses an inactivated H5N1 virus from Vietnam, said an official for Sinovac Biotech, which developed the vaccine along with the Chinese Centres for Disease Control ... The virus has infected 376 people in fourteen countries since late 2003 and killed 238 of them, or 63 per cent. An eventual vaccine to protect people against a flu pandemic would probably be made only four to six months after the start of such a disaster, after the culprit virus strain had been identified. But some form of protection would still be needed for the initial months of a pandemic, and drug companies, including Sinovac, are in a race to design what are know as 'pre-pandemic' vaccines. Sinovac is conducting tests to see if its bird flu vaccine offers cross-protection against other strains of the virus found in Indonesia, Turkey and Abhui province in China ... On 2 March [2008] GlaxoSmithKline company said a vaccine it had designed to protect people against H5N1 might be effective in warding off a few different subtypes of the virus.

(www.iht.com, 3 April 2008)

Japan is to become the first country in the world to vaccinate thousands of officials against bird flu. Six thousand health workers and other staff will be inoculated over the next few months and the programme might be extended to cover millions more. Although bird flu has caused 240 deaths since 1993, none has been in Japan. But there are fears that an outbreak elsewhere in Asia could spread quickly in Japan, which has some of the world's most densely populated areas ... Japan has already stockpiled 20 million doses of so-called 'pre-pandemic' bird flu vaccine for use after a major outbreak. The vaccine has been made using the deadly H5N1 strain of the disease collected in Vietnam and Indonesia ... The plan is to initially use 6,400 doses of vaccine to inoculate doctors, quarantine inspectors and other health and immigration officials. If successful, the government aims to expand the programme to others ... [an additional] 10 million people who are in medical occupations or other key jobs such as at utilities ... By taking this action Japan is taking bird flu precautions to levels not seen anywhere else in the world ... Japan is probably the only Asian country which has the resources to do this ... The WHO does not sound convinced that it would improve the chances of Japan weathering a major bird flu outbreak ... WHO spokesman Gregory Harti: '[The planned vaccinations are] a big roll of the dice. Obviously, the Japanese think there's some benefit to be had from this and we are not going to prevent an individual country from using their resources.'

(www.bbc.co.uk, 16 April 2008)

Chinese officials have reported that the country's fifth outbreak of the H5N1 avian flu this year [2008] is killing chickens in poultry markets in the southern city of Guangzhou. Although this particular outbreak is not known to have infected humans, China has already reported three human avian flu deaths this year. Far more worrisome is the 3 April confirmation by the government of Pakistan and the WHO of three cases in a family cluster in Pakistan's North West province late last year [2007], suggesting limited human-to-human transmission ... China's prodigious effort to vaccinate 14 billion chickens annually has been chaotic, compromised by the appearance of significant amounts of counterfeit vaccines and the absence of protective gear for vaccination teams – who might actually spread the disease by carrying faecal material on their shoes from one farm to another.

(www.feer.com, 30 April 2008)

'A three-year-old boy has died of bird flu in Indonesia, raising the death toll from the disease there to 108, the health ministry said yesterday [30 April]' (*FT*, 1 May 2008, p. 10).

South Korean officials say they have killed the entire poultry population of Seoul to curb the spread of bird flu ... The cull began just hours after the authorities recorded Seoul's second outbreak of the virus in a week ... Tests are being carried out to determine if the South Korean outbreak was the deadly H5N1 strain. The virus was detected in southern parts of the country last month [April] ... [For] the first time the virus has been found in Busan – South Korea's second largest city ... The outbreaks brought the number of confirmed detections of the virus in South Korea to twenty-eight.

(www.bbc.co.uk, 12 May 2008)

European medical regulators have approved the first human vaccine against bird flu intended for use before or in the early stages of a pandemic, Glaxo-SmithKline, its maker, said Monday [19 May]. The vaccine, Prepandrix, activates an immune response to the H5N1 strain of bird flu ... The company has previously announced plans to donate 50 million doses of the pre-pandemic vaccine to the WHO ... The official licence comes from the European Commission, the executive arm of the EU.

(*IHT*, 20 May 2008, p. 19)

The Hong Kong government ordered a mass cull of all poultry on Wednesday [11 May] in a bid to stop the spread of the H5N1 virus among birds in hundreds of markets scattered across the territory. Last week officials found the bird flu virus at a poultry stall in one of the city's many so-called wet markets and ordered the culling of 2,700 birds during the week. On Wednesday government officials said that the virus had since spread among the island's poultry population and mass cullings were now necessary as a precaution. Cheng Siu-hin (director of agriculture, fisheries and conservation): 'We have not found any dead chickens – not yet. We have not had any human cases' ... Since the H5N1 virus resurfaced in Asia in 2003 it has killed 241 people in a dozen countries, according to the WHO. The largest number of human fatalities has been in Indonesia, with at least 108 confirmed deaths.

(www.iht.com, 11 June 2008)

The government [of Hong Kong has] decided to preclude future problems with its drastic decision to end live-chicken trade ... The government has offered $128 million to put the whole business out of its misery. That is the cost of a plan unveiled on 20 June to buy back all the licences allowing live chickens to be sold. The latest bout of bird flu was first detected in four wet markets in Hong Kong on 11 June [2008].

(*The Economist*, 28 June 2008, pp. 76–7)

'Authorities in Brussels yesterday [10 October] confirmed two "risk areas" had been set up in Germany to contain a new outbreak of avian flu on a poultry farm in Saxony' (*FT*, 11 October 2008, p. 9).

'The WTO says there have been 246 confirmed cases of the disease in humans since 2003 [including seven in Cambodia]' (www.iht.com, 12 December 2008).

More than 370,000 chickens have been culled in China's eastern province of Jiangsu after an outbreak of the H5N1 strain of bird flu ... The outbreak is thought to be the first in mainland China since June. Meanwhile a man has reportedly contracted the virus in Cambodia, while Taiwan is investigating suspected infection among birds. The death of a teenage girl from H5N1 was announced in Egypt on Tuesday [16 December] and a bird cull is also underway in India. More than 200 people in a dozen countries have died of the virus since it resurfaced in Asia in 2003 ... China's ministry of agriculture said it received notification that the H5N1 virus had been found in two areas of Jiangsu on Monday [15 December] ... Officials say they think migrating birds might have been the source of the disease ... China is among a number of countries experiencing a return of the virus this season. Authorities in the Indian state of West Bengal are implementing a cull after tests on poultry from two villages yielded positive results. In Cambodia another cull is underway after the WTO and government confirmed a young man had the virus ... Authorities in Taiwan say they are investigating the cause of the sudden death of poultry in Luzhu, Kaohsiung county ... Earlier in the week Egyptian authorities announced the death of a sixteen-year-old girl from the virus. The discovery of infected birds in Hong Kong last week sparked a cull of more than 80,000 birds.

(www.bbc.co.uk, 17 December 2008)

A woman suspected of being infected with bird flu has died in Beijing, the local health bureau said today [6 January 2009]. It would be the first bird flu death in the country in almost a year. The woman died yesterday [5 January] ... Xinhua news agency said the woman, from eastern Fujian province, had bought nine ducks at a market in Hebei province, which surrounds Beijing, and then gutted the birds ... The last known reported fatality in China was in February last year [2008] when a forty-four-year-old woman died in the southern province of Guangdong. At least twenty people have died of bird flu in China to date.

(www.independent.co.uk, 6 January 2009)

A [nineteen-year-old] woman has died from bird flu in a Beijing hospital, the government reported Tuesday [6 January], but the WHO said the case did not appear to signal a new public health threat ... Tests confirmed she had the H5N1 bird flu virus ... [She] became ill after buying and cleaning nine ducks in December at a market in Hebei province, which borders Beijing. It was the first reported death in China from the illness in nearly a year ... According to the latest WHO tally, bird flu has killed 248 people worldwide since 2003, including twenty-one in China ... In northern Vietnam an eight-year-old girl has tested positive for the disease – the first human case reported there in almost a year, health officials said Tuesday. The girl from Thanh Hoa province was admitted to a hospital on 27 December with a high fever and other symptoms after eating a sick goose raised by the family ... The H5N1 bird flu virus continues to devastate poultry stocks around the world. China, which raises more poultry than any other country, has vowed to aggressively fight the virus.

(www.iht.com, 7 January 2009)

'China has issued an alert against bird flu following the death of a nineteen-year-old woman from the disease ... Since the outbreak of bird flu in 2003 twenty-one people in China have died. Worldwide 247 people have died' (www.bbc.co.uk, 7 January 2009).

'Nepal said that it had found the H5N1 bird flu in poultry, the first time the deadly virus has surfaced in the Himalayan nation, prompting widespread culling operations in the country's south-east region' (*The Times*, 17 January 2009, p. 46).

A two-year-old girl in northern China is in critical condition after testing positive for bird flu, state media said Sunday [18 January]. It is China's second confirmed case of the virus this month. The girl fell ill on 7 January in the central Hunan province and was taken to her home province of Shaanxi in northern China ... Since the end of 2003 the H5N1 virus has infected numerous species of birds in more than sixty countries in Asia, Europe and Africa. It has not been found in North or South America, including the Caribbean, according to the Food and Agriculture Organization ... [China] reported its first human infection case in 2005. So far thirty cases have been confirmed. Twenty of them have been fatal, Xinhua said. China announced it was setting up a nationwide network to test for the virus.

(www.cnn.com, 18 January 2009)

A Chinese woman has died from bird flu in the eastern Shandong province ... Aged twenty-seven ... [she] died at the weekend after becoming infected with the H5N1 strain of avian influenza ... The three new cases are the first to be reported in China in almost a year ... The toll from bird flu in China is now reported by the state media as twenty-two since 2003 ... The ministry of agriculture said on Sunday [18 January] ... [that] China now faces 'a grim situation' in bird flu prevention, threatened by frequent outbreaks in neighbouring countries ... Bird flu often resurges in the winter months in China, but not every case is fatal ... [The] H5N1 [strain] resurfaced in Asia in 2003, killing at least 247 people.

(www.bbc.co.uk, 19 January 2009)

China has recorded its third bird flu death this year [2009] after a sixteen-year-old boy died in central China on Tuesday [20 January] ... On Saturday [17 January] a twenty-seven-year-old woman from eastern China died of bird flu, making her the second person to die this year ... On 5 January a nineteen-year-old woman died of bird flu after handling poultry.

(www.cnn.com, 20 January 2009)

Shu Yulong, from the National Centre for Disease Control and Prevention ... said that the country is likely to experience an epidemic of human bird flu cases in the next month or two ... Winter and spring are prime bird flu seasons, when more than 70 per cent of cases occur. Millions of Chinese people are heading home for Chinese New Year, increasing the chances of infection ... and in spring birds carry the virus over great distances ... A two-year-old toddler reported to have been in critical condition with the H5N1 virus has now recovered and is described as 'stable' ... In Hong Kong consumers have been told not to eat poultry brought in from the Chinese mainland.

(www.bbc.co.uk, 20 January 2009)

A woman from China's far north-west ... in Xinjiang Uighur Autonomous Region ... has died from bird flu, health authorities said Saturday [24 January], making her the country's fourth fatality from the deadly avian influenza so far this year. The thirty-one-year-old woman ... died Friday morning [23 January] ... Test were positive for H5N1, the department said.

(www.cnn.com, 24 January 2009)

A twenty-nine-year-old man in south-west China is in critical condition after testing positive for bird flu, making him the country's sixth confirmed case of the virus this month, state media said Sunday [25 January] ... The man fell ill on 15 January.

(www.cnn.com, 25 January 2009)

A twenty-one-year-old woman in central China has been infected by the H5N1 strain of bird flu in the country's eighth reported case of the disease this year [2009], the health ministry said Sunday [1 February], as Hong Kong reported that three birds found at local beaches had died of bird flu ... China has reported seven other cases of H5N1 since January, five of which were fatal ... Hong Kong said the carcasses of a goose and two ducks found in the city had tested positive for bird flu ... [but] said it was not clear yet which strain the fowl carried. There are several subtypes of H5 bird flu, including the H5N2 strain, which is not known to be harmful to humans. The more virulent H5N1 strain has killed 254 people worldwide since 2003, including twenty-five in China, according to the WHO. While the disease remains hard for humans to catch, scientists have warned that if outbreaks among poultry are not controlled, the virus may mutate into a form more easily passed between people, possibly triggering a pandemic that could kill millions worldwide ... India has reported no human infections ... [but] the latest outbreak of the virus in poultry is the sixth since 2007 in West Bengal, where more than 4 million birds were culled early last year [2008] in what the WHO called India's worst bird flu outbreak ... Hundreds of thousands of birds were also culled in the north-east of India after the virus was detected there in November [2008].

(www.iht.com, 1 February 2009)

Bird flu is becoming less deadly ... [but] scientists fear that this is the very thing that could make the virus more able to cause a pandemic ... This paradox – emerging from Egypt, the most recent epicentre of the disease – threatens to increase the disease's ability to spread from person to person by helping it achieve the crucial mutation in the virus ... The WHO is to back an investigation into a change in the pattern of the disease in Egypt, the most seriously affected country outside Asia. Although infections have been on the rise this year [2009] ... they have almost all been in children under the age of three, while twelve months ago it was mainly adults and older children who were infected. And the infections have been much milder than usual; the disease normally kills more than half of those infected; all of the eleven Egyptians so far infected this year are still alive. Experts say that these developments make it more likely that the virus will spread. Ironically, its very virulence has provided an important safeguard. It did not get much chance to infect other people when it killed its victims swiftly, but now it has much more of a chance to mutate and be passed on ... [An expert who works with the WHO in Egypt] stressed that there was still no evidence of the disease passing from person to person.

(www.independent.co.uk, 12 April 2009)

Swine flu: influenza A(H1N1 or 2009 H1N1)

'Swine flu is a contagious respiratory disease that affects pigs and can jump to humans' (www.cnn.com, 30 April 2009). 'Mexico is the epicentre of the outbreak' (www.cnn.com, 3 May 2009).

> Hong Kong, the epicentre of a SARS outbreak six years ago, announced some of the toughest measures anywhere on Sunday [26 April] in response to a swine flu outbreak in Mexico and the United States ... One legacy of SARS is that Hong Kong may now be better prepared for a flu pandemic than practically anywhere else in the world. Fearing that SARS might recur each winter, the city embarked on a building programme to enlarge its capacity to isolate and treat those affected with communicable respiratory diseases. The city has also expanded its flu research labs, already the best in the world and leaders in tracking the H5N1 avian flu virus. The so-called bird flu virus ... is different from the H1N1 flu virus causing illnesses in Mexico and the United States.
>
> (www.iht.com, 27 April 2009)

'Pork producers question whether the term "swine flu" is appropriate, given that pigs so far do not seem to be falling ill' (*IHT*, 29 April 2009, p. 5). 'The strain, scientists say, is a mixture of swine, human and bird viruses' (*IHT*, 9 May 2009, p. 3).

> China has banned imports of pork products from Mexico and several US states as part of attempts to prevent a deadly flu virus entering the country. Japan, Hong Kong, Singapore, Malaysia and Indonesia announced plans to screen travellers for symptoms of swine flu. Asian governments are on high alert after the WHO warned of a possible pandemic ... Beijing has banned pork imports from Mexico and the US states of Texas, Kansas and California ... China's ministry of health has warned its citizens to be vigilant although it also noted that so far there is no evidence that the new flu virus can be spread through food ... In Hong Kong ... all travellers will be screened on arrival and any ill person will be quarantined. Japan, Singapore, Malaysia and Indonesia have announced similar plans, with many airports using devices that were put in place to monitor SARS and bird flu over the last few years. H1N1 is the same strain that causes seasonal flu outbreaks in humans but the newly detected version contains genetic material from versions of flu which usually affect pigs and birds.
>
> (www.bbc.co.uk, 27 April 2009)

('A declaration from the WHO [stated] that "there is no risk of infection from this virus from consumption of well-cooked pork and pork products"': *IHT*, 29 April 2009.)

'China and Russia are moving to quarantine visitors with suspicious symptoms. Asian airports have turned on their heat-sensing equipment to detect sick incoming passengers – kit they had installed after earlier scares resulting from outbreaks of avian flu and SARS' (www.economist.com, 27 April 2009).

142   *Political developments*

> New Zealand on Tuesday [28 April] became the first country in the Asia-Pacific region to confirm cases of swine flu ... In China Hans Troedsson, the WHO representative in China, said he believed a school in the province of Shaanxi has been closed down after several students had shown symptoms of respiratory infections ... Earlier on Tuesday the State Council said it would strengthen supervision of and public information about swine flu ... Local media reported over the weekend that up to 100 students of a primary school in northern Shaanxi province suffered from flu symptoms and the school had been shut ... On Monday [27 April] the WHO increased its alert on the H1N1 virus to an unprecedented phase 4, saying that it posed a 'significant risk', intensifying fears that the flu could become a global pandemic. Aside from Mexico, from where the disease spread, there have been confirmed cases of swine flu in the United States, Canada, Spain and the UK.
>
> (www.ft.com, 28 April 2009)

'Chinese officials said on Wednesday [29 April] they would work with Taiwan in controlling any spread of swine flu' (www.ft.com, 29 April 2009).

'On 29 April the WHO upgraded the status of swine flu's spread to grade five [Phase 5] out of six, indicating that a global pandemic is thought to be imminent' (www.baltictimes.com, 30 April 2009).

'The level five designation means infection from the outbreak that originated in Mexico has been jumping from person to person with relative ease' (www.cnn.com, 30 April 2009).

> Phase 6, the highest level in the WHO's alert system, is a pandemic ... The term describes the geographic spread of a disease, not its severity. There can be a pandemic of a mild disease ... Phase 5 means that the disease is spreading in communities – not just within households or in returning travellers – in two countries in one of the WHO's six regions, in this case the United States and Mexico. Phase 5 also means a pandemic is imminent. To move up to Phase 6 community spread would have to occur in at least one other country in another region.
>
> (www.iht.com, 3 May 2009)

'To reach Phase 6 there would need to be evidence that the virus was spreading in a sustained way in a country outside the Americas' (*IHT*, 9 May 2009, p. 3).

> In the clearest sign yet of how seriously China is taking swine flu, President Hu Jintao convened a meeting on Thursday morning [30 April] of the Standing Committee of the Politburo – the nine men who run China – and the meeting was immediately announced. It is rare for China's authorities to disclose any meeting of the Standing Committee, and particularly to do so as soon as the meeting ended ... After struggling to cope six years ago with an outbreak of SARS, the Chinese leadership is taking a much more visible approach now to swine flu ... Government officials hid the [SARS] outbreak for four months, even concealing patients at closed military hos-

pitals, before the disease spread to Hong Kong and then around the world ... On Tuesday morning [28 April] ... President Hu Jintao announced that China was stepping up its inspection and quarantine procedures for people and imports of pigs and pork products ... East Asia, Central Asia and South Asia have not yet had a laboratory-confirmed case of swine flu, although suspected cases are being tested, notably in South Korea and Hong Kong. But flu experts predict that the disease will arrive in the region soon, if it has not already ... The novel form of flu now moving around the globe is politically more palatable for China because it made its first appearance far from China's shores. The new flu does have a genetic segment that has been identified as coming from pigs in Eurasia, prompting the Mexican ambassador to China to suggest that his country should not be blamed for the disease. But flu specialists say that the disease appears to have jumped to people in Mexico. China's agriculture ministry said on Wednesday that swine flu had not been found in the country's pigs and that China had not been the origin of the virus ... [There has been] heavy media attention to the issue in Hong Kong.

(www.iht.com, 30 April 2009)

'The first case of swine flu in Asia was confirmed by the Hong Kong government today ... A Mexican citizen who had flown to the territory with a stopover in Shanghai had developed a fever after arriving yesterday [30 April]' (www.iht.com, 1 May 2009).

Hong Kong authorities quarantined the man at a local hospital ... [and] immediately quarantined the hotel where the traveller had stayed on Thursday night [30 April] ... The man did not leave the airport while in Shanghai ... Hong Kong has begun requiring all travellers to fill out health declarations before entering the territory.

(*IHT*, 2 May 2009, p. 5)

Six years after SARS paralysed this city and killed 299 of its citizens, Hong Kong is not taking chances with swine flu. Within minutes of the confirmation on Friday evening [1 May] of Asia's first swine flu case – a twenty-five-year-old traveller from Mexico – the police had cordoned off the hotel where the young man stayed for fewer than seven hours on Thursday afternoon and evening [30 April]. More than 200 guests will be quarantined in the building for a week ... Roughly 100 hotel staff members will also be quarantined for at least one night at the hotel, and then at government vacation camps that are being converted into quarantine centres Everyone who sat in the five rows closest to the Mexican traveller on a flight from Shanghai to Hong Kong at midday on Thursday is being contacted and will be quarantined for a week, along with the aircraft's flight crew ... Hong Kong has fifteen times as many beds for severe respiratory illnesses as it uses for those illnesses on an everyday basis ... In Beijing authorities suspended all regularly scheduled flights between mainland China and Mexico until further notice. Hong Kong does not have direct flights to Mexico ... Even before lab tests confirmed Friday evening [1 May] that the traveller had swine flu, Hong Kong authorities sent vans of police officers and health workers to the hotel.

(www.iht.com, 2 May 2009)

'China says it will quarantine all those who travelled on a flight from Mexico with a man suffering from swine flu ... Beijing said it would put his fellow passengers under week-long observation. It also suspended flights from Mexico' (www.bbc.co.uk, 2 May 2009).

On Saturday [2 May] Canadian health officials said that the virus has been found in sick pigs on one farm in Alberta, the first report of the swine flu actually being found in swine. Previously there has been heated debate about whether the virus could infect pigs, even though its genetic makeup clearly points to its having originated in swine at some point. But people were infecting each other, and, until Saturday, no pigs had been found with the virus – a fact that the pork industry used to bolster its argument that the virus should not even be named for swine. The news from Canada changes things. But it has a somewhat unexpected shift: a person appears to have spread the disease to pigs, and not the other way around. A worker at the farm had travelled to Mexico, fallen ill there and unknowingly brought the disease back to Canada last month [April]. The worker has recovered. About 10 per cent of the 2,200 pigs on the farm got sick ... All recovered without treatment. The entire herd remains under quarantine as a precaution.

(www.iht.com, 3 May 2009)

On Sunday ... [Mexico] said that the virus appeared to have peaked between 23 April and 28 April ... [Mexico has] 101 suspected deaths, twenty-two confirmed ... Outside Mexico the effects of the virus do not appear to be severe ... More than 100 people, including many Mexicans, have been quarantined in China ... Mexican officials say more than seventy Mexican citizens have so far been isolated ... About fifty are being held in quarantine in Shanghai ... with ten in Beijing. Mexican nationals are also being held in the city of Wenzhou.

(www.bbc.co.uk, 4 May 2009)

The WHO reported Monday [4 May] that the disease had widened globally, with twenty countries reporting 985 laboratory-confirmed cases, compared to 898 confirmed cases in eighteen countries on Sunday [3 May] ... [Mexico has] 60 per cent of the world's total confirmed cases and the United States 23 per cent of the total ... Twenty-five deaths from the disease have been confirmed in Mexico ... In the United States there has been one death, a toddler from Mexico City who died in Texas. No deaths have been reported in other nations.

(www.iht.com, 4 May 2009)

'On Sunday [4 May] a group of twenty-five Canadian exchange students were confined to a hotel in the northern city of Changchun' (*IHT*, 5 May 2009, p. 4).

> The Mexican and Chinese governments sent chartered flights to each other's countries on Tuesday [5 May] to pick up their respective nationals stranded or quarantined because of the global swine flu outbreak. By Tuesday the number of confirmed cases stood at 1,085 in twenty-one countries, according to the WHO. Twenty-five people have died of the virus in Mexico; one died in the United States. An AeroMexico flight was making several stops throughout China to collect nearly seventy citizens who were being held in quarantine ... As a result of the flight suspensions 200 Chinese citizens were stranded in Mexico City and Tijuana. A China Southern Airlines flight was expected to fetch them Tuesday ... Mexican officials have bitterly criticized China for putting Mexican citizens in isolation. They said Mexicans were being singled out because of their passports, despite showing no signs of the virus. China has denied discriminating against Mexicans, saying it is exercising proper precaution to prevent the spread of the virus.
>
> (www.cnn.com, 5 May 2009)

'[A Chinese] foreign ministry spokesman denied there was any discrimination: "The measures concerned are not targeted at Mexican citizens. This is purely a medical quarantine issue"' (www.bbc.co.uk, 5 May 2009).

'Key developments on swine flu outbreaks: deaths, twenty-six in Mexico and one in the United States, a toddler from Mexico who died in Texas; confirmed sickened worldwide 1,447 (802 in Mexico; 380 in the United States)' (www.iht.com, 5 May 2009).

'A Texan with H1N1 flu died this week, only the second death outside Mexico ... The Texan woman [was] in her thirties ... US health officials said she had chronic health problems' (www.independent.co.uk, 6 May 2009).

> An aircraft carrying ninety-eight Chinese stranded in Mexico by the flu outbreak arrived in Shanghai today [6 May] and all appeared healthy but will have to spend a week in quarantine. An AeroMexico plane had arrived in Shanghai a day earlier to pick up dozens of Mexicans ... None of the forty-three Mexicans that China had quarantined showed symptoms of H1N1, prompting Mexico to accuse China of discrimination.
>
> (www.independence.co.uk, 6 May 2009)

> More than 2,000 people in twenty-three countries worldwide now have confirmed cases of the new strain of the H1N1 flu, the WHO said on Thursday [7 May 2009]. Over half of the 2,099 laboratory-confirmed cases are in Mexico ... where forty-two people are confirmed to have died of the disease ... Thirty per cent of the WHO confirmed cases are in the United States, where authorities say the virus is now widespread and two deaths have been reported ... Serious cases of the virus have particularly struck young people for reasons that are still not fully understood ... In Shanghai on Thursday [7 May] travellers from Mexico began to be released after spending a week in

quarantine, while some 350 guests of a quarantined hotel in Hong Kong were due to be released Thursday night.

(www.iht.com, 7 May 2009)

'Hong Kong officials isolated 286 guests and staff at a hotel there after a Mexican guest fell ill' (www.iht.com, 11 May 2009).

The WHO is considering an overhaul of its pandemic ratings system ... The WHO's system of pandemic alerts provides no indication of the danger of the virus. Even if the A(H1N1) virus in Mexico proves no more lethal than a typical seasonal flu, it could soon trigger the highest level 6 WHO pandemic alert once it has been identified as spreading widely between humans in different parts of the world.

(www.ft.com, 7 May 2009)

Nearly 300 guests and staff at a hotel in Hong Kong have been released after being held in quarantine for a week ... Although critics called the quarantine an over-reaction, officials were keen to avoid a repeat of the 2003 SARS epidemic. That outbreak killed 300 people in Hong Kong and 800 worldwide after a single carrier spread the disease in a city hotel. The Mexican man who sparked the scare is in a stable condition at a hospital in Hong Kong. It is not clear when he will be released.

(www.bbc.co.uk, 8 May 2009)

According to the latest WHO tally, 2,384 people in twenty-four countries have been infected with the strain ... Mexico [on Friday 8 May] confirmed another death from swine flu, bringing the national death toll to forty-five ... [while] the total number of people made ill by the virus [rose] to 1,317. The United States has 1,639 cases of the H1N1 flu in forty-three states, with two deaths.

(*IHT*, 9 May 2009, p. 3)

'Canada reported its first death linked to swine flu on Friday [8 May] ... She died on 28 April ... [but it was] not clear to what extent H1N1 may or may not have contributed to her death' (www.iht.com, 9 May 2009).

'China, Indonesia, Russia and a dozen more countries ... [have banned] imports of pork products from the United States and others touched by the virus ... Even before the flu outbreak China had deployed several arguments to keep out American pork' (www.iht.com, 10 May 2009; *IHT*, 11 May 2009, p. 8).

There have been few more dramatic moments at the WHO than the latenight gathering on 29 April, when Dr Margaret Chan, its powerful director-general, declared: 'It really is all of humanity that is under threat during a pandemic' ... In her announcement on 29 April Dr Chan made clear that she alone had decided to raise the pandemic level ... In the days since her announcement, concerns about the swine flu outbreak have eased around the globe ... Coverage of the flu outbreak no longer dominates cable news shows ... But Dr Chan has yet to relax the alert level of the organization, the public health arm of the United Nations. That is because the warning system is based on how far the virus has spread, not its lethality. While most praise the actions of Dr Chan and the WHO in the current outbreak, some have said that the organization needs to adjust its warning system to reflect what is known about the severity of the spreading illness ... Dr Chan said she had been guided in her recent decisions by her experiences during the 2003 SARS outbreak in Hong Kong, where she led the health department. Rules adopted in 2005 by the WHO, based in Geneva, have made Dr Chan perhaps the most powerful international health official in history. She no longer must beg for co-operation from national authorities but can demand information about threats to global health ... In 2005 rules adopted by the WHO gave the director-general complete authority to change the global pandemic alert level ... She faced a terrible decision in 1997 when an outbreak of avian influenza threatened the population. Fresh poultry is a Hong Kong staple, but Dr Chan ordered the region's population of 1.4 million chickens and ducks slaughtered. The outbreak ended. Public health experts who witnessed her handling of SARS gave her high marks ... Dr Chan was later criticized by some in Hong Kong for failing to respond quickly enough to the 2003 SARS epidemic, although a panel of experts supported her leadership. Her rapid and urgent response to an infectious threat from Mexico last month grew out of that experience, several who knew her said ... Initial reports from Mexico suggested that swine flu was both lethal and highly infectious. Only when the disease spread to the United States did it become clearer that it was not as dangerous as feared.

(www.iht.com, 10 May 2009; *IHT*, 11 May 2009, pp. 1, 4)

WHO experts say it is not possible to create a scale giving a scientific assessment of the severity of the outbreak, on the lines of hurricane warnings or the Richter scale for earthquakes. That is because the new flu affects people differently in various countries, depending on their stage of development, healthcare systems and experience in dealing with epidemics.

(www.iht.com, 14 May 2009)

A Chinese man returning from studying at a US university has become the first suspected case of swine flu in mainland China, the health ministry said Sunday [10 May]. The ministry identified the patient as a thirty-year-old student ... He was being treated in a hospital in Chengdu and had been placed in isolation ... Twenty-nine countries have now officially reported 4,379 cases of swine flu, the WHO said Sunday ... Mexico has reported 1,626 confirmed human cases, including forty-five deaths, while the United States has reported 2,254 laboratory-confirmed cases, including two deaths. A third swine-flu-related death was confirmed in the United States over the weekend.

(*IHT*, 11 May 2009, p. 4)

Chengdu city officials said they had located and quarantined more than 130 of the estimated 150 other passengers who had travelled with the infected man on a connecting flight from Beijing to Chengdu, the capital of Sichuan province ... His father and girlfriend, who met him at Chengdu airport, have been placed in quarantine, as has the taxi driver who took him to the hospital ... All three reported deaths in the United States to this point have involved victims with health problems, as has the single fatal case in Canada.

(www.iht.com, 11 May 2009)

China has confirmed the first case of swine flu on the Chinese mainland and is searching for people who could have had contact with the infected man ... The authorities say he travelled from St Louis [in the United States] to Tokyo, then to Beijing and finally landed in Chengdu on Saturday [9 May] ... About 130 people from the patient's flight to Chengdu have already been quarantined.

(www.bbc.co.uk, 11 May 2009)

Mexico has complained that the Chinese measures unfairly target its citizens, and announced Sunday [10 May] that thirty Mexican companies would boycott an international food industry event in Shanghai next week at which they were to have been guests of honour.

(www.iht.com, 11 May 2009)

'The WHO reported Monday [11 may] that thirty countries have officially confirmed 4,694 cases of the new influenza infection. The United States, with 2,532 cases, has now surpassed Mexico with 1,626 cases. Mexico has reported forty-eight deaths from swine flu' (www.iht.com, 11 May 2009).

The number of confirmed case of the new influenza A(H1N1) flu has climbed to 6,497, including sixty-five deaths, the WHO said on Thursday. The number of countries reporting confirmed cases remains at thirty-three ... Other countries with confirmed cases but no deaths ... [include] China (four).

(www.iht.com, 14 May 2009)

'As of 17 May 2009: deaths: global total of seventy-five ... [including] sixty-eight in Mexico, five in the United States ... Confirmed cases: the WHO says thirty-nine countries have reported more than 8,480 cases, mostly in the United States and Mexico' (www.iht.com, 17 May 2009).

'As of 18 May China had three confirmed cases and one suspected case of swine flu and Hong Kong had three, all in people travelling from the United States, Mexico and Canada' (*IHT*, 20 May 2009, p. 2).

'There have been no reports of deaths from H1N1 flu in China. Among nearly 19,000 infections worldwide 117 people have died' (www.bbc.co.uk, 8 June 2009).

The WHO raised its alert on swine flu to the highest level [Phase 6] on Thursday [11 June], in its first designation of a global pandemic in forty-one years ... But the pandemic is 'moderate' in severity ... with the overwhelming majority of patients experiencing only mild symptoms and a full recovery, often in the absence of any medical treatment ... The WHO released a report Wednesday [10 June] saying that seventy-four countries had reported 27,737 cases of the disease and 141 deaths since April ... The last pandemic, the Hong Kong flu of 1968, killed about 700,000 people worldwide. Ordinary flu kills 150,000 to 500,000 people each year ... On Wednesday a fifty-five-year-old man became the first person to contact the disease locally in Hong Kong, according to health officials. So far the city has had no fatalities ... China confirmed ten new flu cases on Thursday [11 June], bringing the total number of infections on the mainland to 111. Health officials say all of the country's flu cases have involved people returning from abroad.

(www.iht.com, 11 June 2009)

The WHO ... emphasized that it was acting because of the geographic spread of the virus to seventy-four countries, not because it had proved particularly lethal ... According to WHO rules, the organization should declare a pandemic upon finding evidence of widespread 'community transmission' – meaning beyond travellers, schools and immediate contacts – on two continents ... Since the outbreak started in Mexico in April, the virus has been heavily concentrated in the Americas, but the rise in cases in Australia and elsewhere appears to indicate community-wide spread in other regions.

(*IHT*, 12 June 2009, p. 5)

'The WHO [said that] ... increasing the alert to Phase 6 does not mean that the disease is deadlier or more dangerous than before, just that it has spread to more countries' (www.cnn.com, 11 June 2009).

'The last pandemic in 1968 killed about 1 million people' (www.bbc.co.uk, 11 June 2009).

Contrary to the popular assumption that the new swine flu pandemic arose on factory farms in Mexico, [US] federal agriculture officials now believe that it most likely emerged in pigs in Asia, but then travelled to North America in a human. But they emphasized that there was no way to prove their theory and only sketchy data underpinning it.

(www.iht.com, 24 June 2009)

H1N1 swine flu has killed more than 700 people around the world since the outbreak began four months ago, says the WHO ... This represents a jump of at least two-thirds from the last official death toll of 429, published by the WHO on 6 July.

(www.bbc.co.uk, 21 July 2009)

More than 1,000 people worldwide have died from swine flu since it emerged in Mexico and the United States in April, according to the latest figures from the WHO. As of 31 July the total number of victims killed by the H1N1 virus, also known as swine flu, stood at 1,154 – an increase of 338 since the WHO's previous update on 27 July. The virus has spread around the world with unprecedented speed, spreading as widely in six weeks as common influenza viruses spread in six months, according to the WHO.

(www.cnn.com, 5 August 2009)

'Chinese health authorities have approved a vaccine that they say prevents swine flu with a single dose ... More than 5,000 cases of swine flu have been confirmed in China. The WTO says the situation in the country is "quite stable"' (www.bbc.co.uk, 3 September 2009).

The new H1N1 flu virus has killed at least 2,837 people [globally] but it is not causing more severe illness than initially feared and has not mutated, the WHO said Friday [4 September] ... About a quarter of a million cases have been laboratory-confirmed worldwide, but this is far fewer than the true number, according to the WHO, which has stopped requiring its 193 member states to report individual cases. Its previous update of 28 August showed at least 2,185 deaths ... The virus could eventually infect 2 billion people, or a third of the world's population, according to WHO estimates.

(*IHT*, 5 September 2009, p. 2)

China's health minister says the nation is facing a grim situation as it tries to contain a rapid surge in swine flu. Chen Zhu said a vaccination programme would start this week, prioritizing those taking part in events to celebrate National Day on 1 October ... China is the first country in the world to use swine flu vaccines, after conducting successful clinical trials ... About 6,000 people have fallen ill with swine flu.

(www.bbc.co.uk, 8 September 2009)

China has developed a vaccine for swine flu and is set to become the first country in the world to begin mass inoculations ... The single-shot vaccine has been approved ... More than 5 million doses will be ready by the end of September ... Health minister Chen Zhu ... [has said] that some 200,000 people taking part in the [1 October] anniversary celebrations will be the first to receive the vaccine ... Chen said on Tuesday [8 September] that there have been 5,592 recorded cases of H1N1 in China's thirty-one inland provinces, but no one has yet died from the illness. He said: 'Due to the rising number of cases, especially since late August, we have indeed started seeing some serious cases' ... There are plans to vaccinate 65 million people before the end of the year [2009].

(www.cnn.com, 10 September 2009)

China has detected eight cases of swine flu mutation, a health official said Wednesday [265 November] ... Last week the WHO said it was investigating samples of swine flu variant linked to two deaths in Norway. But the director of the Chinese National Influenza Centre told Xinhua that the mutated swine flu virus found in China had shown an 'isolated' spread in the mainland, was not resistant to drugs and further infection could be prevented by vaccines.

(*IHT*, 26 November 2009, p. 10)

North Korea on Wednesday [9 December] acknowledged an outbreak of swine flu, as relief officials in South Korea reported that the virus had killed dozens of people in [North Korea] ... North Korea's official news agency, KCNA, said nine cases had been confirmed in the capital of Pyongyang and in Sinuiju, a town near the border with China. It did not say whether there had been any deaths. But the Seoul-based aid group Good Friends said about forty people had already died after swine flu broke out in the North last month [November]. Such reports compelled the South Korean president, Lee Myung Bak, on Tuesday [8 December] to offer to send swine flu medication to North Korea ... Good Friends, which gleans information on North Korea through inside informants, also said that the North Korean government was strengthening customs inspections on the border with China in an apparent attempt to contain the virus. It also said the authorities were instructing schools to start a winter vacation earlier than usual.

(www.iht.com, 9 December 2009)

On Thursday [10 December], in a rare admission of a domestic problem and a sign of new openness, North Korea accepted a South Korean offer to ship swine flu medication, South Korean officials said. A day earlier the North had acknowledged nine cases of H1N1 influenza in Pyongyang and Sinuiju, a town on the Chinese border. But Good Friends, a relief agency based in Seoul, reported that the outbreak was far more serious and has caused dozens of deaths. The South Korean president, Lee Myung Bak, offered Tuesday [8 December] to send vaccine, and on Thursday South Korea's unification minister, Hyun In Taek, said the country was prepared to ship enough Tamiflu and other medications to treat 500,000. It was unusual for the North to accept Mr Lee's offer so quickly. Pyongyang has denounced him for his tough stance against its nuclear programme.

(www.iht.com, 10 December 2009; *IHT*, 11 December 2009, p. 9)

A convoy of South Korean trucks crossed the border into North Korea on Friday [18 December] to deliver medicine to combat swine flu ... North Korea acknowledged for the first time last week that swine flu had broken out in the country after Seoul offered unconditional aid to help contain the spread of the virus. North Korean officials did not mention any virus-related deaths, but a civic group in Seoul said the disease had killed about fifty people in the North since early November. South Korea sent enough doses of the antiviral drugs Tamiflu and Relenza for 500,000 North Koreans.

(www.iht.com, 18 December 2009)

South Korea has sent medicine for swine flu to North Korea, after the North said it had nine cases of the virus ... The shipment of Tamiflu and Relenza, worth $15 million and enough to treat 500,000 people, was taken over the border to the North's town of Kaesong in refrigerated trucks ... [South Korean] officials say they believe the flu virus to be more widespread in the North than reported so far and do not want to see it spread further with the onset of winter.

(www.bbc.co.uk, 18 December 2009)

2 The economy

Economic background

'One of the major tasks after reunification was to socialize the economy of the South' (*The Economist*, 28 March 1992, p. 73).

'In the past couple of years China, Vietnam and the Philippines have been conducting an unprecedented joint survey of the South China Sea to probe its oil and gas reserves' (*The Economist*, 15 December 2007, p. 72).

'Vietnam is blessed with the world's third largest reserves of bauxite, the raw material for aluminium' (*The Economist*, 25 April 2009, p. 64).

The economic system

The general features of command planning and the general issues involved in economic transition are to be found in *North Korea: A Guide to Economic and Political Developments* (Jeffries 2006a).

'The government [is] committed to "market-orientated socialism with Vietnamese characteristics"' (www.iht.com, 28 January 2008).

'Vietnam is following ... [a] path of export-led growth based on a mix of natural resources and foreign investment in low technology industries ... Vietnam has two decades before an ageing population becomes a restraint' (Philip Bowring, www.iht.com, 4 November 2009; *IHT*, 5 November 2009, p. 7).

'Vietnam has imposed a series of price controls on transportation and gasoline in the past week' (*IHT*, 8 April 2008).

'In an ... attempt to limit price distortions as oil surged above $100 a barrel, the government slashed fuel subsidies in February [2008]' (*The Economist*, Survey 2008, p. 5).

> Since the beginning of this century, Vietnam has held third place on average annual GDP growth, just behind China and India, and has been most successful in poverty reduction. It has become a major exporter, ranking fortieth in the world ... Its biggest market is the United States ... Many of the 'boat people' or their progeny now return, bringing valuable capital, know-how and networks. The country also has dynamic demographics: with a

current population of 90 million, it will pass 100 million by 2011, and benefit from a youth dividend ... In pursuing reform and liberalization, the Vietnamese government aims to achieve the status of an industrialized nation by 2010 ... This year [2010] marks the thirty-fifth anniversary of the 'fall of Saigon', which brought to an end the Vietnam War and led in 1976 to the unification of the country as the Socialist Republic of Vietnam. The first decade after that was marked by repression, economic stagnation leading to collapse and the outpouring of refugees. By 1986, however, emboldened by the example of China's opening, Hanoi embarked on a reform programme known as *doi moi*, or 'renovation'. The programme raised hopes and foreign investors flocked in, but initial results were disappointing as implementation of the reforms lagged. In the 1990s foreign investors turned away ... Then came a second wind at the beginning of this century. Foreign investors and many boat people returned and the economy boomed.

(Jean-PierreL ehman, *IHT*, 12 July 2010, p. 6)

Financial and exchange rate policy: developments since October 2006 (including the global financial crisis)

The finance ministry has just produced a draft personal taxation law, expected to be approved in January [2007], that offers more tax breaks for the wealthy than the United States does. Inheritances among immediate family members will be entirely exempt from taxation. So will interest on all but the largest bank accounts.

(www.iht.com, 24 October 2006; *IHT*, 25 October 2006, p. 13)

State-owned banks, which account for about 70 per cent of banking system assets, are already burdened with high levels of debt from poorly performing companies ... While the state's share of fixed investment has risen to 52 per cent – up from 43 per cent – during the past decade, its share of economic output has fallen slightly, reflecting an inefficient use and allocation of capital.

(*FT*, 8 January 2007, p. 15)

Inflation reached 12.6 per cent in December [2007], driven by higher prices for food, fuel and construction material. The rise was the highest for a decade and exceeded those in other emerging markets in Asia ... On 16 January [2008], in an anti-inflationary effort, the central bank ordered banks to maintain their reserves at 11 per cent of their dong and dollar deposits for as long as twelve months. The central bank had already tweaked its currency policy late last year [2007], allowing the dong to appreciate against the US dollar.

(www.iht.com, 28 January 2008)

Vietnam's central bank yesterday [30 January 2008] said that it was raising its three key interest rates by up to 1.5 percentage points as of 1 February.

The move reflects the authorities' struggle to tame the surging inflation rate that has fuelled labour unrest among factory workers. It would be the first interest rise in Vietnam since December 2005 ... Hanoi estimated this week that consumer prices in January would be 14.1 per cent higher than a year ago, up from a 12.6 per cent inflation rate in December [2007]. The UN estimates that the real inflation rate for the poor, who spend a greater proportion of their income on food, is even higher ... In a statement yesterday the State Bank of Vietnam said that its base rate – used by commercial banks to calculate their local currency lending rates – would rise by 50 basis points to 8.75 per cent, while the discount rate – used by the central bank in buying securities from commercial banks – would rise to 6 per cent from 4 per cent. The rediscount rate – at which the central bank lends to banks – will go up to 7.5 per cent from 6.5 per cent. Previously, the central bank had said it wanted to rein in credit growth, which jumped by about 37 per cent last year [2007].

(*FT*, 31 January 2008, p. 7)

The government this week said the annual inflation rate had hit 14.1 per cent, its highest since 1995. On 30 January the central bank raised its official interest rates by up to 1.5 per cent to try to prevent an inflationary spiral ... Until this week's rise they were barely above zero in real terms ... The country is suffering from the worldwide surge in the cost of fuels and foodstuffs – food prices are up by a whopping 22 per cent year-on-year. But the inflationary spike is also partly the consequence of a prolonged boom: Vietnam's economy grew by around 8.5 per cent last year [2007], one of Asia's most impressive rates, having grown by an average of 7.5 per cent annually in the previous decade ... The rising cost of living has caused a rash of strikes and worries that food might be scarce over the Tet lunar new year holiday this month ... Vietnam's inflation target is not very exacting: the aim is only that it should fall below the rate of economic growth. But even this proved too hard last year, when inflation was around 4 percentage points higher than growth ... China and Thailand have responded to public discontent at rising food costs with further price controls on some staple items. So far Vietnam, which is intent on liberalizing its economy after joining the WTO last year, has not followed suit. Indeed, the government talks only of further relaxing its grip on prices: it plans soon to start letting the market set the prices of fuels, though it has not named a date ... Rising inflows of FDI and speculative money have put the dong under strong upward pressure. Early last year the central bank responded by selling dong for dollars ... In December [2007] the central bank switched tactics and increased the flexibility of its currency regime. The dong can now fluctuate within 0.75 per cent of a central rate reset each day, supposedly in response to market pressures. However, the bank still seems to be managing the central rate, which has not moved far.

(*The Economist*, 2 February 2008, pp. 61–2)

Vietnam's inflation rate jumped to 15.7 per cent in February [2008], its highest rate in twelve years ... The sharp rise in prices was pushed by a 25.2 per cent increase in the cost of foodstuffs and a 16.4 per cent rise in housing and building materials driven by the construction boom ... Hanoi decided to track the dollar down, which means they imported inflation from China [whose currency has begun to revalue against the dollar]... [since] the price of imports becomes more expensive ... Inflation has been fuelled further by the surge in credit growth on rapid lending by banks.

(*FT*, 28 February 2008, p. 8)

[Globally] the primary cause of the stubbornly high food and energy prices is demand from fast-growing emerging economies like China, along with the rise of ethanol, which is gobbling up a big chunk of the US corn crop and diverting acreage from wheat.

(*IHT*, 3 March 2008, p. 14)

'Rising prices, especially of foodstuffs, have fuelled a wave of labour unrest, with factory workers striking to protest against wages that they say are insufficient to make ends meet' (*FT*, 3 March 2008, p. 8).

'Borrowing conditions in international markets have suddenly deteriorated, forcing the postponement of a sovereign bond issue' (www.iht.com, 21 March 2008).

[There has been] a marked surge in inflation-fuelled labour unrest, which has primarily affected the garment and footwear sectors. There have been around 600 strikes in the past fifteen months ... Vietnam's annual inflation rate has soared to 19.4 per cent year on year in March [2008], from 15.7 per cent in February, hitting double figures for a fifth consecutive month. Food price inflation, which holds around a 40 per cent weighting in the consumer price index and has been accelerating rapidly since mid-2007, continues to be the main factor driving up the general price level. The cost of food and foodstuffs surged by 30.6 per cent year on year in March, up from a 25.2 per cent gain in February ... The government has begun to target consumer price inflation aggressively. In March it lowered import duties on certain products, raised interest rates and introduced a comprehensive strategy to fight rising prices. A key part of that strategy has been to require commercial banks to buy a total of $1.26 billion in compulsory Treasury bills, which has decreased liquidity in the market, and to cap dong deposit rates. In addition, the State Bank of Vietnam (SBV) has raised the discount rate to 6 per cent (from 4.5 per cent previously) and the base rate to 8.75 per cent (from 8.25 per cent). The SBV has also lowered its target for credit growth in 2008, saying it will closely monitor banks' lending activities ... In addition to draining liquidity from the market, the SBV has widened the trading band within which the dong is allowed to fluctuate on a daily basis, from 0.75 per cent to 1 per cent. The dong has been appreciating against the dollar in recent months ... This latest move by the SBV is intended to allow the currency to strengthen further in order to alleviate inflationary pressures ... [by making] imports cheaper ... Vietnam has announced plans to cut rice exports by up to 1 million tonnes this year [2008].

(www.economist.com, 4 April 2008)

[In March] the official year-on-year inflation rate rose to 19.4 per cent led by a worrying 31 per cent increase in food prices. The first quarter 2008 trade deficit came in at $7.4 billion, four times higher than in the first quarter of 2007 ... A property bubble drove prices of prime real estate assets to double or triple in the space of one year ... Interest rates are a blunt instrument when directed credits to SOEs make up a quarter of the stock of loans and when banks are organized into an explicit cartel to avoid outbreak of competition ... In 2007 investments a share of GDP exceeded 40 per cent, half of which was undertaken in the public sector and partially financed by state banks ... The government's response to the inflationary pressure was to increase the reserve requirements of the banks by 100 basis points in February 2008, adding a 500 basis point hike (in May 2007). SVB [the State Bank of Vietnam] also required the larger banks to buy 20.3 billion dong in state Treasury bills carrying a yield of 7.8 per cent by mid-March. For a time SBV limited purchases of dollars to control money growth. All of these encouraged the banks to hoard Vietnam dong liquidity, forcing up inter-bank lending rates as high as 43 per cent in late February. Fearing the effect of a wave of margin calls on the balance sheets of smaller banks, the government also narrowed the intraday trading band of the stock market to 1 per cent from 5 per cent.

(Pincus and Ahn 2008: 28–30)

On 13 February the State Bank of Vietnam [SBV] ordered forty-one banks and credit organizations to buy $1.26 billion worth of one-year Treasury bills by 17 March – a tactic designed to halt price increases. In 2007 inflation had already reached a decade-high of 12.6 per cent year on year. By February [2008] it reached 15.6 per cent ... Banks began to tighten purse strings, rejecting myriad loan applications. In the end the SBV had to inject almost $2 billion into the banking system. It also widened the inter-bank trading band for the dong twice allowing the dong to rise steadily against the dollar ... The government increased tariffs on cars twice in April to 83 per cent from 60 per cent ... Prime minister Nguyen Tan Dung made a choice in April to keep the exchange rate 'in favour' of exports. Until the trade deficit situation improves the exchange rate will no longer be used to combat inflation. The prime minister also called to postpone 'unnecessary' construction projects ... The ministry of finance has ordered local government agencies to stop buying cars and building offices, minimize spending on ceremonies and conferences, and cut annual budgets by 10 per cent.

(Thuy 2008: 34–5)

Vietnam's central bank even had to order the country's commercial banks to resume buying dollars within the tight range of exchange rates set by the government; many banks had started betting on dollar depreciation and refusing to accept large sums in dollars, to the point that multinational companies and exporters had trouble wiring money into the country to pay their employees' salaries.

(*IHT*, 8 April 2008, p. 13)

The central bank of Vietnam said it will try to rein in inflation by limiting loans to consumers and investors in stocks and property as the country faces the prospect of a widespread credit rating downgrade ... On Friday [2 May] Standard & Poor's cut its outlook for the Vietnamese sovereign rating to 'negative' from 'stable', heightening concerns that other ratings agencies would follow suit, a move that would deal a blow to a country dependent on foreign capital inflows. Vietnam runs a large current account and trade deficit because of infrastructure spending and high oil prices. Annual inflation rates have been running at double-digit rates for six consecutive months ... Nguyen Van Giau (governor of the central bank, the State Bank of Vietnam, speaking on Monday 5 May): 'Strict control will be applied to monitor credit growth as well as credit quality and measures to curb loans to stock trading, real estate investment and consumer finance will continue to ensure the safety of commercial banks' ... The central bank will conduct foreign exchange policy with the objective of keeping the dong stable and favourable for exports this year [2008] and not let the currency fluctuate too widely ... Annual inflation rose to 21.42 per cent in April, among the highest rates since 1991 and among the highest in Asia. The January-to-April [2008] trade gap surged to $11.1 billion, a fourfold increase from a year earlier. The central bank's latest moves follow a series of policy directives in March ... [which] included raising commercial banks' reserve requirements, requiring banks to buy Treasury bills and cutting the Vietnamese 2008 economic growth target to 7 per cent from 8.3 per cent last year [2007].

(www.iht.com, 5 May 2008)

Vietnam's annual inflation rate accelerated to 25.2 per cent in May, its highest since 1992 ... The surge ... was driven by a 67.8 per cent year-on-year rise in the price of grain – the staple food which accounts for 42.8 per cent of the basket of goods and services Hanoi uses to calculate its inflation rates ... The rapid rise in the cost of living has fuelled labour unrest, with factory workers striking for higher wages ... Hanoi has said that fighting inflation is its top economic priority. It has sought recently to slow down credit growth by raising bank reserve requirements and paring credit growth targets. Last week Vietnamese banks also began to raise dong deposit rates after the central bank lifted a 12 per cent ceiling on interest rates.

(*FT*, 28 May 2008, p. 10)

On 4 May [2008] the finance ministers of thirteen East Asian countries agreed on the sidelines of the annual meeting of the Asian Development

Bank in Madrid to set up a pool of foreign exchange reserves. The members of the Association of South-east Asian Nations [Asean] together with China, Japan and South Korea decided that at least $80 billion of the region's foreign reserves are to be funnelled into a regional fund to protect regional currencies against speculative attacks and provide countries in crisis with liquidity. Of the funds 20 per cent are to be provided by the ten Asean members and the remaining 80 per cent by the 'Plus Three' countries (China, Japan and South Korea) ... To ease concerns that the IMF's position would be damaged, the ministers agreed to inclued an 'IMF link', which allowed only 10 per cent of the credit lines to be disbursed without the borrowing country having a lending programme with the IMF. In 2005 the portion that could be disbursed without an IMF programme was increased to 20 per cent.

(www.feer.com, 18 June 2008)

Vietnam's foreign business community is warning that rapid inflation, growing labour unrest and a real estate bubble could erode the country's appeal as an investment destination ... The warning comes just after news that inflation surged to 25.2 per cent in May, its highest level since 1992, spurred on by steep rises in the cost of food, construction and housing.

(*FT*, 2 June 2008, p. 6)

Vietnam's central bank yesterday [10 June] raised its benchmark interest rates for the third time this year [2008] – to 14 per cent from 12 per cent – to fight soaring inflation that is eroding confidence in the dong. The bank simultaneously reduced the official dong exchange rate by 1.96 per cent against the US dollar ... The dong is little traded internationally ... The dong in the black market ... [has weakened] in recent months ... Inflation began to rise rapidly late last year [2007], but Hanoi's growth-orientated authorities responded tepidly. The central ban finally raised interest rates in February [2008], followed by a further rise in May. Hanoi plans to put about $125 million worth of public investment projects on hold to slow the economy. But economists say the government must do more to rein in public spending.

(*FT*, 11 June 2008, p. 9)

'In 2007 ... [there was a budget] deficit of 4.9 per cent of GDP ... Vietnam has operated a policy that pushes the dong slightly lower against the dollar each year' (*IHT*, 19 June 2008, p. 15).

The central bank has announced a 2 per cent devaluation [of the dong] ... It also raised its base interest rate from 12 per cent to 14 per cent ... Like the stock market, property prices have tumbled, leading to fears about the country's banks, which lent heavily for speculation in both assets. The government is already thought to be providing discreet liquidity support to a dozen small banks ... The government is trying to curb currency speculation by restricting foreign exchange booths from selling dollars. To reduce imports, it is said to be allowing the central bank to sell dollars only to businesses that have its approval for their foreign purchases (such as buying capital goods). This, however, may push others towards the black market or offshore, further undermining the credibility of the official exchange rate ... Despite the recent increases, real interest rates remain negative. Meanwhile, a draft law bans banks from pricing loans at more than 150 per cent of the base rate and this has all but stopped lending.

(*The Economist*, 21 June 2008, p. 104)

Authorities have suspended all gold imports in an effort to tackle the country's spiralling trade deficit and help support the depreciating dong. With Vietnamese investors rushing into gold as a hedge against soaring inflation, Hanoi – which sets an annual quota for gold imports – had temporarily withdrawn licences for further imports, market players said yesterday [23 June]. The decision comes as record imports of gold bars have made Vietnam the world's largest market for gold bullion, surpassing India and China and helping deepen Vietnam's trade deficit ... The rising deficit has put pressure on the dong, which was in effect devalued by 2 per cent on 11 June as part of a readjustment in the official exchange rate. Despite the devaluation, the dong trades at a further discount on the black market. Hanoi has closely regulated gold imports for years. But the recent collapse of the local equity and property markets, inflation that hit 24 per cent in May [2008] and concern about the weakness of both the US dollar and the dong have spurred a significant increase in local demand for gold this year [2008].

(*FT*, 24 June 2008, p. 8)

Vietnam yesterday [4 August] announced tough measures to contain rampant inflation, warning companies that they could be prosecuted for passing on higher commodity costs to customers. The government said it would prosecute or revoke the licences of companies that increased the prices of their goods without sufficient justification, part of a plan to freeze prices for the rest of the year on goods ranging from coal to public transport. The focus on energy follows recent efforts to control the cost of food, which accounts for two-fifths of Vietnam's consumer price index. Inflation accelerated to 27 per cent in July [2008], overtaking Sri Lanka as the fastest rate in Asia ... The ministry of planning and investment last week unveiled curbs on the construction of golf courses, which had been encroaching on agricultural land. Since early 2006 new golf courses had been licensed at a rate of more than one a week, threatening an already shrinking rice acreage. Vietnam's was the first central bank in South-east Asia to raise interest rates this year [2008] ... The government ... itself has been trying to cut its looming subsidy bill by raising retail fuel prices.

(*FT*, 5 August 2008, p. 5)

With inflation rising to 27 per cent last month [July] – the highest in Asia – and food prices rising to 74 per cent above those of a year ago, Vietnam is suffering its first serious downturn since it moved from a command economy to an open market nearly two decades ago. Last month the government raised the price of gasoline by 31 per cent to an all-time high of $1.19 a litre. Diesel and kerosene prices rose still higher. The country's fledgling stock market, which had been booming a year ago, has fallen in volume by 95 per cent and is at a virtual standstill ... Hundreds of strikes at the factories that have been an engine of Vietnam's growth are one of the sharpest signs of discontent ... After a steep reduction in the poverty rate from 58 per cent of the population in 1993 to around 15 per cent last year [2008], some people ... are slipping back again below the poverty line. Prime minister Nguyen Tan Dung told the National Assembly in May [2008] that the number of households going hungry had doubled in one year.

(www.iht.com, 19 August 2008; *IHT*, 20 August 2008, p. 11)

Vietnam has outlined a series of tax breaks and other measures as it fights to live up to its target of 6.5 per cent economic growth next year [2009] despite the slowdown in its main export markets. The government announced this week that it would expand a proposed $1 billion economic stimulus package largely through increasing tax breaks for importers, manufacturers and consumers. It also laid out further plans in a resolution passed last week, but released on Tuesday [16 December].

(www.ft.com, 18 December 2008)

Vietnam devalued the dong by 3 per cent in an attempt to keep its export-dependent economy afloat. The government said that 2008 economic growth had shrunk to 6.23 per cent from 8.5 per cent last year [2007] and there were signs it was likely to slow further in 2009 ... Hanoi's move comes after spending most of the year trying to maintain the currency's strength to slow spiralling inflation.

(*FT*, 27 December 2008, p. 6)

'Inflation soared to more than 20 per cent in the last quarter of 2008' (www.bbc.co.uk, 2 January 2009).

The government ... plans to boost spending this year [2009] by 23 per cent (almost $6 billion, about 6 per cent of GDP). Of this about $1 billion will subsidize loans to cash-strapped exporters ... An estimated 500,000 workers lost their jobs last year [2008] and the government reckons a further 400,000 may be laid off in 2009 ... [Vietnam] needs 1 million new jobs every year to absorb its growing work force, now around 45 million people ... GDP expanded by 6.2 per cent in 2008, the slowest rate for nine years ... Most observers, including the IMF, think it will be lucky to reach 5 per cent this year [2009]. Yet the government's target is still 6.5 per cent.

(*The Economist*, 7 March 2009, pp. 62, 64)

'This week Vietnam increased import tariffs on dairy products, after raising duties on paper last month [February]' (*The Economist*, 14 March 2009, p. 67).

162　*The economy*

> Growth stumbled to its slowest rate in a decade in the first quarter [of 2009], falling to 3.1 per cent year-on-year as its export-driven economy is strangled by tumbling global demand and inward investment. The new estimates, released by the government on Thursday [26 March] represent a sharp slowing from growth of 7.4 per cent in the first quarter of last year [2008], and partially reflects both the 5 per cent fall in exports in the first two months of this year [2009] and rapidly diminishing foreign investment. FDI pledges fell 70 per cent in the first three months. The first quarter figures were lower than many analysts were expecting. The government is still hoping for annual growth of between 5 per cent and 6 per cent, down from its estimate of 6.5 per cent at the end of last year. Its estimates are in line with the World Bank's 5.5 per cent, and slightly above the IMF's recently revised estimate of 4.75 per cent growth ... Exports are forecast to contract by 7 per cent this year, down from growth of 2.6 per cent last year. But some analysts say that there might be a silver lining for Vietnam, one of the world's lowest cost producers. They believe that as consumers move downmarket to save money, countries like Vietnam will be hit less hard than its more expensive export competition.
>
> (www.ft.com, 26 March 2009)

'Vietnam extended its commercial loan subsidy programme, which was originally expected to last only until the end of this year [2009], to the end of 2011' (www.ft.com, 8 April 2009).

'In Vietnam 100,000 garment workers lost their jobs in January and February [2009]' (www.economist.com, 14 April 2009).

> Elements of Vietnam's economic stimulus package have become clearer in recent weeks ... The package, which was announced earlier in 2009 ... is being implemented ... [at a] rapid pace ... One of the main components of the economic stimulus [is] a 4 percentage point interest rate subsidy ... All companies except those operating in a relatively short list of 'negative sectors' (including stockbroking, consumer imports and property development) are eligible for the subsidy ... Another component of the government's economic stimulus is a new credit-guarantee scheme to support commercial bank lending to small and medium-sized enterprises ... Unusually, guarantees issued by the Vietnam Development Bank ... the sole delivery vehicle ... can cover up to 100 per cent of the loan, and can be for either dollar-denominated or dong-denominated loans. Eligible firms must have fewer than 500 employees and chartered capital of less than 20 billion dong ($1.1 million), and must also be free of overdue debts or tax arrears. Unlike the interest rate subsidy, however, the Vietnam Development Bank has discretionary powers to decide which companies will receive the guarantees. The government's latest announcement, in 18 April, presented a series of stimulus measures targeting the interest-free loans for purchases of farm equipment and subsidized loans for fertilizer and other agricultural inputs. Vietnam's agricultural sector employs more than two-thirds of the country's

population and accounts for a major proportion of exports ... In an effort to raise additional funds for projects included in its stimulus package, the government has recently embarked on US dollar-denominated domestic bond issues, with the aim of trying to issue as much as $1 billion of bonds of various tenors in 2009 ... Japan's government has resumed development assistance to Vietnam, following the belated arrest of at least two Vietnamese government officials suspected of having received bribes in connection with a water and road project near Ho Chi Minh City. The Japanese executives who paid the bribes admitted their guilt in a court in Japan some months ago ... As official development assistance takes on greater importance amid shrinking foreign direct investment flows and falling export earnings, Vietnam's development partners are likely to enjoy greater leverage to push the economic reform agenda than they have had in recent years, during which Vietnam has received ample private investment, and policy-makers' appetite for reform has waned.

(www.economist.com, 22 April 2009)

Thirteen East and South-east Asian countries agreed Sunday [3 May] to set up a $120 billion emergency fund for use in the economic downturn, the first independent effort by Asia to shield itself from financial crisis. Japan also announced a plan to supply up to $60.5 billion to support its neighbours in a downturn. While Asian banks largely avoided the credit crisis that tore through Wall Street and much of Europe, the region has since been hit by the downturn in the West, which has eroded demand for Asian automobiles, electronics and other exports.

(*IHT*, 4 May 2009, p. 17)

Japan offered $100 billion yesterday [3 May] to help Asian states hit by the financial crisis ... Tokyo announced at a meeting of the finance ministers of the ten countries of Asean in Indonesia [Bali] that it would set up a $60.5 billion bilateral currency swap scheme, on top of a $38.4 billion commitment to the multilateral Chiang Mai initiative. The Chiang Mai deal, a $120 billion currency scheme that has been under discussion for years, was formally agreed yesterday by the Asean countries during a meeting with the finance ministers of Japan, China and South Korea ... The Chiang Mai scheme, which had originally been envisaged as a series of bilateral currency swaps limited to $80 billion, is due to come into force before the end of the year [2009] ... The thirteen countries have also agreed to put $500 million as initial capital into a new trust fund to guarantee local currency bond issues by Asian countries.

(*FT*, 4 May 2009, p. 8)

Vietnamese exports have been fairly resilient. While economies such as Singapore and Taiwan have seen declines of 30 per cent or 40 per cent in shipments, Vietnam was down a modest 3.7 per cent in the first four months of this year [2009] against the same period in 2008.

(*FT*, 27 May 2009, p. 9)

Vietnam's government has coped well with the global crisis but needs to rein in its plans if it is not to overshoot, a new report by the World Bank says. The World Bank's 2009 GDP growth forecast of 5.5 per cent is at the optimistic end of the scale, but even the pessimists believe Vietnam's position as a low-cost producer, combined with an aggressive stimulus programme, will prevent it falling into recession.

(www.ft.com, 10 June 2009)

'Vietnam will see a 3.9 per cent growth in GDP for the first half of the year [2009], helped by a rise in rice exports' (*FT*, 26 June 2009, p. 8).

Vietnam has come through the worst of the economic crisis and the trail has provided new opportunities, according to Vu Van Ninh, finance minister. The national general statistics office on Wednesday [1 July] said GDP growth accelerated to a year-on-year rate of 4.5 per cent in the second quarter [of 2009] from 3.1 per cent in the first.

(www.ft.com, 1 July 2009)

'In Vietnam banks have been ordered to cap new lending to head off inflation' (*FT*, 28 July 2009, p. 5).

The central banks of Russia and Vietnam have signed a deal for bilateral trade in national currencies, the Russian regulator said in a statement yesterday [14 September]. The statement said: 'In order to carry out payments and settlements in national currencies, the authorized Russian and Vietnamese banks can carry out the purchase and sale of roubles and dong, as well as mutual lending.'

(*FT*, 15 September 2009, p. 8)

At the start of the year [2009] the prognosis for Vietnam's economy looked as bleak as – if not bleaker than – that for other export-orientated poor countries. There were widespread fears of a surge in unemployment and an increase in poverty and social disorder. Yet the economy is now forecast to grow robustly over the next couple of years. Credit is cheap and flowing; and the stock market has more than doubled in value in the past six months. But there are fears that the impressive V-shaped rebound may be storing up trouble. The doom-mongers were right in foreseeing a sharp downturn. Exports fell by 14 per cent year-on-year in the first eight months of 2009; the number of families suffering food shortages rose by a fifth; and the value of foreign direct investment tumbled by 82 per cent. But the contraction proved short lived, Crédit Suisse, an investment bank, forecasts GDP growth of 5.3 per cent this year [2009] and 8.5 per cent next [2010]. Like other governments, Vietnam's served up a big fiscal stimulus to stave off job losses. The central element was an interest rate subsidy worth 17 trillion dong ($1 billion), which seems to have succeeded in stemming the feared tide of factory closures ... Officials are now debating whether they can end the interest rate subsidy in December [2009], as scheduled, without destroying the businesses they have been trying to help. Economists are growing increasingly concerned about the sustainability of the recovery, fuelled as it is by government spending and cheap credit. The Asian Development Bank (ADB) predicts that Vietnam's budget deficit will widen from 4.1 per cent of GDP in 2008 to 10.3 per cent this year [2009]. Financing the gap may not be easy. Investors these days are averse to risky emerging market government debt. Foreign currency reserves fell from $23 billion at the end of December [2008] to $17.3 billion at the end of June [2009], according to the ADB. This month [September] the government secured a $500 million budget support loan from the bank. There are two big worries among foreign economists. The first is that, unless the government can find the will to rein in spending, restrain credit growth and cut the budget deficit, it will be hard to ease persistent and perhaps self-fulfilling fears about the return of inflation. This reached its peak of an annual rate of 28 per cent in August 2008, leading to the hoarding of rice and panic buying of gold. Second, the focus on the government's fiscal stimulus has distracted it from reform, the pace of which has disappointed some since Vietnam joined the WTO in 2007. Victoria Kwakwa, the World Bank's country director, has said the government should not get 'sidetracked' by the short-term rebound, but focus instead on 'the fundamental constraints to the economy's competitiveness'. That means micro reforms such as opening up the telecoms and retail industries to foreign competition. But it also means streamlining the clunky, all-pervasive state-owned enterprises, and, more generally, tackling the corruption and red tape. Without such reforms, Vietnam will find it hard to rise above its present niche as a low-cost manufacturing base into the more diversified, richer economy it could become.

(*The Economist*, 26 September 2009, p. 70)

'Vietnam's economy is expected to expand some 5 per cent this year [2009]' (*FT*, 13 October 2009, p. 22).

Vietnam's central bank said on Wednesday [25 November] that it would devalue the dong for the third time since June 2008 and narrow its trading band. The central bank also said it would raise its benchmark interest rate to 8 per cent from 7 per cent on 1 December. The one-time devaluation will see the currency's mid-point weakened by 5.44 per cent, effective from Wednesday afternoon ... The currency's trading band against the dollar will be narrowed to 3 per cent from 5 per cent, effective Thursday [26 November]. The devaluation came just a week after Vietnam's president and finance minister said that the country was taking steps to reduce the economy's reliance on the US dollar and would not devalue the dong. The dong has slumped against the dollar on Vietnam's unofficial markets this year [2009], fuelling speculation the government might devalue it for the third time since June 2008. The immediate reason for the dong's weakness, traders say, is that demand for dollars has risen because the spread between gold prices in Vietnam and in foreign markers has widened. Vietnam lifted an eighteen-month ban on gold imports on 12 November in a bid to curb panic buying that had sent the dong plummeting. In addition, the global downturn has hit foreign investment flows and remittances from workers abroad and exports, further reducing dollar supplies. The dollar is also the reserve currency of choice for Vietnamese businesses and households, prompting officials to complain about dollar hoarding. Between June 2008 and March 2009 Vietnam authorities widened the trading band of the dong three times to relieve pressure on the currency. It also conducted two devaluations. After each move the official exchange rate almost immediately gravitated to the weak end of the trading ban, and the black market rate fell further ... Vietnam's foreign exchange reserves fell in August to about $16.5 billion from $23 billion at the end of 2008, World Bank data showed.

(www.iht.com, 25 November 2009)

Hanoi has devalued its currency by 5.4 per cent against the dollar and raised interest rates by a full percentage point in an effort to cut inflation and end weeks of damaging uncertainty which has seen ever increasing pressure on the currency.

(www.ft.com, 25 November 2009)

'Vietnam plans to stop its interest rate subsidy scheme at the end of the year [2009], becoming the first Asian nation to start unwinding its post-crisis stimulus programme, the government announced on Wednesday [2 December]' (www.ft.com, 3 December 2009).

Vietnam's elegantly V-shaped recovery would be a terrible thing to spoil on the way to the Communist Party's Eleventh National Congress in early 2011. With that in mind, the government long denied any intention of devaluing the currency. On 25 November [however] ... the state bank lowered the official dong–dollar exchange rate by 5.2 per cent. In the same stroke Vietnam became the first country in Asia to increase interest rates since the financial crisis began, lifting the base rate from 7 per cent to 8 per cent in an attempt to slow credit growth and attract more dong-denominated deposits ... In the first half of 2008, when speculation and inflation threatened to surge out of control, the government was forced to rein in excesses. But it was to reverse itself only months later, as the global slowdown made itself felt. As the government followed the lead of other Asian nations trying to spend its way out of trouble – largely through a 17 trillion dong ($1 billion) interest rate subsidy programme – it began to build itself a new series of problems. Current account and budget deficits widened, foreign currency reserves shrank, and economists began to question the wisdom of a recovery based on government spending and cheap credit. Currency traders argued that its loose monetary policy would bring back inflation, which hit a six-month high of 4.35 per cent year-on-year in November. Their view was shared by many ordinary Vietnamese who, having been bruised by hyperinflation in the past, rushed to convert their dong-denominated savings into dollars and gold, the preferred stores of value in a country where only one person in ten has a bank account. Skittish foreign investors withdrew their money and cautious state-owned enterprises hoarded greenbacks; together, they created a persistent shortage of dollars. With too little hard currency to back it, in the past few months the dong went limp in the black market. The threat of a currency crisis loomed. Hence the government's volte-face. After lowering the exchange rate and tightening its monetary belt, it went on to egg state-owned enterprises into converting their stake in the dollar – estimated to be worth $10.3 billion – into the wilting dong to support its value and alleviate the shortage of harder currency ... This is Vietnam's third devaluation since the summer of 2008 ... Already 42 per cent of the total money supply is held in gold or dollars.

(www.economist.com, 10 December 2009)

Vietnam's strategy for competing in the global arena – and a relatively successful one until recently – had been to carve out niche markets where it could deliver, say, quality products like handicrafts or specialized clothing that China could not. But all of Vietnam's main export markets are heavily dependent on the United States. In 2009 the United States was the biggest importer of Vietnamese goods, absorbing about a fifth of the country's exports. Furniture companies, to take one industry, have had a huge drop in orders after the rapid downward spiral in sales of new homes in the United States ... Vietnam's economy grew 4.6 per cent for the first nine months of 2009, compared with the same period in 2008, according to the World Bank, in part because of government stimulus measures ... Vietnam in recent years had been able to sustain an average growth rate above 7 per cent ... In the first ten months of 2009 Vietnamese exports declined 13,8 per cent compared with the period in 2008, the World Bank said ... In order to square off against China, many manufacturers try to rely on niche industries and specialties rather than competing on price or low labour costs ... As Vietnam's tourism market grows, particularly attracting new golf resorts and vacationers from nearby countries in South-east Asia and elsewhere, furniture manufacturers are turning to supply such resorts.

(www.iht.com, 25 December 2009)

Vietnam's economy grew at its fastest rate in two years in the fourth quarter [of 2009], helped by government spending. Hanoi's statistics office said economic growth expanded by 6.9 per cent in the final three months of the year. That compares to 6.04 per cent in the previous quarter. In a statement it said the economy 'had passed the most difficult period'. The government took measures worth about $8 billion to boost growth, including subsidies in order to encourage banks to lend. Overall in 2009 the rate of expansion slowed to 5.32 per cent, the lowest rate since 1999. That was put down to weaker demand for exports in the first part of the year. The government also said it must 'firstly continue to actively prevent the return of hyperinflation and the existing potential inflationary factors'. In November the central bank raised rates and devalued the currency in an attempt to control inflation, which ran at a rate of 6.52 per cent in December. Last year [2008] an overheating economy pushed it up to 28 per cent.

(www.bbc.co.uk, 31 December 2009)

Vietnam has ordered all gold trading floors to close by the end of March [2010], ending a business that turns over $1 billion a day but which the government feared was spinning out of control ... The order also bans using overseas accounts, but does not affect jewellery or retail gold sales. The government said it was concerned that some investors had been drawn into over-leveraging their positions by low interest rates and the increasing price of gold ... The government said that in some cases, investors had only been required to put up 7 per cent of the value of their portfolio ... The trade has become a lucrative source of income for many of the banks and trading houses that have opened the exchanges ... Analysts say it could free liquidity that might flow back into stock markets ... Vietnam's big appetite for gold has put pressure on the dong and was a key factor in forcing the country to devalue the currency by 5 per cent in November [2009].

(*FT*, 2 January 2010, p. 23)

Over the past two years there have been violent swerves from austerity to stimulus and back again as the economy moved through inflation, the global crisis and now renewed signs of overheating. But for an economy that has relied on exports and foreign direct investment for much of its growth over the past decade, Vietnam has survived the global slowdown remarkably well. Statistics released last week show the economy grew 5.32 per cent last year [2009], down from its average of more than 7 per cent over the preceding four years, but still substantially stronger than the expectations of many of its competitors ... [There is] a rising budget deficit that the World Bank estimates will hit 9.7 per cent of GDP this year [2010] after expenditure on a stimulus programme which the World Bank estimates has cost the country almost $4 billion, or 4 per cent of GDP.

(*FT*, 5 January 2010, p. 7)

[The] central bank said yesterday [10 February 2010] it was devaluing the dong for the second time since November [2009], slashing its reference rate by more than 3 per cent. Today the dong's mid-point reference rate will be 18,544 per cent, 3.36 per cent down from 17,941, where the State Bank of Vietnam has kept it since 10 December [2009].

(*FT*, 11 February 2010, p. 9)

The consumer price index rose by 2 per cent in February ... GDP grew by 5.3 per cent last year [2009] ... The government ... is believed to have spent over $1 billion in 2009 (over 1 per cent of GDP) to prop up the economy, mainly by subsidizing banks' loans to businesses. As a result the credit supply expanded by 37 per cent, driving up the black market price of dollars ... The loan-subsidy programme largely benefited well-connected state-owned enterprises ... On 10 February ... the central bank devalued the dong by 3.4 per cent, following a devaluation of 5.4 per cent in November [2009]. The aim was to entice holders of dollars to buy dong. A dollar shortage has been starving Vietnam's exporters of the currency they need to purchase imported parts and materials ... The government has reluctantly raised state-controlled commodity prices: petrol, electricity and coal are all to be more expensive ... The finance ministry has been circulating a draft decree that would allow the government to impose price controls on a wide range of essential goods. The European Chamber of Commerce has warned that such measures may well lead to nothing but 'shortages' and 'hoarding'.

(*The Economist*, 6 March 2010, p. 69)

In a series of recent announcements, government officials have introduced plans for price controls and import restrictions that have drawn foreign investors, who are normally discreet in their criticism of the government, into the open ... One proposal that has drawn particular ire would formally re-establish the government's ability to set prices for key commodities, including petrol, steel, concrete, milk and pharmaceuticals. There was little sign of reform in a recent speech by Nong Duc Manh, General Secretary of the Communist Party. He said the government was trying to maintain political stability and 'struggle against all the manoeuvres of hostile forces by preventing them from profiting from matters such as democracy, human rights, multi-partyism and pluralism to sabotage the Vietnamese revolution' ... There is concern among conservatives that economic progress is loosening the grip of the party ... Mr Manh who must step down early next year [2011] at the end of his term, is a conservative whose support for Nguyen Tan Dung, the reformist prime minister, has been equivocal ... The party congress [is] scheduled for early next year.

(*FT*, 4 March 2010, p. 7)

'Russia's GDP grew the most of any major economy in dollar terms over the last decade, followed by Indonesia and Vietnam, according to a report released last week by Goldman Sachs' (www.iht.com, 11 January 2010).

[In] 1986 Vietnam adopted its *doi moi* programme of economic liberalization – commonly translated as 'renovation ... What Vietnamese fear is not that their government has developed an Athenian affinity for deficits and debt – Hanoi's deficits are relatively modest, and it has not been in international financial markets long enough yet to rack up any serious IOUs. What makes them nervous is the suspicion that the governing Communist Party will do anything to hit its economic growth target in advance of a party congress early next year [2011], even if that means letting inflation get out of control. To hedge against that possibility, Vietnamese have been vacuuming up gold and US currency. So many dollars have been scooped up, in fact, that the country's central bank, the State Bank of Vietnam, is at risk of running out of them, analysts warn. Any shock, like a double-dip global recession that hits exports or foreign investment, and Vietnam could find itself without enough dollars to pay for critical imports like fuel, they say ... In 2008 the country managed to sidestep the global recession, growing 5.3 per cent and pulling its GDP *per capita* above $1,000 while keeping incomes more evenly distributed than in the United States. But the balance of payments predicament is only the latest in a series of hard knocks the country has endured ... A recurring feature of the Vietnam War, hyperinflation returned in the late 1980s and early 1990s along with an investment boom that followed *doi moi*. Now any new sign of it sends the public scurrying for more dollars, creating a vicious circle that puts downward pressure on the dong and pushes prices even higher. In the past two years the Vietnamese currency has fallen 15 per cent amid such concerns ... The result is what economists refer to as the dollarization of Vietnam's economy. Things as varied as hotel rooms and cameras are priced in dollars ... Where do all these greenbacks go? Many go into low-yielding US dollar deposits at banks. But another portion – no one knows how many dollars are circulating in Vietnam – gets stashed at home ... High savings are a persistent feature of Asian economies, one that economists say helps to perpetuate global trade imbalances and may have been in part to blame for the global crisis. Like other economies in the region, Vietnam is also a big exporter, the world's second largest exporter of rice and coffee, for instance. And like many of its neighbours, it fixes the official exchange rate of its currency against the dollar. But Vietnam is still at such a comparatively low level of development that it has to import many of the more highly manufactured goods it needs to keep going, such as construction material. And while it exports oil, it has to import refined products for fuel. As a result, the country runs a net trade deficit. So while other Asian nations accumulate dollars to keep their currencies from rising, Vietnam has been shedding dollars to keep the dong from falling and thereby worsening inflation, even though letting the dong depreciate freely would make its exports even cheaper. Vietnam was one of the few economies to avoid global recession, but by the end of last year [2009] it had become clear that Asia as a whole was recovering quickly and that Vietnam was back to the races. With inflation surging, the government faced new pressure on the dong. In November [2009] the central bank raised interest rates to quell inflation. And, unable to pull the dong's street value back up to the official exchange rate, it lowered the official rate so it could stop selling dollars at what amounted to a discounted rate. In February [2010] it lowered the official rate yet again. The dong has stabilized somewhat now, and credit growth has cooled. But Vietnamese investors and analysts remain sceptical that the situation has entirely stabilized, largely because efforts to keep inflation under control are accompanied by statements from Hanoi supporting faster economic growth. Early next year [2011] the Communist Party is due to hold its Eleventh National Congress, a key period of political jockeying, analysts say. For government officials, the analysts say, achieving growth targets is a key test. Last month

[June] prime minister Nguyen Tan Dung predicted that GDP would not only reach the government's target but exceed it. Yet the central bank's own efforts sometimes seem to be at cross purposes. While the central bank has imposed a discouraging 1 per cent ceiling on dollar savings accounts to discourage demand for the US currency among its citizens, it is also trying to buy dollars to buttress its own reserves [said one analyst].

(Wayne Arnold, www.iht.com, 8 July 2010; *IHT*, 9 July 2010, p. 17)

The central bank on Tuesday [17 August] devalued the dong by 2 per cent to 18,932 against the US dollar to help stem the country's ballooning trade deficit. Yesterday [18 August], on the black market, it fell to 19,480 from 19,320 the previous day. Vietnam's trade deficit hit $7.4 billion in the first seven months of this year [2010], double the rate for that period last year [2009] ... Vietnam has an export-orientated economy, and runs large annual trade surpluses with the United States, Japan and the EU. But its export industries must import many of their components, so businesses have a large appetite for dollars, which grows as the economy expands. In recent weeks businesses have been unable to find enough dollars to meet their needs, and many have turned to the black market ... The country's trade deficit stems almost entirely from imports from China, with which it runs an annual deficit that has outpaced its surpluses with richer countries. Vietnam exports mainly raw materials to China, while importing high value-added consumer and industrial goods. That, too, created a demand for dollars ... Demand was also driven higher by traders trying to arbitrage the large gap in interest rates on dollar- and dong-denominated bank accounts. Early this year [2010] the government limited interest on dollar accounts to roughly 5 per cent to discourage dollarization of the economy, while account rates are 10 per cent or higher.

(*FT*, 19 August 2010, p. 4)

Vietnam's foreign minister ... Pham Gia Khiem ... has dismissed IMF concerns that a lack of clarity in government macroeconomic policy is damaging confidence among international investors. The government has been forced into a series of rapid shifts in macroeconomic policy over the past three years as it was buffeted by high inflation, the global slowdown and, most recently, fears of a possible currency crisis. The central bank has devalued the dong three times since November [2009] in a bid to stem downward pressure on the currency, which has been driven by concerns about Vietnam's large trade and budget deficits. In an annual review of Vietnam's economic policy released on Thursday [9 September] the IMF paid tribute to the government for managing to ride out a number of difficult challenges but warned that 'the current macroeconomic stability does not appear robust'. The IMF said 'inadequate clarity' on government policy had 'undermined market confidence' and recommended that 'transparency in government intentions, based on higher quality data published timely, should be further advanced to provide market players [with] predictability'

... The IMF noted that this year [2010] the government had set goals for GDP, inflation, credit growth and money supply, while targeting a stable exchange rate. The IMF said: 'It may be difficult to convince the market [it] can achieve all these objectives with relatively blunt policy tools.'

(*FT*, 10 September 2010, p. 10)

The state sector

The government is pumping vast sums of money into some state enterprises, hoping to create national champions similar to the South Korean *chaebol*. Sectors targeted include insurance, minerals, oil, shipping, telecoms and electricity. Hanoi has set up a state holding company – ostensibly along the lines of Singapore's Temasek – to manage its investments and maximize returns ... While the state's share of fixed investment has risen to 52 per cent – up from 43 per cent – during the past decade, its share of economic output has fallen slightly, reflecting an inefficient use and allocation of capital.

(*FT*, 8 January 2007, p. 15)

In the early 1990s concern over the poor performance of state-owned industrial enterprises led the government to try a new approach. General corporations and conglomerates were created out of existing firms, supposedly following the model of the Japanese *keiretsu* and [South] Korean *chaebol*. The idea was that larger firms would realize economies of scale and scope, which would enable them to compete internationally. The gap in the logic was that most of the conglomerates – firms like the mining corporation Vinacomin, the shipper Vinalines, the electricity producer EVN and the state oil company PetroVietnam – earned their money from mineral rents or preferential access to the domestic market. Rather than wade into the treacherous waters of international competition, most preferred to build on their market power in Vietnam to move into lucrative domestic ventures in the property market, financial services, telecommunications and tourism ... SBV [State Bank of Vietnam] has recently granted banking licences to three conglomerates (FPT, the insurer Bao Viet and PetroVietnam) and more are in the queue. These companies are replicating the familiar South-east Asian pattern of creating diversified corporate empires around a cash-generating monopoly and a bank to provide easy access to capital ... In early April [2008] ... prime minister Nguyen Tan Dung ... ordered all state general corporations to invest at least 70 per cent of their capital in their core businesses ... The private and foreign-invested sectors account for nearly all of the job growth recorded over the past seven years. Welded to this competitive but low margin economy is a separate system of capital-hungry state firms concentrated in natural resource exploitation and producing goods and services for the domestic market. These firms account for the bulk of borrowing from state-owned banks and have begun to borrow overseas. They have leveraged their political influence to diversify into the lucrative domestic property and financial markets ... The conglomerates have been allowed to open banks and non-bank finance companies. The developing world is full of examples of the hazards of interlocking corporate and banking interests. From Chile's *grupos* to South Korea's *chaebol* and Indonesia's *konglomerat*, the melding of banks and powerful corporations has led to imprudent intra-group lending, loss of control over monetary policy and ultimately financial instability.

(Pincus and Ahn 2008: 31–3)

Privatization and stock markets

Vietnam's finance ministry has expressed alarm at the volume of bank lending being used to finance the purchase of shares on the country's tiny ... stock market ... [which] has risen 85 per cent this year, as investors ... discover the practice of margin trading ... A letter sent to the State Bank of Vietnam ... warned that share prices ... were spiralling because of speculative buying partly financed by credit from commercial banks. The letter said some Vietnamese investors were using their newly acquired shares as collateral to obtain loans to buy more, which could result in a surge of bad debt ... Vietnam's formal stock market has thirty-five stocks and a market capitalization of about $1.8 billion. Investors can also buy unlisted shares of state companies that have been partly privatized. Shares in private Vietnamese companies are also traded in the informal, over-the-counter market.

(*FT*, 20 April 2006, p. 23)

'The state-owned banks, which have been on a lending orgy, are saddled with bad loans – rating agencies put the damage at about 17 per cent to 20 per cent of total loans' (p. 18).

'The stock market, with just thirty-six listed companies, has risen about 90 per cent so far this year [2006]' (*FT*, 24 April 2006, p. 7).

After a feeble start in 2000, with five listed stocks ... Vietnam's stock market ... now has thirty-five. Still while foreign money managers have acquired a renewed taste for Vietnam, only a handful of foreign funds have succeeded in investing in the market, leaving the market capitalized at a paltry $2 billion. The government is trying to strengthen the market by gradually eliminating the barriers to foreign portfolio investment. As one lure, it has raised the limits of foreign ownership of listed companies to 49 per cent. Government moves to cut brokerage fees and cool speculation in the local property market have also fuelled a fad for investing among Vietnamese.

(*IHT*, 27 April 2006, p. 17)

'The five-year economic plan calls for the country to scrap restrictions on investment by foreign companies ... Foreign investment in Vietnamese companies is capped at 49 per cent' (*IHT*, 20 April 2006, p. 17).

Wall Street has extended its advance into Vietnam's business capital, Ho Chi Minh City, with Merrill Lynch acquiring a coveted 'trading code' needed to buy and sell shares directly on Vietnam's small but growing stock market. Merrill Lynch obtained the right to directly hold Vietnamese shares last week ... Citigroup, one of the largest foreign financial institutions operating in Vietnam, obtained a trading code last year [2005] and is already marketing Vietnamese equities to foreign investors. Also jumping into the fray is JPMorgan, which will soon initiate coverage of Vietnamese equities. Until recently foreign participation in Vietnam's six-year-old stock market was led by boutique fund managers, such as Dragon Capital and PXP Vietnam Asset Management, which focus exclusively on the communist country. With just listed companies and a total capitalization of $2.7 billion, the formal exchange in Ho Chi Minh has a daily turnover of just $4 million to $5 million. Yet Vietnam's $750 million maiden sovereign bond issue last October [2005] raised international interest in one of South-east Asia's fastest growing economies ... Like India, Vietnam requires all foreign investors buying listed equities to have trading codes, which officials use to track foreign ownership in listed firms and ensure that foreign ownership equity limits – 49 per cent for most listed companies and 30 per cent for banks – are not breached. But the protocols needed for obtaining such codes are geared more to individuals than foreign institutions, which slowed major foreign players' advance into the market.

(*FT*, 14 August 2006, p. 23)

The national stock exchange, the six-year-old Ho Chi Minh Securities Trading Centre, list forty-nine stocks with a market value of $3.1 billion ... The Vietnam stock index has surged 66 per cent this year [2006] in dollar terms, the best performance of 413 Asian indexes tracked by Bloomberg. Chinese indexes are the next best performers. In July [2006] Sacombank became the first Vietnamese lender to trade on the stock exchange, raising the market's value by 50 per cent ... The stock market started in July 2000 with just two listed companies and a total value of $16.8 million ... Overseas investors are restricted to a 49 per cent stake in companies listed on the Ho Chi Minh City bourse and a 30 per cent holding in Sacombank.

(*IHT*, 22 September 2006, p. 19)

FPT, Vietnam's largest information technology company yesterday [24 October 2006] said it plans to list all of its 60.8 million shares before the end of this year [2006]. The news came as the company said it had sold a stake to Texas Pacific Group, the US private equity firm, and Intel Capital, the venture capital arm of chipmaker Intel ... None of the companies involved would say what proportion of FPT's value the stake represents ... Local bankers estimate that FPT, founded as the Corporation for Financing and Promoting Technology in 1988, is 80 per cent owned by its employees. About 8 per cent is state-owned, with the remainder held by investment houses based in Vietnam ... The government has announced a 50 per cent tax reduction for companies which list before 1 January 2007.

(*FT*, 25 October 2006, p. 26)

The [stock] market remains nascent. The stock exchange lists fifty-one stocks with a market value of $3.2 billion and the value of companies traded in the over-the-counter market in Vietnam may be as much as $6 billion ... The companies listed on the stock exchange in Thailand, by contrast, have a market value of $136 billion ... The Vietnamese government has been privatizing state-owned businesses and encouraging the more than 3,000 companies traded on the over-the-counter market to move to the main board.

(www.iht.com, 26 October 2006)

Vietnamese companies are rushing to list their shares on the country's two small stock exchanges to take advantages of tax incentives due to be phased out at the end of the year [2006] ... The stampede began in September, after Hanoi announced that a two-year, 50 per cent tax reduction for newly listed companies that was used to entice firms onto the exchanges would not apply after 31 December ... [One theory is that] the ending of the tax waiver might be part of Hanoi's preparations for the partial privatization and listing of big state enterprises, including Bao Viet insurance, Vietcombank, a brewery and a mobile phone operators. Hanoi cannot afford tax breaks for such large groups, which are vital contributors to government revenue ... Just fifty-two companies are listed on the six-year exchange in Ho Chi Minh City, with another sixteen or so listed on the newer Hanoi market. By contrast shares of at least 150 companies trade in the unregulated, over-the-counter market. Both listed and OTC companies are generally small and medium-sized former state enterprises that have been semi-privatized, with shares distributed to management, staff and the public.

(*FT*, 6 November 2006, p. 25)

The government planned to restructure about 900 state enterprises in 2006, turning 600 into shareholding companies (and thus continuing the effort at the same pace as in 2005). It planned to equitize another 1,500 state enterprises by 2010, leaving only 554 state enterprises by the end of the decade.

(*Asian Survey*, 2007, vol. XLVII, no. 1, p. 169)

Nguyen Tan Dung, the prime minister, has approved a list of seventy-one state-owned enterprises, including national carriers Vietnam Airlines, that will be partially privatized between now and 2010, the government said yesterday [2 January 2007]. The decision will require the companies to submit plans to sell equity shares to the public to the prime minister for his approval. Vietcombank and Vietnam Insurance are among the companies that will offer shares to the public this year [2007]; twenty-six others, including Vietnam Airlines, will be public in 2008. Another nineteen will offer shares in 2009 and six more in 2010. The government will maintain a controlling stake of at least 51 per cent in each of the companies.

(*FT*, 3 January 2007, p. 7)

'Other companies listed for share sales in 2008 include Vietnam's national garment and textiles company, with the national steel company scheduled for 2009' (*IHT*, 3 January 2007, p. 12).

'Over the past decade just 12 per cent of total state enterprise capital – mostly in small companies – has been turned into shares and just half of that has passed into private hands, mostly to managers and employees of the enterprises' (*FT*, 8 January 2007, p. 15).

> The number of listed companies ... [on] the Ho Chi Minh City stock exchange ... increased to 106 from about 30. December [2006] alone saw forty-nine new listings ... Share values on the young stock exchange rocketed 144 per cent last year [2006] – making it one of the world's best performing equity markets.
>
> (*FT*, 8 January 2007, p. 15)

Vietnam, which plans to accelerate the privatization of hundreds of state-run firms this year [2007], will retain full control of companies that operate energy projects, the national railroads and flight-control operations, prime minister Nguyen Tan Dung said ... [Vietnam] will also continue to hold full control over military firms, the media and currency, Dung said in a directive that came to light on Wednesday [28 March 2007] ... The main Ho Chi Minh Securities Centre and the over-the-counter Hanoi Securities Trading Centre have about 200 listed companies. The combined market capitalization of $22 billion represents 38 per cent of GDP. The directive, which is expected to take effect in April [2007], lists enterprises in which the state will hold a 100 per cent stake, including the following: production and supply of explosives, toxic chemicals, radioactive substances, equipment for national defence; the national power transmission grid and major electric generation projects; national and urban railroads, airports, large seaports, flight control; the marine safety agency; postal services, radio and television, publishing houses and the media, the state lottery; money printing, coin minting, tobacco production, irrigation projects and dikes, planting of forests, and money lending to fulfil the government's socio-economic development targets. Enterprises in which the state will hold more than 50 per cent include the following: maintaining the national railroad system, urban drainage and public lighting systems, geographic and meteorological surveys; production of vaccines; power plants with a capacity of 100 megawatts or more; mining coal, bauxite, copper ore, iron ore, zinc ore, gold and gemstones; exploring and processing crude oil and natural gas; building and repairing the air transport system; providing telecommunications infrastructure; steel mills with a capacity of more than 300,000 tonnes per year; cement plants with a design capacity of more than 1.5 million tonnes a year;

key chemicals, fertilizers and pesticides; planting and processing rubber and coffee; breweries with a capacity of more than 100 million litres per year; producing paper for newspapers or high quality writing paper; wholesale food, gasoline, oil products, medicine and pharmaceuticals; purifying and supplying water; international marine transport, railroad and air transport; money trading and insurance. The government imposes a 49 per cent foreign ownership cap in non-bank businesses listed on the Ho Chi Minh and Hanoi stock markets. The foreign ownership ceiling in listed and unlisted banks is 30 per cent, with a 10 per cent cap for individual investors. The state-run Industrial and Commercial Bank, Vietnam's fourth largest bank with assets of $8.6 billion, said it plans an initial public offering in October [2007]. It did not say how much it aimed to raise.

(www.iht.com, 28 March 2007)

The Ho Chi Minh Securities Trading Centre's VN index is up 39 per cent for 2007, even with a recent decline, after rising 145 per cent in 2006 ... The VN index's gain is second in Asia only to the Chinese benchmark CSI 300 index's 49 per cent climb. Still, the Vietnamese measure had fallen 11 per cent from its record high reached on 12 March ... The value of the Ho Chi Minh trading centre's shares has risen to $14.8 billion from about $500 million at the end of 2005. The number of listed companies on the six-year-old market has more than doubled over the past six months to 107. Almost all were initially state-owned. The goal is to eventually keep [state] control of just 100 to 200 'strategic' companies.

(*IHT*, 11 April 2007, p. 15)

'The Ho Chi Minh stock exchange for the past two years has been among the fastest growing in Asia. [But] it has fallen 12 per cent so far in 2008 after gaining 23 per cent in 2007' (www.iht.com, 28 January 2008).

Vietnam will ease restrictions on the amount of money banks can lend to local stock market investors, the central bank and state media said [on 30 January 2008], sending the index up almost 4 per cent. The central bank plans to limit bank loans to stock investors at 20 per cent of registered capital, a change from rules keeping lending at 3 per cent of loans. The VN index jumped 3.9 per cent to 843.10 at close of market ... The central bank would impose a new cap of 15 per cent to 20 per cent of registered capital; banks with a capital adequacy ratio of at least 8 per cent and bad debt of less than 5 per cent would qualify.

(*FT*, 31 January 2008, p. 7)

The central bank this week loosened some restrictions on lending for share purchasing, imposed last year [2007] to discourage investors from borrowing to bet heavily on the then soaring stock market. The measures were, it seems, too successful: the main VN share index ended the year 21 per cent below its March [2007] peak.

(*The Economist*, 2 February 2008, p. 61)

Vietnam's stock market rose 144 per cent in 2006, but has cooled considerably since. It ended 2007 up just 23 per cent and is down almost 12 per cent so far this year [2008]. The Hanoi government has also decided to slow the privatization process, postponing several big initial public offerings amid poor market sentiment.

(*FT*, 14 February 2008, p. 27)

'Last week the Ho Chin Minh City stock exchange [was] down 16 per cent' (*IHT*, Friday 29 February 2008, p. 21).

'[The] stock market bubble has now burst leaving prices at roughly half their peak levels' (www.iht.com, 21 March 2008).

The Ho Chi Minh City stock market caught fire, with the index reaching a peak of 1,170 in March [2007], up 140 per cent year on year ... On 25 March [2008] the stock market bottomed out at 496, a fall of 57 per cent off the peak of a year earlier.

(Pincus and Ahn 2008: 28)

'Stock prices ... are off 53 per cent in Vietnam' (www.iht.com, 2 April 2008).

Ho Chi Minh City's market ... fell 44 per cent over the [first] quarter [of 2008] ... The IMF urged the country's regulators to cool the market, They did, instructing banks to stop lending to people and companies to speculate on shares. This let some air out of the bubble and, in January this year [2008], the measure was partly rescinded ... To rein in roaring inflation – almost 20 per cent in the year to March – the authorities have had to impose lending curbs, this time much broader ones than those to reduce speculation ... The government told the State Capital Investment Corporation (SCIC), which holds the state's remaining stakes in part privatized firms, to buy back shares to bolster the market ... The idea met with resistance from the SCIC. So on 27 March a more drastic measure was introduced, restricting daily price movements of individual shares to just one percentage point either way. Banks were also ordered to stop selling shares that they had received as collateral. The measures, intended to be temporary, succeeded in halting the market collapse. On 3 April it was announced that the trading ban would be widened to two points. There are perhaps half a million stock market investors in a country of 85 million.

(*The Economist*, 5 April 2008, p. 92)

The Ho Chi Minh stock exchange is the worst performer in Asia this year [2008], losing 43 per cent, after being one of the top performers a year ago. The share price slump prompted government intervention in March to buy back shares and restrict the intra-day trading band to 1 per cent. The market rose sharply on Monday [7 April] after regulators doubled the intra-day trading band to 2 per cent ... Property prices have fallen about 10 per cent to 15 per cent after quadrupling in cities last year [2007].

(www.iht.com, 7 April 2008)

The privatization programme has moved in fits and starts ... The number of state firms, about 12,000 in the early 1990s, has dropped spectacularly, Counting them is tricky because many are bunched into holding companies, subsidiaries and sub-subsidiaries, but Vu Tien Loc, the chairman of Vietnam's Chamber of Commerce, says only about 2,000 are still fully owned by the state. By 2010 only some 500 will be left, mainly in sensitive areas such as defence. Late last year [2007] the government launched an initial share offering in Vietcombank, one of five state-owned commercial banks. The rest will follow in the next few years ... Until 2000 the country had no stock market, but by the end of last year [2007] 221 firms (including partly privatized ones) ... had listed on the Ho Chi Minh market and the smaller one in Hanoi. A slew of recent laws will remove the current bias in favour of state firms, making it easier for private companies to raise capital ... Private firms are bounding ahead despite bureaucracy, corruption, poor regulation, a feeble legal system and a creaking infrastructure. In the World Bank's latest annual league table measuring the ease of doing business in different countries, Vietnam does not come out well, though overall it beats Indonesia, the Philippines and India ... The corruption index produced by Transparency International, a not-for-profit organization, shows Vietnam as a poor performer, but better than some of its local competitors.

(*The Economist*, Survey, 26 April 2008, pp. 8–9)

'A slew of ambitious larger firms is coming to the stock market' (p. 4).

'This week ... Vietnam's Ho Chi Minh index lost 3 per cent ... taking its loss for the year to 60 per cent' (*FT*, 14 June 2008, p. 26).

It has been one of the worst ever stock market runs. Ho Chi Minh fell every trading day in May and early June ... By the time the stock market had finished its twenty-five-day slide last week the index was down 60 per cent from the start of the year [2008], making it the world's worst performer ... On four of the past five trading days Ho Chi Minh has risen, gaining nearly 4 per cent in total.

(*FT*, 19 June 2008, p. 40)

The plunge in the country's stock market has been as stunning as its ascent. The benchmark VN index surged 144 per cent in 2006 and an additional 56 per cent last year [2007] ... Since hitting a high of 1,179 in March 2007, the main index has sunk by more than 60 per cent, sinking to a two-year low of 370.45 last week.

(*IHT*, 17 June 2008, p. 16)

'[On 19 June] Vietnam's small market fell a further 2.4 per cent to take year-to-date losses to 60 per cent' (www.iht.com, 19 June 2008).

'Bao Viet, Vietnam's biggest insurer, has been given permission to list its shares on the Ho Chi Minh Exchange next week ... The share sales mark an important step in the revitalization of Vietnam's stalled privatization programme' (www.ft.com, 18 June 2009).

Vinashin, Vietnam's prized shipbuilder and export group, this week appointed its third boss in two months as the government scurries to avoid a debt default and salvage its vision of state-led development. Vinashin's troubles, stemming from the confluence of a global downturn and the proclivity of Vietnamese state companies to wander into unfamiliar lines of business, are even threatening the career of Nguyen Tan Dung, the prime minister. With Vinashin at the fore, Mr Dung has championed a development strategy that envisioned turning big state companies into communist versions of the *chaebol*, the South Korea conglomerates like Samsung which drove that country's rise from poverty to the ranks of Asia's wealthiest. Some $750 million from the country's first sovereign bond issue was channelled to Vinashin. Mr Dung, who has been in office since 2006, hopes to be elected next year [2011] to the post of Communist Party General Secretary, Vietnam's most powerful job ... Carl Thayer said: '[Vinashin's troubles have] added weight to a growing internal party consensus to keep Nguyen Tan Dung in place as prime minister' ... Vinashin's troubles are worrying foreign banks and investors, who hold a $187 million bond issue and $600 million in outstanding loans. But Nguyen Hong Truong, the deputy transport minister overseeing the company's restructuring, says banks have been directed to extend credit to Vinashin again. He said: 'If banks cannot provide enough credit, the government will issue new bonds [to meet the company's obligations]' ... Many say the company was handicapped by Pham Thanh Binh, the founding chief executive whose vow to make Vietnam the world's fourth largest shipbuilder turned into expansionist hubris ... The government sacked Mr Binh on 1 July [2010] after an audit found $4.6 billion of debt at Vinashin against assets reported at $4.8 billion. He was expelled from the Communist Party and arrested for mismanaging state assets. Last Friday [27 August] the government sacked Mr Binh's replacement, citing his failure to resolve problems at a subsidiary unable to complete a floating storage unit for PetroVietnam, the national oil company. This week the government named the company's chief business officer as acting chief executive. Vinashin's rise was only slightly slower than its fall ... The corporate structure sprawled into twenty-eight shipyards and 200 subsidiaries. One subsidiary took on the Tam Dao Belvedere, a resort hotel north of Hanoi. The 2008 global downturn's impact on Vinashin was compounded by its dependence on imported components for 70 per cent of the value of its ships. As new orders dried up, the company began running out of foreign currency to pay for components to complete existing contracts. By last September [2009] customs officers were refusing entry for components for Vinashin because it had fallen so far behind on paying dues ... Salary arrears were up to $13 million in arrears. After the July audit, the government announced it would be breaking up Vinashin. Six big subsidiaries were assigned to PetroVietnam and seven to Vinalines, a state shipping conglomerate.

(*FT*, 1 September 2010, p. 7)

Exports of textiles and garments rose by 17 per cent in the first seven months of this year [2010] to $5.8 billion, suggesting that investors still favour Vietnam as a base for cheap manufacturing. Its advantages have been amplified by recent labour unrest and rising costs in southern China's factories. In Hanoi there is renewed talk of 'China Plus One' as a strategy for multinationals keen to spread their bets. Vietnam could gain handsomely, thanks to its labour which is cheaper than China's and its neighbours' [Malaysia, Thailand, Philippines and Indonesia being mentioned in a chart] ... Even after a pay rise, the monthly wage for a textile worker starts at $84, says Nguyen Tung Van, head of the Communist Party-run textiles workers' union ... The industry employs around 1.7 million people, makers of footwear, furniture and more also gain from supplies of cheap labour ... GDP per head was below £100 in 1990 but is now well over $1,000 says the World Bank. But with workers getting richer, more will need to move into higher skilled work, becoming better educated and using capital and technology more efficiently ... Vietnam's creaky infrastructure (power cuts are still common, even in the capital) and inefficient bureaucrats make it hard for exporters to compete. A wish to develop poorer provinces has led to some questionable choices: Vietnam's only oil refinery, for example, is in central Quang Ngai, far from either oil wells or industrial cities. The government, too, needs to give up on short-term fixes. The dong has been devalued three times since 2009. Fiscal weaknesses and policy flip-flops led Fitch, a credit-rating agency, to cut Vietnam's sovereign rating in July [2010]. Foreign reserves have been run down. Many Vietnamese opt to hoard dollars, not bank them. Inflation, at 8.2 per cent, is a worry. More could be done to develop a domestic market, too, in a population of 86 million. One problem is dominant state-owned enterprises. Some competition has appeared in sectors like banking, but too often big state firms are morphing into conglomerates, helped by cheap credit and political ties. Party leaders speak warmly of South Korea's *chaebol*, but Vietnam's versions are unlikely to develop a competitive edge. Note, for example, Vinashin, a deeply indebted shipbuilding company, where the powerful ex-boss, who had been appointed by the prime minister, was arrested in August for mismanagement.

(www.economist.com, 2 September 2010; *The Economist*, 4 September 2010, p. 66)

Foreign trade

Exports to the United States jumped to $6.5 billion last year [2005] from $800 million in 2001, making the United States Vietnam's largest export market and trading partner. Vietnam's economy has become the fastest growing in Asia behind China, expanding 8.4 per cent last year [2005].

(*IHT*, 27 April 2006, p. 17)

Since 1990 Vietnam's exports have increased faster than China's ... [Vietnam] alarmed the Brazilians by becoming their main competitor in growing coffee. Vietnam is now ramping up its exports of everything from shrimps to ships to shoes ... It has just become the world's largest exporter of pepper and aims soon to overtake Thailand in rice. It is even selling tea to India. Foreign-owned factories are chalking up the fastest gains ... Agriculture's share of economic output continues to shrink – from about 25 per cent in 2000 to 21 per cent last year [2005]. By 2010 it may be down to 15 per cent.

(*The Economist*, 5 August 2006, p. 49)

EU nations agreed Wednesday [4 October] to impose long-term tariffs on leather footwear from China and Vietnam. But the deal bitterly divided the EU, which will now look into changing the way it imposes such duties ... The shoe issue opened a rift in the EU between North and South, with countries like Germany, Britain and the Nordic members opposing the tariffs, while Italy along with France, Spain and Portugal lobbied hard for them. The Italians argued that their shoemakers – small-scale and often family-run businesses with high labour costs – were being unfairly smothered by their huge-scale Asian counterparts. The northern European faction – with backing from shoe sellers hungry for low-cost products – contended that the measures were not protection but protectionism. After tough negotiations the twenty-five EU member states reached a compromise Wednesday, agreeing to tariffs on the shoes for two years rather than the full five-year period that the European Commission ... had recommended ... An EU study this year said that China and Vietnam were dumping – or selling at below-cost prices to win market share – in Europe by unfairly helping their leather shoe manufacturers with favourable financing deals and low rents ... The Commission had imposed temporary tariffs, but those expire Friday [6 October]. The new tariffs, of 16.5 per cent against China and 10 per cent against Vietnam, go into effect Saturday [7 October] on most categories of leather shoe imports.

(*IHT*, 5 October 2006, p. 16)

'China supplied about half of the 2.5 billion pairs of shoes sold in Europe last year [2005]. China has about 9 per cent of the EU market for leather shoes' (*IHT*, 6 October 2006, p. 16).

Imports of leather shoes from China and Vietnam to Europe will continue to face steep punitive tariffs under a deal reached by EU governments on Wednesday [4 October]. In future imports from China will face tariffs of 16.5 per cent and imports from Vietnam will face a 10 per cent levy ... Earlier this year [2006] ... the European Commission, said there was 'compelling evidence of serious state intervention in the leather footwear sector in China and Vietnam' ... Wednesday's compromise deal means that the new tariffs will enter force for just two years and not the five recommended by the Commission.

(www.bbc.co.uk, 4 October 2006)

'The EU confirmed that Vietnam was dumping leather shoes, based on what it costs Brazil – the chosen surrogate – to make them ... [In 2005] it imposed duties on Vietnamese bicycles after comparing them with bikes made in Mexico' (*The Economist*, 4 November 2006, p. 100).

'Vietnam is a big net beneficiary of the surge in commodity prices as an exporter of oil, coal, rice, rubber, coffee and seafood, and output of high value agricultural crops continues to grow rapidly' (www.iht.com, 21 March 2008).

> Vietnam and India on Friday [28 March 2008] tightened limits on rice exports, joining India and Cambodia in trying to conserve scarce supplies for domestic consumption at the risk of triggering further increases in global prices, which have roughly doubled since the start of this year [2008] ... A plant virus has damaged the harvest in Vietnam ... Vietnam, the world's second largest rice exporter after Thailand, announced Friday that it would reduce rice exports by 22 per cent in the hope of curbing the rapidly accelerating inflation rates in the country.
>
> (www.iht.com, 29 March 2008)

> Rising prices and a growing fear of scarcity have prompted some of the world's largest rice producers to announce drastic limits on the amount of rice they export. The price of rice, a staple in the diets of nearly half the world's population, has almost doubled in the last three months ... The moves by rice exporting nations over the last two days – meant to ensure scarce supplies will meet domestic needs – drove prices on the world market even higher this week ... Vietnam's government announced on Friday that it would cut rice exports by nearly a quarter this year. The government hoped that keeping more rice inside the country would hold down prices. The same day India effectively banned the export of all but the most expensive grades of [basmati] rice. Egypt announced on Thursday [27 March] that it would impose a six-month ban on rice exports, starting on 1 April, and on Wednesday [26 March] Cambodia banned all rice exports except by government agencies ... Vietnam, Egypt and India all limited rice exports last year [2007], but the limits were much less drastic and were imposed much later in the year, after much more rice had been stopped ... The government of Thailand, the world's largest rice exporter followed by Vietnam, has not yet limited exports. But a national debate has started in Thailand over whether to do so ... In Vietnam an obscure plant virus has cause annual output to start levelling off; it had increased significantly each year until the last three years ... Together with rising prices for other goods, like wheat, soybeans, pork and cooking oil, higher rice prices are also contributing to inflation in many developing countries. Retail rice prices have already jumped by as much as 60 per cent in recent months in Vietnam, trailing increases in wholesale prices but leading a broader acceleration in inflation. Prime minister Nguyen Tan Dung of Vietnam announced Wednesday that the government's top priority now was fighting inflation. Overall consumer prices are more than 19 per cent higher this month [March 2008] than last March

[2007] and the inflation rate has nearly tripled in the last year. Rice is unusual among major agricultural commodities in that most of the major rice-consuming countries are self-sufficient or nearly so. Only 7 per cent of the world's rice production is traded across international borders each year, according to figures from the United Nations Food and Agriculture Organization in Rome. Nguyen Van Bo, the president of the Vietnam Academy of Agricultural Sciences, which oversees government farm research institutes, said that the government expected rice production to rise further by 2010 despite the rapid expansion of residential housing and factories into what had been prime rice-growing land. But the government needs to train farmers to alternate corn with rice to defeat rice pests like the virus, he said.

(www.iht.com, 30 March 2008)

'Exports plus imports equal 160 per cent of GDP, making the economy one of the world's most open' (*The Economist*, Survey, 26 April 2008, p. 3). '[Vietnam is] a fairly poor country that nevertheless strongly supports freer trade. In the absence of progress on the Doha round ... of world trade talks ... Vietnam is seeking bilateral and regional trade deals' (p. 14).

The world's second largest exporter of rice yesterday [18 June] dashed hopes of a significant reduction in prices of the grain in the short term when Vietnam imposed a minimum export price of $800 a tonne for new contracts. The minimum export price came as Hanoi yesterday lifted a ban on the signing of contracts that was imposed earlier this year [2008]. However, it said that it would allow limited sales and reiterated a limit of 3.5 million tonnes of exports for the first nine months of the year. Vietnam this year cut its 2008 export target from 4 million tonnes. Last year [2007] it sold about 4.8 million tonnes of rice ... The price of rice surged last month [May] to a record high of $1,100 a tonne, up from $300 a year ago.

(*FT*, 19 June 2008, p. 6)

When the clock strikes midnight on New Year's Eve, China and then Asean nations will usher in the world's third largest free trade area ... Trade between China and the ten states that make up Asean has soared in recent years, to $192.5 billion in 2008, from $59.6 billion in 2003. The new free trade zone will remove tariffs on 90 per cent of traded goods ... The zone will rank behind only the European Economic Area and the North American Free Trade Area in trade volume. It will encompass 1.9 billion people ... Existing tariffs are already low ... Some manufacturers in South-east Asia are concerned that cheap Chinese goods may flood their markets once import taxes are removed ... Indonesia, for example, is so worried that it plans to ask for a delay in removing tariffs from some items like steel products, textiles, petrochemicals and electronics ... Asean and China have gradually reduced many tariffs in recent years. However, under the free trade agreement – which was signed in 2002 – China, Indonesia, Thailand, the Philippines, Malaysia, Singapore and Brunei will have to remove almost all tariffs in 2010. Asean's newest members – Cambodia, Laos, Vietnam and Myanmar – will gradually reduce tariffs in coming years and must eliminate them entirely by 2015. Most of the goods that will become tariff-free in January [2010] – including manufactured items – are currently subject to import taxes of about 5 per cent. Some agricultural products and parts for motor vehicles and heavy machinery will still face tariffs in 2010, but those will gradually be phased out. In recent years China has overtaken the United States to become Asean's third largest trading partner after Japan and the EU. The overall trade balance has shifted slightly in China's favour, although there are significant differences among South-east Asian countries' trade balances ... Singapore, Malaysia and Thailand have only small trade deficits with China, while Vietnam's has grown substantially in recent years. In 2008 Vietnam exported items worth $4.5 billion to China but imported about $15.7 billion worth of Chinese goods ... [It has been argued that] countries like Vietnam that focus on the production of inexpensive consumer goods are more likely to be hurt ... [but that] China will import more agricultural goods, like tropical fruit, from countries like Thailand, Malaysia and Vietnam when the trade area takes effect.

(www.iht.com, 28 December 2009; *IHT*, 29 December 2009, p. 14)

'The free trade area is expected to help Asean nations increase exports, particularly those with commodities that resource-hungry China desperately wants' (www.iht.com, 1 January 2010).

The China–Asean deal takes effect following the completion last summer [2009] of an agreement on investment rules, the last leg of an eight-year negotiating marathon that produced earlier agreements on goods and services. Tariffs have been falling since 2005, with 90 per cent of goods due to be tariff-free from yesterday [1 January 2010] for the six core members ... The target is 2015 for the other four (Laos, Cambodia, Burma and Vietnam) ... The deal remains short of genuine free trade. The trade in goods agreement provides for each country to register hundreds of sensitive goods on which tariffs will continue to apply, in many cases until 2020. Sensitive goods include various types of electronic equipment, motor vehicles and automotive parts and chemicals, as well as items such as popcorn, snowboarding equipment and toilet paper ... The deal creates the third largest regional trading agreement by value after the EU and the North American Free Trade Agreement, covering countries with mutual trade flows of $231 billion in 2008 ... China is already South-east Asia's third largest trading partner, with about 11 per cent of total two-way trade ... Indonesia led opposition to the pact, seeking to delay its implementation because of fears that sectors from steel to petrochemicals to cosmetics and herbal medicines would face overwhelming competition from cheap Chinese imports.

(*FT*, 2 January 2009, p. 6)

186 *The economy*

The World Trade Organization (WTO)

Vietnam has reached an agreement with the United States that paves the way for the country to join the WTO, US and Vietnamese officials said Sunday [14 May] ... The two sides reached agreement in principle ... [and] the official signing will be conducted soon ... in early June [it is expected] ... probably in Ho Chi Minh City ... [But] several issues remain unresolved ... [In April] Vietnam concluded talks with Mexico, making the United States the last country with which it needed to complete negotiations ... The agreement will substantially lower tariffs on US industrial and agricultural products and lift non-tariff trade barriers on American service providers ... It also calls for further political and economic reform in Vietnam, including increasing transparency in commerce ... A sticking point in the talks was a Vietnamese government decision to spend $4 billion on subsidies to its garments and textile industry ... The two sides agreed that Vietnam would scrap the plan joining the trade body and immediately stop subsidizing local garment and textile companies when the two countries sign the agreement ... The US Congress needs to grant Vietnam the status of 'permanent normal trade relations', the last step before Vietnam can become a member of the Geneva-based trade body ... Bilateral trade has steadily increased since the two countries signed a comprehensive trade accord in 2001. Trade reached nearly $8 billion last year [2005], with Hanoi showing a surplus.

(www.iht.com, 14 May 2006)

'The agreement lowers tariffs on US industrial and farm products and removes non-tariff barriers that block US service providers from working in Vietnam ... Vietnamese exports to the United States rose to more than $6.5 billion in 2005' (*IHT*, 15 May 2006, p. 12).

All foreign banks will for the first time be allowed to open 100 per cent owned subsidiaries and branches in Vietnam under an agreement reached between US and Vietnamese negotiators. The last bilateral accord Vietnam needed to sign before joining the WTO will limit individual foreign banks to holding a 30 per cent stake in any Vietnamese-controlled bank, up from the current 10 per cent. It also provides for a significant opening up of Vietnam's insurance and securities markets, and smaller concessions in telecommunications ... The deal offers a boost to Vietnam's fast-growing garment industry, because the United States has agreed to lift all quotas on imports, becoming the last country in the world to do so ... Foreign manufacturers and farmers will benefit from reduced tariffs in Vietnam. Foreign companies will be able to engage immediately in the wholesale and retail sectors throughout Vietnam ... The deal calls for Vietnam to end all subsidies to its garment industry immediately, with a one-year provision for emergency curbs if subsidies are not halted. Like China, however, Vietnam will remain a 'non-market economy' until 2018, which makes it easier for US companies to bring anti-dumping cases that allow for higher tariffs on imports.

(*FT*, 16 May 2006, p. 8)

The United States and Vietnam signed a trade pact Wednesday [31 May] that removes one of the last major hurdles to Hanoi's bid to join the WTO. The deal further dismantles trade barriers between the two countries by ending US quotas on Vietnamese textiles and garments and giving American companies greater access to the growing Vietnamese market. Bilateral trade rose 21.6 per cent to $7.8 billion last year [2005] ... A historic trade pact ... in 2001 pushed two-way trade from less than $1 billion a year to nearly $8 billion last year – most of it exports from Vietnam. The new pact will lower barriers even further, with Vietnam agreeing to reduce tariffs to 15 per cent or less on US manufactured and agricultural goods and to open up its telecommunications, financial and energy services to foreign companies. Vietnam also agreed to scrap a $4 billion government plan to improve its textile and garment industry, which the United States considered a subsidy ... But a final challenge remains: the US Congress must vote to grant Vietnam permanent normal trading relations.

(www.iht.com, 31 May 2006)

Vietnam said that it planned to cancel state subsidies on all oil products by the end of 2008 as it moved to liberalize its fuel market in line with WTO commitments. The fuel subsidy this year [2006] will cost the government about $808 million, equivalent to around 1.4 per cent of the country's GDP of around $57 billion.

(*IHT*, 11 August 2006, p. 14)

Terms for ... Vietnam's entry into the WTO ... were approved late Thursday [26 October 2006] by trade negotiators from around the world [meeting in Hanoi] ... The agreement [is] subject to final approval on 7 November by a special meeting of trade ambassadors from the organization's 149 members ... The agreement Thursday was concluded by a WTO working party ... It requires Vietnam to reduce or appeal many import duties, eliminate a long list of textile industry subsidies and allow foreign banks to incorporate wholly owned subsidiaries in Vietnam beginning 1 April [2007]. In exchange, quotas on Vietnam's garment exports will be lifted and Vietnam will gain the right to challenge foreign countries' trade barriers before WTO tribunals in Geneva. Vietnamese membership will leave Russia, Iran and Ukraine as the three biggest countries that have not yet joined the WTO ... American companies rank ninth in foreign investment in Vietnam, with only a quarter as much approved investment as Taiwan or Singapore. There could be another delay this winter [2006]. The US Congress is scheduled to vote in mid-November on whether to grant permanent status to its trade relations with Vietnam. If the House of Representatives or the Senate defeats the measure, or if either chamber delays action, Vietnam would still join the

WTO, but its rules would not apply to bilateral trade between the United States and Vietnam until Congress acted ... Vietnam is a modest exporter of oil now but expects to become a net importer in seven or eight years. Vietnam has responded by making plans to build its first nuclear power plant ... Vietnam passed an investment law this year [2006] guaranteeing foreign-owned companies equal treatment with domestic companies. But with WTO membership some of the biggest changes will start coming next 1 April [2007]. That is the date that Vietnam has accepted in WTO negotiations for allowing foreign banks to set up 100 per cent foreign-owned subsidiaries ... But Vietnam will retain the right to approve acquisitions of existing banks.

(*IHT*, 27 October 2006, p. 12)

While Vietnam's competitive clothing manufacturers will benefit from fewer restrictions on their exports to the United States and Europe, other sectors in the still heavily state-dominated economy will face stiffer competition from foreign suppliers and the removal of many government subsidies ... Hanoi has pledged an immediate end to all WTO-inconsistent state subsidies in the textiles sector and other industries. It has also agreed to special provisions as a 'non-market economy' that will make it easier for trading partners to impose anti-dumping and anti-subsidy duties on its imports.

(*FT*, 27 October 2006, p. 7)

The 149 member countries of the WTO voted yesterday [7 November 2006] to admit Vietnam ... [as the 150th member and] the organization's twenty-second since the organization [replaced GATT] ... Every existing members can veto every applicant unless it agrees to reform trade law ... [The] documents for Vietnam's accession oblige it to dismantle trade barriers, end many subsidies, allow for foreign companies to buy Vietnamese ones and protect intellectual property rights. Trading partners have insisted on treating Vietnam as a 'non-market economy' for up to twelve years, making it easier to impose emergency tariffs to block Vietnamese imports they deem to be subsidized or sold below cost price. The United States is a particularly determined gatekeeper. On top of its traditional export interests of financial services and farm goods, it increasingly demands not just laws to protect patents and copyrights but guarantees they will be enforced.

(*FT*, 8 November 2006, p. 13)

Almost twelve years of talks ... have picked over many bones of contention, including Vietnam's textile subsidies, which it has promised to eliminate, and its banking system, which it has pledged to open up by next April [2007] ... As one price of entry Vietnam has agreed to remain on a list of so-called 'non-market economies', alongside China and several other WTO members, most of them former Soviet republics ... [making] it harder for

Vietnam to defend itself against the charge of dumping. Dumping occurs when an exporter sells a product abroad for less than it charges at home or for less than it costs to make ... [The United States] comes up with its own calculation of 'normal value' based on costs in other 'surrogate' countries. America is Vietnam's biggest market and one of the more prolific users of anti-dumping duties ... [The decision in 2003 to impose duties on] Vietnamese catfish, or 'basa' fish as they are now labelled, not to upset fish farmers in the Deep South ... [was calculated on] what Vietnam's fillets would cost if they were reared on a fish farm in Bangladesh.

(*The Economist*, 4 November 2006, p. 100)

The [US] House of Representatives ... [in] a surprising result [on 14 November] ... defeated a measure backed by President George W. Bush that would normalize trade relations with Vietnam. The setback, four days before Bush was scheduled to leave for his first visit to Vietnam, may be only temporary, however. The legislation embodies approval by Congress of 'permanent normal relations' with Vietnam, with the aim of making it easier for Hanoi to join the WTO. The legislation received a majority vote but fell short of the two-thirds needed for the passage under special rules that speeded up its consideration in the House. The vote came on the first day of the lame-duck session [after mid-term elections] in which the outgoing House, still controlled by a Republican majority, met to pass crucial bills by the end of the year [2006] ... The White House still hopes for the bill's approval this week ... The loss, however temporary, was also a portent that trade bills could face tougher odds in the lame-duck session and in January, when Democrats take control of the House and Senate ... The legislation is necessary because Cold War-era legislation known as the Jackson–Vanik law, which requires an annual review of Vietnam's political and economic practices and an annual granting of trade preferences, must be rescinded under WTO rules.

(*IHT*, 15 November 2006, p. 15)

Prospects for congressional approval of several free trade bills backed by the administration have been thrown in doubt by House Republican leaders, who abruptly withdrew the one aimed at Vietnam. The failure of the Vietnam bill late Tuesday [15 November] was a deep disappointment and embarrassment for the White House ... Though the bill could come back to the House before the end of the year [2006] some legislative aides said that its future was in doubt, along with that of several other bills lowering trade barriers with poor countries in Asia, Africa and Latin America ... Failure of the measure does not bar Vietnam from joining the WTO. Rather, it would place the United States out of compliance with the organization, because the Jackson–Vanik Amendment, passed in 1975, requires an annual review of Vietnam's political and economic practices, which is not allowed under the WTO's rules.

(www.iht.com, 15 November 2006)

American figures show US–Vietnam trade reached $8.1 billion in 2006, out of which $7.2 billion represented Vietnamese exports to the United States. This compares with two-way trade worth just $1.1 billion in 2000, of which Vietnam's exports to the United States were less than $400 million.

(*FT*, 8 January 2007, p. 15)

'In 2007 the United States accounted for more than $100 billion, or one-fifth of Vietnam's exports' (*IHT*, 3 March 2008, p. 8).

Vietnam joined the WTO on 11 January 2007.

The EU's executive is proposing extending anti-dumping duties on Chinese and Vietnamese shoe exports for a minimum of fifteen months, a compromise that aims to satisfy shoemakers and retailers alike in Europe. The European Commission, under pressure from shoe-making countries like Italy, first imposed duties on imports in 2006 for two years ... But the issue has divided the bloc, with countries such as Sweden ... arguing the duties hurt consumers by pushing up prices. The Commission reimposed the tariffs on a temporary basis last October [2008] pending a review ... The proposal is expected to be adopted by the full Commission in the next few weeks, and then goes to national governments, which must decide whether to accept or reject it ... The Commission recommended that most Chinese shoes continue to face duties of 16.5 per cent, while it said 10 per cent duties would be applied to products of all Vietnamese companies. The Commission could have proposed an extension of up to five years, but limited it to fifteen months – for now ... If approved by EU member states, the new measures would take effect from 3 January.

(www.iht.com, 13 October 2009; *IHT*, 14 October 2009, p. 14)

('EU nations agreed Wednesday [4 October 2006] to impose long-term tariffs on leather footwear from China and Vietnam. But the deal bitterly divided the EU, which will now look into changing the way it imposes such duties ... The shoe issue opened a rift in the EU between North and South, with countries like Germany, Britain and the Nordic members opposing the tariffs, while Italy along with France, Spain and Portugal lobbied hard for them. The Italians argued that their shoemakers – small-scale and often family-run businesses with high labour costs – were being unfairly smothered by their huge-scale Asian counterparts. The northern European faction – with backing from shoe sellers hungry for low-cost products – contended that the measures were not protection but protectionism. After tough negotiations the twenty-five EU member states reached a compromise Wednesday, agreeing to tariffs on the shoes for two years rather than the full five-year period that the European Commission ... had recommended ... An EU study this year said that China and Vietnam were dumping – or selling at below-cost prices to win market share – in Europe by unfairly helping their leather shoe manufacturers with favourable financing deals and low rents ... The Commission had imposed temporary tariffs, but those expire Friday [6 October]. The new tariffs, of 16.5 per cent against China and 10 per cent against Vietnam, go into effect Saturday [7 October] on most categories of leather shoe imports': *IHT*, 5 October 2006, p. 16. 'China supplied about half of the 2.5 billion pairs of shoes sold in Europe last year [2005]. China has about 9 per cent of the EU market for leather shoes': *IHT*, 6 October 2006, p. 16. 'Imports of leather shoes from China and Vietnam to Europe will continue to face steep punitive tariffs under a deal reached by EU governments on Wednesday [4 October]. In future imports from China will face tariffs of 16.5 per cent and imports from Vietnam will face a 10 per cent levy ... Earlier this year [2006] ... the European Commission ... said there was "compelling evidence of serious state intervention in the leather footwear sector in China and Vietnam" ... Wednesday's compromise deal means that the new tariffs will enter into force for just two years and not the five recommended by the Commission': www.bbc.co.uk, 4 October 2006.)

> The EU has voted to extend tariffs on shoes from China and Vietnam ... The tariffs, which were first introduced in 2006, will last for a further fifteen months ... The tariffs on Chinese shoes will remain at [a maximum of] 16.5 per cent, and those on Vietnamese shoes will remain at 10 per cent ... A number of countries in the EU were opposed to the extension ... The extension has also proved unpopular among some retail groups in Europe ... UK Business Secretary Lord Mandelson: 'A small majority of member states did not oppose the measures.'
>
> (www.bbc.co.uk, 22 December 2009)

> The charges add 9.7 per cent to 16.5 per cent to the import price of Chinese shoes and 10 per cent to Vietnamese shoes ... European importers and retailers had called for an end to the charges ... European governments said that they had voted by a majority to extend the duties at a meeting Tuesday [22 December]. They did not say how the twenty-seven member countries had voted. The EU introduced the trade charges in October 2006.
>
> (www.iht.com, 22 December 2009)

> The extension of the duties, as high as 16.5 per cent on leather shoes, was a compromise with a group of northern European countries, which opposed extending the levies for the usual five-year period ... The trade protectionism, begun in 2006, helped reduce Chinese and Vietnamese exporters' combined share of the EU shoes market to 28.7 per cent in the twelve months through June 2008 from 35.5 per cent in 2005. The 2006 decision to impose the levies for two years was itself a compromise because such anti-dumping measures usually last five years. The levies are 16.5 per cent against all Chinese exporters except Golden Step, which faces a 9.7 per cent duty, and 10 per cent against all Vietnamese exporters. In April 2008 the EU extended the 16.5 per cent duty to Macao after finding that Chinese exporters were shipping leather shoes to Europe via Macao or were assembling them there to evade the duty.
>
> (*IHT*, 23 December 2009)

The Asian financial crisis

As a lesson from the Asian crisis, Asian countries have not only tried to strengthen their financial systems and accumulated foreign reserves; they have also entered a regional policy dialogue on monetary and financial co-operation. In contrast to the last crisis, where virtually no financial co-operation mechanisms were in place, China, Japan, Korea and the ten Asean countries have now set up a pool of foreign exchange reserves for provision of short-term liquidity in case one of them runs into trouble. The sums involved so far are small, but for a country like Vietnam, where fear of a currency crisis similar to the one that shattered the Thai miracle in 1997 now spreading, regional support could be crucial.

(www.feer.com, 22 September 2008)

Foreign debt and aid

In 1993 Vietnam's *per capita* income was $180. It climbed to $640 for 2005 and is expected to reach $1,000 by 2010, when Vietnam will no longer qualify for concessionary loans from the World Bank [according to the World Bank] ... Vietnam has eschewed heavy reliance on foreign aid; less than 15 per cent of public spending for the last couple of years came from aid, the bank said.

(www.iht.com, 19 June 2006; *IHT*, 20 June 2006, p. 2)

The Asian Development Bank agreed Friday [21 September] to loan Vietnam nearly $1 billion to build a coal-fired power plant ... about 190 kilometres (120 miles) east of Hanoi ... as the booming country scrambles to keep up with its surging demand for power ... ADB and Vietnamese officials say the plant is necessary to help Vietnam avoid blackouts ... They say they will use state-of-the-art equipment to minimize pollution from the plant, which is located in the same province as Halong Bay, a major tourist attraction and one of Vietnam's greatest natural treasures. The board voted unanimously Friday to release the first $28 million toward construction of the $931 million project. This is the biggest loan from the Manila-based ADB for a power plant. The money will be used to finance one of two plants on the site. The second will be financed by a private company working with the Vietnamese government. The Mong Duong plant is expected to begin generating power by 2012 ... Vietnam now relies quite heavily on hydro-power, as well as on natural gas and oil. It has nearly exhausted its ability to bring more hydro plants on line. During the dry season, from March through May, the country is vulnerable to power outages. The government wants to diversify its power sources and plans to build more gas- and coal-fired plants over the next decade. It also hopes to add nuclear power to the mix, and is planning to open a nuclear plant by 2020 ... Vietnam signed and ratified the Kyoto Protocol that seeks to limit global warming. But because it is a developing nation with very low *per capita* carbon dioxide emissions.

Vietnam is not restricted by provisions designed to reduce emissions in developed countries. Even with the plant, Vietnam will not be among the world's top 100 carbon dioxide producers.

(www.iht.com, 21 September 2007)

Vietnam no longer really needs the multilateral organizations' aid. Multilateral and bilateral donors together have promised the country $5.4 billion in loans and grants this year [2008], but with so much foreign investment pouring in, Vietnam's currency reserves increased by almost double that figure last year [2007].

(*The Economist*, Survey, 26 April 2008, p. 4)

Tokyo has suspended all new aid lending for Vietnam – and 65.3 billion yen in already pledged funds – after a corruption scandal involving a Japanese consulting company contracted to aid-funded road projects in Ho Chin Minh City. A donors' meeting ended in Hanoi yesterday [5 December] with pledges of $5 billion in aid. Without Japan, which pledged $1.1 billion last year [2007], the total fell short of the previous conference's $5.4 billion ... Former officials of Pacific Consultants International, a Tokyo-based project contractor, and the company itself, pleaded guilty in a Tokyo court last month [November] to providing $820,000 in bribes to an official overseeing infrastructure projects in the Vietnamese city in relation to contracts dating back in 2001 ... Vietnamese authorities have vowed to co-operate with Japan in investigating the case ... Vietnamese state media reported the suspension of a transport and water official in connection with the case ... [Japan] said the 65.3 billion ($710 million) in loans affected by the suspension were to fund a water project and rail system in Hanoi and urban improvement of the northern port city of Haiphong ... The IMF said at the conference it expects Vietnam's growth to slow to 5 per cent in 2009, down from 6.25 per cent in 2008 and 8.5 per cent the year before ... [Vietnam has] a large current account deficit.

(*FT*, 6 December 2008, p. 8)

A suspension of Japanese development assistance [took place] after the discovery of a multi-million-dollar bribery scheme that diverted aid funds from Japan, until now Vietnam's largest donor, ... Two reporters were arrested last year [2008] for writing about the skimming of aid not only from Japan but also the World Bank. One journalist is in jail and the other is in re-education.

(www.iht.com, 14 January 2009)

Foreign direct investment

'Foreign investment [was] running at $5.8 billion last year [2005]' (*The Economist*, 28 January 2006, p. 66).

'Vietnam attracted $10 billion in foreign direct investment last year [2006] and is on track to exceed that figure this year [2007]' (www.iht.com, 23 August 2007).

'Net foreign direct investment in 2006 was $2.3 billion, a 20 per cent increase over the previous year, and is expected to rise again this year [2007]' (*FEER*, September 2007, p. 45).

> Chinese and American investments in Vietnam last year [2005] were about equal – a little more than $2 billion each, according to government figures ... China's investments have been mostly in raw materials like coal and bauxite, and in building roads and rails that will connect the long coast of Vietnam to southern China.
> (www.iht.com, 19 June 2006; *IHT*, 20 June 2006, p. 2)

'Singapore [is] the biggest overseas investor in Vietnam ... [with] $7.57 billion' (www.iht.com, 26 September 2006).

'Government estimates show that foreign direct investments will jump 25 per cent to $10 billion in 2008 from last year [2007]' (www.iht.com, 7 April 2008).

The problems of attracting foreign direct investment and measures taken to tackle these problems

> Since late December [2005] wildcat strikes have swept through Ho Chi Minh City. Tens of thousands of workers joined the protest over wages and conditions ... The government issued a decree earlier this month [January 2006] raising the minimum wage in foreign-owned factories ... by up to 40 per cent ... starting 1 February [2006] ... [This is] the first mandated rise in several years ... Most strikers have now returned to work, but some have not ... Workers in Vietnam have staged walkouts before, particularly over alleged mistreatments by foreign managers, but the scale and co-ordinated nature of the latest strikes are, well, striking ... Most of the affected factories are owned by East Asian companies, the biggest investors in Vietnam. At Song Than industrial zone, on the outskirts of Ho Chi Minh City, 80 per cent of the factories are owned by Taiwanese, producing clothing, shoes, furniture and bicycles for export ... On 15 December [2005] Taiwan said it was building a landing strip on one of the [Spratly] islands.
> (*The Economist*, 28 January 2006, p. 66)

> Prime minister Nguyen Tan Dung has told the authorities to quickly bring to trial a case in which the Dutch bank ABN AMRO is accused of having conducted illegal foreign currency deals ... [It was reported on 31 October 2006] that initial inspections by the state bank and the ministry of public security had found that ABN AMRO 'had seriously violated Vietnamese laws and international practices' ... The case, which has prompted diplomatic protests from the Netherlands, centres on foreign currency deals that ABN AMRO carried out for Industrial and Commercial Bank of Vietnam, known as Incombank, which says it lost $5.4 million in the process. The police have detained four ABN AMRO employees since March [2006] and

demanded that the bank pay back the money, saying that it should have known that it was dealing with an unlicensed trader in Incombank and had breached local banking regulations ... The suspected [Incombank] trader is suspected of having used a stolen computer password to execute the transactions ... ABN AMRO has denied wrongdoing and said it has followed normal trading practices. The case has raised concerns among foreign business executives here about police intrusion into what many see as a routine banking dispute.

(www.iht.com, 1 November 2006)

Two of ABN's local staff have been jailed and two others arrested ... Prime minister Nguyen Tan Dung recently ... hinted that the ABN staff might escape criminal charges if the bank compensated the state for the loss ... ABN has fallen foul of an archaic national law that makes causing economic losses to the state a criminal offence potentially punishable by death ... The law is a damaging anachronism. As well as being a deterrent to foreign investors, it is a serious obstacle to Vietnam's economic development. By tying the hands of government officials in negotiations with prospective private investors in power generation projects, it has already contributed to delays in plans for the capacity expansion needed to relieve Vietnam's worsening electricity shortages.

(*FT*, editorial, 3 November 2006, p. 16)

At the weekend Vietnamese police told the state-controlled *Thanh Nien* newspaper that ABN AMRO had deposited $4.5 million in a police custody account at the state treasury as compensation for 'illegal profits' and as a deposit against future liabilities. The Dutch bank yesterday [27 November 2006] declined to comment.

(*FT*, 28 November 2006, p. 25)

Vietnam plans to allow expatriates to buy and sell houses to attract foreign investment to the sector, real estate dealers said Monday [16 July 2007]. The ministry of construction plan applies to foreigners who will stay in Vietnam for a year. They will be allowed to buy and own one house per person over fifty years. Many of the expatriates are executives in foreign-invested companies ... The proposal allows foreign owners to sell without restrictions and use the property as collateral for bank loans in Vietnam but forbids them from renting the home. In Vietnam the state owns the land but gives infinite freehold to its citizens ... About a quarter of the 81,000 currently living in Vietnam would be eligible to buy houses ... Last year [2006] the consulting firm Mercer ranked Hanoi the world's thirty-second most expensive city for expatriates, mainly for high rents that could go up to $3,000 per month for a three-bedroom serviced apartment. Real estate prices, especially condominiums in big cities like Ho Chi Minh City, have gone up about 50 per cent in the past year.

(www.iht.com, 16 July 2007)

Further aspects of foreign direct investment

Intel, the world's largest make of computer chips, said Friday [10 November 2006] that it would more than triple its initial investment in Vietnam to $1 billion, greatly expanding the size of a chip assembly and testing plant that it is building here ... Construction is expected to begin in March [2007] on what is Vietnam's first semi-conductor factory and Intel's sixth testing centre in Asia ... Intel, which is based in Santa Clara California, talked of 1,200 jobs when it announced $300 million investment in February [2006].

(www.iht.com, 10 September 2006)

Nike set up shop in Vietnam in 1995 ... [and is now] the second largest manufacturer on Nike-branded products after China. About 160,000 Vietnamese now work making Nike shoes and apparel, accounting for about 30 per cent of the US company's global supply and around 9 per cent of Vietnam's manufactured exports ... Intel last week unveiled plans to build a $1 billion semi-conductor assembly and testing facility in Ho Chi Minh City, the largest investment by a US company.

(*FT*, 17 November 2006, p. 9)

Hanoi is to raise the ceiling on the stake a strategic, non-bank foreign investor can have in a domestic bank to 15 per cent from 10 per cent ... The ownership limit for a foreign bank in a Vietnamese bank remains unchanged at 10 per cent and the total foreign ownership limit in a domestic bank will also remain at 30 per cent, the government said in a statement Saturday [21 April 2007]. In exceptional cases the government could allow a strategic, non-bank foreign investor to own up to 20 per cent of a Vietnamese bank if proposed by the State Bank of Vietnam, the central bank, said the statement, which cited a decree signed on Friday [20 April]. A strategic foreign investor can only transfer the Vietnamese bank shares five years after purchase ... A non-bank foreign investor that is not a strategic investor will only be allowed to hold 5 per cent, down from 10 per cent now, the statement said, without giving a definition for 'strategic investor' ... The decree is likely to take effect in May, given the time needed for procedures such as its official publication. Vietnam caps the foreign ownership in a domestic bank at 30 per cent, with a 10 per cent limit for an individual investor, regardless of status. The central bank had asked the government to double the 10 per cent cap to 20 per cent. Foreign banks with stakes in Vietnamese banks are ANZ, Standard Chartered, HSBC Holdings, OCBC, BNP Paribus, United Overseas Bank and Deutsche Bank. Each of the foreign banks has a 10 per cent stake in a Vietnamese bank, except for Standard Chartered's 8.56 per cent in Asia Commercial Bank, one of Vietnam's two listed banks. The other listed lender is Saigon Thuong Tin Commercial Bank, which has ANZ among its shareholders ... The government decree also doubled the registered capital requirement for a Vietnamese bank to 1 trillion dong, or $65 million, if it wants to be qualified to sell shares to foreign investors. It said that a foreign bank must have at least $20 billion in total assets in the year before it registers to buy Vietnamese bank shares.

(www.iht.com, 22 April 2007)

Investing in the emerging market economy in Vietnam carries risks like a shortage of skilled workers, poor infrastructure and shortcomings in the legal system, prime minister Nguyen Tan Dung said Thursday [23 August]. Dung told an Asean conference of business executives and politicians that many opportunities, but also challenges awaited foreign investors in the country ... Nguyen Tan Dung: 'The first challenge is human resources development that meets the need of rapid economic growth. This is a risk if you want to expand your business but you cannot have sufficient or skilled human resources ... [Poor infrastructure is another risk, but one that the government is working on] ... The third issue I would like to emphasize is the institutional and legal framework. We are in the process of improving the legal framework. We have a policy to get any changes of the legal framework to minimize impact on the interests and benefits of enterprises ... One thing I would like to assure you about is the political stability in Vietnam.'

(www.iht.com, 23 August 2007)

Morgan Stanley has received clearance to open a securities joint venture in Vietnam just weeks after the collapse of plans for a landmark tie-up with a state agency. The US investment bank, the first of its kind from the West to get directly involved in communist-rule Vietnam's securities industry, hopes to profit from a wave of privatizations. Morgan Stanley said its venture with brokerage Gateway Securities would offer a full range of financial services, including investment banking and advisory services, brokerage services, research and principal investing. The new tie-up follows the collapse of Morgan Stanley's plan to set up a securities company with the State Investment Corporation of Vietnam [SCIC], owner of the state-owned companies slated for partial privatization. That proposed joint venture had triggered the wrath of rival investment banks, which feared they could be frozen out of lucrative mandates as Vietnam proceeds with its mass privatization programme. Eventually, SCIC bowed to pressure and pulled out of the deal. Morgan Stanley Gateway Securities, which will be based in Hanoi, will be 49 per cent owned by Morgan Stanley – the maximum foreign investors can hold in a domestic securities firm. However, Morgan Stanley would probably seek to increase its stake after 2011, when Vietnam's World Trade Organization commitments oblige it to open the securities business to majority foreign-owned firms ... In December [2007] Morgan Stanley paid $217 million for a 10 per cent stake in PetroVietnam Finance Corp., which works as a de facto bank financing energy projects for the company.

(*FT*, 14 February 2008, p. 27)

'Vietnam remains a beneficiary of Taiwanese and [South] Korean manufacturers diversifying away from southern China because of rising cost and a need to spread risk' (www.iht.com, 21 March 2008).

Vietnam has become the darling of foreign investors and multinationals. Firms that draw up a 'China-plus-one' strategy for new factories in case things go awry in China itself often make Vietnam the plus-one. Wage costs remain well below those in southern China and productivity is growing faster, albeit from a lower base. When the UN Conference on Trade and Development asked multinationals where they planned to invest this year [2008] and next, Vietnam, at number six, was the only South-east Asian country in the top ten.

(*The Economist*, Survey, 26 April 2008, p. 4)

VietJetAir ... the first private airline in Vietnam ... [is preparing] for launch at the end of the year [2008] ... Vietnam changed its legislation in 2006 to admit privately owned airlines, and granted VietJetAir its licence last December [2007] ... The leading shareholders in the airline are two industrial conglomerates, TMC and Sovico, which own 49 per cent and 33 per cent, respectively. Other private investors hold the rest ... The new airline will compete with Vietnam Airlines, the national airline, and Pacific Airlines, an offshoot of Vietnam, Airlines in which Qantas of Australia has a minority stake.

(*FT*, 1 May 2008, p. 28)

Vietnam still offers foreign investors a corporate tax rate of zero for the first four years, and half the usual rate of 10 per cent for the next four years ... Foreign direct investment ... over the past three years ... soared more than eightfold in Vietnam ... A recent survey by Grant Thornton, the global accounting and consulting firm, found that companies were more worried about attracting and retaining key staff members in Vietnam than elsewhere in the world. [China was a close second.) ... Infrastructure is likely to be another impediment ... Like most countries in Asia, Vietnam has not improved transportation links as quickly as China. Traffic jams slow down shipments and drive up costs.

(*IHT*, 18 June 2008, p. 14)

Vietnam's great war hero, General Vo Nguyen Giap, has stood up to defend his country once again, this time against what he says would be a huge mistake by the government – a vast mining operation run by Chinese company. Now ninety-seven, the commander who led his country to victory over both France and the United States has emerged as the most prominent voice in a broad popular protest that is challenging the secretive workings of the country's Communist leaders. In an unusual step, the government has taken note of the criticisms in recent weeks and appears to be making at least gestures of response, saying it will review the project's environmental impact and slow its full implementation. The project, approved by the Communist Party's decision-making Politburo in late 2007, calls for an investment of $15 billion by 2025 to exploit reserves of bauxite – the key mineral in making aluminium – that by some estimates are the third largest in the world. The state-owned mining group Chinalco has already put workers and equipment to work in the remote Central Highlands under contract to Vinacomin, the Vietnamese mining consortium that is aiming for up to 6.6 million tonnes of aluminium production by 2015. General Giap and other opponents say the project will be ruinous to the environment, displace ethnic minority populations and threaten national security with an influx of Chinese workers and economic leverage ... As the outlines of the project have emerged, a loose coalition of scientists, academics, environmentalists, war veterans and leaders of unofficial Buddhist and Catholic groups have come together to challenge what prime minister Nguyen Tan Dung has called 'a major policy of the party and the state'. Their voices have been amplified in the echo chamber of political blogs, a new voice in public discourse here [in Vietnam] ... In a petition to the National Assembly in April [2009] 135 scholars and intellectuals opposed the plan, saying: 'China has been notorious in the modern world as a country causing the greatest pollution and other problems' ... State-owned Vinacomin [said] ... construction will end in two years and only a small number of Chinese will remain to run the operations ... The government opened itself to its critics in April, convening a seminar at which scientists and economists voiced strong opposition to what one of them said could become a 'major disaster'. Responding at the seminar, deputy prime minister Hoang Trung Hai assured critics that the government would not consider developing the mines without regard to the larger impact and would readjust the projects in an effort to protect the environment. The government now say it will begin with only two of the four planned mining operations, and it is allowing a debate in the National Assembly ... The government might well have brushed off its critics if General Giap had not spoken up, first in January [2009] and twice afterwards, saying the project 'will cause serious consequences to the environment, society and national defence' ... General Giap is the last living comrade of the country's founding father, Ho Chi Minh ... Vietnam was a tributary state of China for 1,000 years and was invaded by China in 1979, and the two countries continue to joust for sovereignty in the South China Sea.

(www.iht.com, 28 June 2009)

(See the entries for 4 and 12 September 2009 in the political chronology.)

Citibank will today [13 October 2009] become the first financial institution to open a retail operation in Vietnam ... The US bank will open a branch in Ho Chin Minh City to provide deposit services to individual customers and remittance services to the broader diaspora ... Vietnam has seen an explosion in the number of banks, and is one of Asia's last great untapped markets with only about 10 per cent of 85 million Vietnamese holding a bank account. Incomes are rising fast. Foreign banks have been expanding operations in the country, attracted by resilient growth – Vietnam's economy is expected to expand some 5 per cent this year [2009] ... Citi also plans to double the number of its ATMs in Ho Chi Minh to thirteen by the end of the year. It has provided corporate and investment banking services in Vietnam since 1993 ... In January [2009] HSBC became the first foreign bank to incorporate in Vietnam and now has three full branches and several transaction offices. Last month [September] it signed a deal with Vietnam Posts to allow clients to use post offices for cash transactions.

(*FT*, 13 October 2009, p. 22)

China ... is increasingly known for shipping out inexpensive labour. These global migrants often toil in factories or on Chinese-run construction and engineering projects, though the range of jobs across 180 countries is astonishing ... But a backlash against them has grown. Across Asia and Africa incidents of protest and violence against Chinese workers have flared. Vietnam and India are among the countries that have moved to impose new labour rules this year [2009] for foreign companies and to restrict the number of Chinese workers allowed to enter, straining diplomatic relations with Beijing ... From Angola to Uzbekistan, and Iran to Indonesia, some 740,000 Chinese workers were abroad at the end of 2008, with 58 per cent sent out last year [2008] alone ... The numbers going abroad this year are on track to roughly match that rate. Chinese workers are not always less expensive, but they tend to be more skilled and easier to manage than local workers, Chinese executives say ... Vietnam had a $10 billion trade deficit with China last year. In July a senior [Vietnamese] official ... said that 35,000 Chinese workers were in Vietnam ... A half-million Vietnamese are working in fourteen countries and territories ... Populist anger erupted this year over a contract that the Vietnamese government gave to Aluminium Corp. of China to mine bauxite, one of Vietnam's most valuable natural resources, using Chinese workers. Dissidents, intellectuals and environmental advocates protested. General Vo Nguyen Giap, the revered ninety-eight-year-old military leader, wrote three open letters criticizing the Chinese presence to Vietnamese party leaders ... Over the summer the central government shut down critical blogs, detained dissidents and ordered Vietnamese newspapers to cease reporting on Chinese labour and the bauxite issue. But in a nod to public pressure, the government also tightened visa and work permit requirements for Chinese and deported 182 Chinese labourers from a cement plant in June, saying they were working illegally. Hanoi generally bans the import of skilled workers from abroad and requires foreign contractors to hire Vietnamese for civil works projects, though that rule is sometimes violated by Chinese companies – well-placed bribes can persuade officials to look the other way, Chinese executives say.

(*IHT*, 21 December 2009, p. 16)

'Vo Nguyen Giap ... lent moral authority to opposition, calling for an environmental survey to be completed first. A final decision on the full project is pending, although a pilot is going ahead' (*FT*, 28 January 2010, p. 13).

'General Giap and other opponents say the project will be ruinous to the environment, displace ethnic minority populations and threaten the country's national security with an influx of Chinese workers and economic leverage' (www.iht.com, 31 March 2010).

> Google ... says it has identified cyber-attacks aimed at silencing critics of a controversial, Chinese-backed bauxite mining project in Vietnam ... Google said malicious software was used to infect 'potentially tens of thousands of computers', broadly targeting Vietnamese-speaking computer users around the world ... Google said the attack may have infected the computers of tens of thousands of people who downloaded Vietnamese keyboard language software ... Infected machines had been used to spy on their owners and to attack blogs containing messages of political dissent, wrote Neel Mehta of the company's security team in a post late Tuesday [30 March] ... McFee, the computer security firm, said: 'The perpetrators may have political motivations and may have some allegiance to the government of the Socialist Republic of Vietnam ... These attacks have tried to squelch the opposition to bauxite mining efforts in Vietnam, an important and emotionally charged issue in the country.'
>
> (www.iht.com, 31 March 2010)

'Computer security firm McFee ... which has been working with Google to uncover the hacking ... suggested the perpetrators could be connected to Vietnam's government' (www.bbc.co.uk, 31 March 2010).

> Vietnamese activists opposed to a Chinese mining investment in their country have been targeted in a cyber-attack, Google revealed on Wednesday [31 March]. The internet company said a virus had been used to attack dissident websites ... The virus created a so-called 'botnet', a network of computers that could be controlled by the writers of the software ... Google said the software was used both to spy on users and to launch strikes against dissident Vietnamese websites ... The bauxite plan has gone ahead on a limited scale.
>
> (www.ft.com, 1 April 2010)

> In a series of recent announcements, government officials have introduced plans for price controls and import restrictions that have drawn foreign investors, who are normally discreet in their criticism of the government, into the open ... One proposal that has drawn particular ire would formally re-establish the government's ability to set prices for key commodities, including petrol, steel, concrete, milk and pharmaceuticals. There was little sign of reform in a recent speech by Nong Duc Manh, General Secretary of the Communist Party. He said the government was trying to maintain political stability and 'struggle against all the manoeuvres of hostile forces by

preventing them from profiting from matters such as democracy, human rights, multi-partyism and pluralism to sabotage the Vietnamese revolution' ... There is concern among conservatives that economic progress is loosening the grip of the party ... Mr Manh, who must step down early next year [2011] at the end of his term, is a conservative whose support for Nguyen Tan Dung, the reformist prime minister, has been equivocal ... The party congress [is] scheduled for early next year.

(*FT*, 4 March 2010, p. 7)

Blackouts this summer [2010] have infuriated businesses, farmers and families but have also built up pressure for the break-up of Electricity Vietnam (EVN) ... With demand for electricity growing at 15 per cent a year, analysts blamed the outages on Vietnam's failure to attract sufficient foreign investment in new power plants. But foreign investors have been discouraged by EVN's monopoly over distribution and government-regulated low electricity prices. In 2007 EVN put forward a plan to privatize the electricity market but this was rejected over concerns that it would have allowed it and other generators to fix the market. The ministry of industry and trade put forward its latest plan last year [2009] ... The government has raised the fines it charges EVN for unexpected power cuts tenfold to a maximum of 40 million dong ($2,100) per outage. Cao Sy Kiem ... former head of Vietnam's state bank and now the head of the country's small and medium enterprise association ... [said] this was far too low to have any effect. Mr Kiem: 'To solve the roots of the problem, we have to break EVN's monopoly' ... Vietnam has attracted some international funds for plants. AES, the US company, signed a deal to invest $400 million in a 1,200 megawatt coal-fired plant in April [2010]. But EVN is the sole investor in the country's first nuclear power plant, which it contracted Russia's Atomstroyexport to build this spring [2010].

(*FT*, 28 June 2010, p. 8)

Total foreign direct investment into Vietnam hit $9.8 billion last year [2009], down from $11.5 billion in 2008, but still significantly better than many experts had predicted during the height of the global crisis ... A recent Japan Bank for International Co-operation (JBIC) survey of Japanese companies with overseas operations found that Vietnam beats China and India as the most promising source of cheap labour ... In the JBIC report investors cited the booming domestic market and cheap labour as attractions, but remained worried about the country's overstretched infrastructure, particularly roads and electricity generation ... Japanese foreign direct investment in Vietnam rose from $153 million in 2005 to $1.1 billion in 2008 before falling back last year to $568 million. That represents 270 per cent growth, in comparison with only 27 per cent growth in investment in China. Inward investment from South Korea paints a similar picture, growing more than 300 per cent from 2005 to 2008 when it peaked at $1.35 billion. Last year investment fell to $590 million ... When Mitsubishi Heavy Industries Aerospace was planning to build a factory to assemble wing flaps for Boeing, it looked to South-east Asia before settling on what is rapidly becoming the region's destination of choice: Vietnam ... Higher value-added investments are increasingly important for Vietnam as the easy pickings of industrialization based on cheap labour are fizzling out ... While MHI was the first aerospace manufacturer to venture into Vietnam, it has already encouraged others to relocate ... MHI clearly has ambitious plans for its Vietnam offshoot. Only half the factory floor is being used, and the company has leased a plot with enough room to build another plant of similar size behind the current building ... [The company says the hope is that] in five or ten years ... Vietnam gets the opportunity to manufacture the parts themselves.

(*FT*, 27 July 2010, p. 21)

[Vietnam's] stock foreign direct investment has tripled since 2000 and its exports have quadrupled. In July Hoya, a Japanese maker of optical glass, announced a $146 million factory near Hanoi to make glass substrates from which hard discs are fashioned. Intel is due to open a $1 billion plant, assembling and testing silicon chips. Vietnam is cheap: its income per person is less than a third of China's. But its pool of workers is not that deep. Strains are already showing in its labour marker. Workers downed tools ninety-five times in the first three months of this year [2010]. The Communist Party has decreed double-digit pay rises and firms are grumbling about a new labour law. Vietnam is not perhaps the sanctuary from strife those fleeing China's coast might wish for.

(www.economist.com, 29 July 2010)

(See the entry for 21 September 2010 in the political chronology for Japanese investment in rare earths.)

TNK-BP, the Russian joint [fifty–fifty] venture [formed in 2003] between BP and a group of Russian billionaires said on Monday [18 October] that it would acquire BP's production and pipeline assets in Vietnam and Venezuela for $1.8 billion. The company will use its own money to finance the acquisitions ... The deal comes as BP plans to sell $30 billion in assets to cover costs linked to the Gulf of Mexico oil spill, the worst such accident in American history.

(www.iht.com, 18 October 2010)

The transaction will leave half the assets' equity on BP's books but give the company an immediate flow of cash for the entire value of the sale ... BP will receive the cash and retain a 50 per cent stake in the reserves .... The agreement with TNK-BP is the first major deal for BP's new chief executive, Robert Dudley, an American who was appointed to run BP midway through the Gulf disaster. BP has said it will raise $30 billion to pay claims relating to the spill, which killed eleven workers and caused tens of billions of dollars in damages. BP has raised more than $11 billion, including the sales announced Monday. That includes $7 billion from the sale of fields in the United States, Canada and Egypt ... and $1.9 billion for the sale of assets in Colombia. For TNK-BP's investors, the sell-off comes at a good time. Taxes at home eat up much of the profits of Russian oil companies ... Until 2008 Mr Dudley had been chief executive of TNK-BP. When he took over from Tony Hayward as chief executive of BP after the Gulf spill, Mr Hayward went to a position on the board of the Russian company.

(www.iht.com, 18 October 2010)

BP has said it will create a $20 billion trust fund to pay claims from the explosion on 20 April on the *Deepwater Horizon* drilling rig ... The spill, which lasted three months, has been described as the largest accidental oil spill in history.

(*IHT*, 19 October 2010, p. 16)

TNK-BP ... will pay $1.8 billion to buy the UK oil group's assets in Venezuela and Vietnam, in a move that marks its most significant diversification outside Russia. The deal will boost BP's bid to raise $30 billion in cash by the end of 2011 to help pay for the costs of the Gulf of Mexico spill. But it also puts TNK-BP on the path of international expansion, propelling a long-standing aim of the company's Russian billionaire shareholders as opportunities for growth in their country diminish due to resource nationalism and a burdensome tax regime. The agreement will cement a peace deal that BP and its Russian partners reached just two years ago after a bruising shareholder battle over control of the company. During the dispute the Russian shareholders complained that BP was blocking the company's international expansion, and Bob Dudley, BP's chief executive, was forced to flee Russia over 'harassment' when he served as TNK-BP's chief. Mikhail Fridman, who leads the Russian shareholders as chairman of Alfa Group and also serves as TNK-BP's interim chief, called the deal 'a milestone in TNK-BP's strategic expansion in the global energy market' ... While the transaction will boost TNK-BP's reserves by only 2 per cent to 3 per cent, it will provide it with a key platform for international expansion as opportunities for growth in Russia decline. Only state-linked companies are reserved access to big new fields in the country, while the tax regime for upstream development 'takes away the impetus for investment', said Valeri Nesterov, oil and gas analyst at Troika Dialog ... Alfa–Access–Renova, the consortium via which the Russian shareholders hold their stake, said the company aimed to procure half of its production outside Russia's borders.

(*FT*, 19 October 2010, p. 21)

Developments in oil and gas

'Last week Beijing warned foreign oil companies against participating in oil exploration in waters off Vietnam. China's border claims extend hundreds of miles to the shores of Vietnam, Philippines, Malaysia, Brunei and Indonesia' (www.iht.com, 22 July 2008).

Shares in Soco International, the Asia-focused oil and gas explorer, fell sharply on Tuesday [12 October 2010] after it said it would abandon an appraisal well off the coast of Vietnam. The well had been seen as key to the company's expansion plans. Soco said that although drilling tests at the Te Giac Den well showed oil and gas in commercial quantities, a lack of reservoir pressure meant it flowed at 'sub-commercial' rates ... The company this year [2010] raised £102 million in a share placing – the first in its thirteen-year history – to fund an ambitious drilling campaign in Asia and Africa. Vietnam was central to those ambitions and in August [2010] Soco predicted its fields there would produce 100,000 barrels of oil a day by 2012 ... [Soco] said that prediction was unaffected ... Nearby wells in Vietnam are still on track for production. Soco's TGT field, in which it holds a 30 per cent stake, is expected to come on stream at 55,000 barrels a day by mid-2011. A further 50,000 barrels a day expansion is scheduled for 2012.

(*FT*, 13 October 2010, p. 19)

Outward investment by Vietnamese firms

Some Vietnamese hope to compete internationally. The largest, PetroVietnam, is already exploring for and producing oil in several countries, from Algeria to Cuba. Its contribution to the government is equal to 30 per cent of the state budget ... Vinamotor, a state-run maker of cars (among other things) is building a bus factory in Dominica and two lorry factories and an asphalt works in Venezuela, but as yet Vietnam is not a mass producer of cars.

(*The Economist*, Survey, 26 April 2008, p. 8)

'Vietnamese firms are investing in Cambodia and Laos' (p. 13).

Agriculture

Agriculture, forestry and fisheries now provide barely half of all jobs in Vietnam, compared with over two-thirds only ten years ago. Even so, over 70 per cent of the population still live in the countryside ... [Land] freehold remains with the central government ... The local officials who managed the land distribution tried to share out the best and worst land fairly, so families often got several tiny scattered plots ... In northern Vietnam the average family has six or seven ... Industrialization is chewing up farmland on the edges of towns ... Recent land reforms have aimed to consolidate holdings to improve productivity ... [The] government has been promoting 'craft villages' specializing in homespun products ... [There has been a] gradual liberalization of farm prices ... Some of the country's diverse ethnic minorities depend on foraging in the forests ... Rather slowly ... minority communities [are being given] patches of forest to tend.

(*The Economist*, Survey, 26 April 2008, pp. 10–11)

> The prime minister has warned rice speculators that they face severe punishment after rising prices led to panic buying over the weekend. The remarks were a sign of the unease felt across Asia to keep the price of the staple food affordable after rice prices soared this year [2008]. Prime minister Nguyen Tan Dung insisted that supplies in Vietnam, the second largest rice exporter in the world after Thailand, were 'completely adequate' for domestic consumption, state media reported late Sunday [27 April]. He warned that any organizations and individuals speculating in the commodity would be 'severely punished'. Crowds flocked to rice markets Sunday in Ho Chi Minh City to stock up on the grain, whose price has more than doubled over the past two weeks ... Price increases in Vietnam have been partly driven by strong demand from neighbouring countries seeking stocks for food security. Last month [March] the government said it would cut rice exports by 1 million tonnes this year to shield the country from the effects of global increases in food prices caused by rising demand in China and India and poor harvests worldwide.
>
> (*IHT*, 29 April 2008, p. 10)

'Much prime paddy land is being converted to factories and housing. Total paddy acreage has dropped from 4.3 million hectares to 4 million hectares in recent years' (*FT*, 29 April 2008, p. 7).

> A proliferation of golf courses is displacing tens of thousands of farmers and devouring the rice fields the country depends on ... The country had only two courses at the end of the war in 1975 ... Development of a single course can cost the land of more than 3,000 farmers, sometimes devouring an entire community ... Until last year [2008], according to experts who have done the calculations, licences for new courses were being issued at an average of one a week, for a total of more than 140 projects around the country ... But a backlash has emerged within the media and among academics and government officials over the social and environmental costs, and the country's leadership has clamped down. In 2008 prime minister Nguyen Tan Dung ordered a halt to new construction pending a review, and four months ago the government ordered the cancellation of fifty of the projects that had already been approved. But most of the others are well under way, to add to the country's thirteen established golf courses ... Kurt Greve (the American general manager of two golf clubs) said: 'Developers and foreign investors want to make the country a tourist destination, and to do that you need to offer more amenities like golf' ... Already, in its drive to industrialize, Vietnam has been losing large amounts of farmland to factories and other developments. According to the ministry of agriculture, land devoted to rice, the national staple and a leading source of export revenue, shrank from 4.5 million hectares (11.1 million acres) to 4.1 million hectares (10.1 million acres) in the years between 2000 and 2006 ... Along with land, golf courses also put a strain on water resources ... Many of the new projects seem to have more to do with raw capitalism than with sport.

Taxes on golf courses are lower than those on other forms of developments, and many of the projects appeared to be disguised real estate ventures.

(*IHT*, 20 October 2009, p. 2)

Economic performance

The effects of the global financial crisis on growth and inflation have already been dealt with.

Table 1 Vietnam: selected economic indicators 2000–10

Economic indicator (projection)	2000	2001	2002	2003	2004	2005	2006	2007	2008	2009	2010
Rate of growth of GDP (%)	6.8	6.9	7.1	7.3	7.8	8.4	8.2	8.5	6.3	5.3	6.5
Inflation rate (consumer) (%)	−1.7	−0.3	4.1	3.3	7.9	8.4	7.5	8.3	23.1	6.7	10.4

Source: Various issues of *World Economic Outlook*; United Nations Economic and Social Commission for Asia and the Pacific, *Economic and Social Survey of Asia and the Pacific*; IMF Country Report 2010.

Unemployment

'More than 1 million young Vietnamese join the labour force each year and 1 million villagers [are] migrating to the cities ... The private sector provides most of the growth in jobs and exports' (*The Economist*, 5 August 2006, p. 50). '[Vietnam] needs to find jobs for over a million people joining the work force each year' (*The Economist*, Survey, 26 April 2008, p. 12).

Poverty and income per head

> Though Vietnam is still, overall, one of Asia's poorest countries, with income per head behind India, its recent growth has been impressively egalitarian. The Asian Development Bank reckons that deep poverty – defined as a daily income equivalent to under $1 – is now only slightly more prevalent than the average for South-east Asia, whereas in 1990 Vietnam's figure was more than twice the regional average. By this measure Vietnam has overtaken China, India and the Philippines and now has only slightly more poverty than Indonesia. Life expectancy has jumped and infant mortality plunged since the 1990s. Vietnam does better on both these counts than Thailand, a far richer country. Almost three-quarters of Vietnamese children of secondary school age are in class, up from about a third in 1990. Again, Vietnam has overtaken China, India and Indonesia.
>
> (*The Economist*, 5 August 2006, pp. 49–50)

[Vietnam's] gradual approach has won praise from the World Bank, which says growth has come fairly equitably, creating fewer divisions between rich and poor than in some developing countries ... In 1993 Vietnam's *per capita* income was $180. It climbed to $640 for 2005 and is expected to reach $1,000 by 2010, when Vietnam will no longer qualify for concessionary loans from the World Bank [according to the World Bank] ... Vietnam has eschewed heavy reliance on foreign aid; less than 15 per cent of public spending for the last couple of years came from aid, the bank said.

(www.iht.com, 19 June 2006; *IHT*, 20 June 2006, p. 2)

Per capita GDP increased from $655 in 2006 to $685 in 2007. According to official data, the percentage of the population living below the poverty line dropped from 59 per cent in 1993 to 35 per cent in 2000 and 18 per cent today.

(*Asian Survey*, 2008, vol. XLVIII, p. 30)

'GDP grew at 8.48 per cent in real terms during 2007 [according to official figures]' (pp. 29–30).

Prosperity is hard to square with the official figure for Vietnam's GDP *per capita*, a mere $839. Even after allowing for higher purchasing power in a low-cost country, the World Bank puts national income per person at only $3,300, below that of several sub-Saharan African states ... [Vietnam has an] age-old tradition of hiding wealth from the authorities ... Plenty of people run micro-businesses alongside their formal jobs ... Deep poverty is confined to small communities of ethnic minorities in remote mountain areas ... [There is] a small but visible underclass, an ever more ostentatious millionaire set and a concerned middle class in between ... A welfare system along European lines is slowly emerging. In 2003 the social security system, providing cover against sickness and work accidents as well as pensions was extended from state employees to private sector workers. A national unemployment insurance scheme is due to start up next year [2009]. A 2006 study by the Vietnamese Academy of Social Sciences concluded that the country could now afford a universal old age pension.

(*The Economist*, Survey, 26 April 2008, pp. 6–7)

Over the past twenty years Vietnam's economy has almost quadrupled in real terms. It has averaged 7.775 per cent annual growth and even last year, at the height of the financial crisis, managed 5.8 per cent. This year [2010] Vietnam expects to achieve another milestone, when GDP *per capita* passes $976 and it officially becomes a middle-income country.

(*FT*, 1 June 2010, p. 22)

'GDP per head was below $100 in 1990 but is now well over $1,000, says the World Bank' (www.economist.com, 2 September 2010; *The Economist*, 4 September 2010, p. 66).

Postscript

Rare earths

> The Chinese government plans a further reduction, of up to 30 per cent, next year [2011] in its quotas for exports of rare earth minerals ... the official *China Daily* newspaper said on Tuesday [19 October] ... Its article attributed the planned quota reduction to an unidentified commerce ministry official ... Another commerce ministry official, Jiang Fan, said at a conference in Xiamen that she was not aware of plans for a further reduction in rare earths.
>
> (www.iht.com, 19 October 2010)

> China, which has been blocking shipments of crucial minerals to Japan for the last month, has now quietly halted shipments of some of those same minerals to the United States and Europe, three industry officials said on Tuesday [19 October] ... The Chinese action involves rare earth minerals ... [The officials] said Chinese customs imposed the broader shipment restrictions Monday morning [18 October], hours after a top Chinese official had summoned international news media Sunday night [17 October] to denounce US trade actions ... Western companies are believed to keep much smaller stockpiles of rare earths than Japanese companies do ... A few rare earth shipments to the West had been delayed by customs officials in recent weeks, industry officials said, but the new, broader restrictions on exports appear to have been imposed Monday morning ... American trade officials announced last Friday [15 October] that they would investigate whether China was violating international trade rules by subsidizing its clean energy industries. The inquiry includes whether China's steady reductions in rare earth export quotas since 2005, along with steep export taxes on rare earths, are illegal attempts to force multinational companies to produce more of their high-technology goods in China.
>
> (www.iht.com, 19 October 2010)

'The Federation of German Industry estimates that Chinese exports of rare earths have declined by as much as 40 per cent worldwide' (*IHT*, 20 October 2010, p. 1). 'The United States uses ... rare earth minerals ... to make advanced equipment like guided missiles' (www.iht.com, 25 October 2010).

While the WTO bans export quotas and export duties, there is an exemption for export restrictions if they are carried out to protect the environment and to preserve supplies of natural resources that might otherwise be exhausted. Chinese officials have said in recent weeks that these are, indeed, the reason behind their rare earth policies.

(*IHT*, 22 October 2010, p. 16)

China could cut rare earth exports by up to 30 per cent next year [2011], state media said on Tuesday [19 October] ... The [Chinese] government has steadily reduced export quotas for the minerals ... The Beijing government lowered export quotas this year [2010] by 40 per cent from last year [2009] and on Tuesday the *China Daily*, citing an unnamed official from the commerce industry, said these would 'continue to be axed' in the first half of next year ... Chao Ning [a foreign trade section chief with commerce quoted in the article] 'Strategic, environmental and economic considerations mean that the country [China] cannot afford to continue shouldering the burden of supplying the world' ... China has long cited environmental concerns as the rationale of its quota cuts ... Japanese prime minister Naoto Kan [19 October]: 'Stockpiling [rare earths] is one option we need to consider' ... The United States is also studying its military dependence on rare earths and considering ways to diversify supply, including reopening rare earth mines outside China.

(www.ft.com, 20 October 2010)

China's commerce ministry has denied a report by the official *China Daily* that it will cut quotas by 30 per cent next year [2011] to stop overmining. The ministry said in a statement: 'The report is completely false. China will continue to supply rare earths to the world, and, at the same time, to protect usable resources and sustainable development. China will also continue to impose restrictive measures on exploration, production and import and export of rare earths.'

(www.bbc.co.uk, 20 October 2010)

The [Chinese] ministry of commerce said in a statement on Wednesday [20 October]: 'China will continue controlling measures on controlling measures on exploiting rare earth, its production and exports, and these measures are not in conflict with WTO regulations. China will continue to supply the world with rare earths' ... Japanese officials say Chinese authorities have blocked shipments of rare earths to Japan ... Japan's chief cabinet secretary said on Wednesday: 'They have been halted' ... According to the US Geological Survey ... China has about 57 per cent of the world's known reserves ... The United States has 9 per cent of global reserves, Australia 4 per cent and the former Soviet Union 14 per cent.

(*FT*, 21 October 2010, p. 16)

German companies say they are being pressed by Chinese officials to increase their investments in China if they want to be assured of access to rare earth minerals and two other obscure elements, tungsten and antimony. China dominates the mining of these metals.

(*IHT*, 22 October 2010, p. 1)

The Japanese trade minister urged China on Sunday [24 October] to restart exports of crucial minerals known as rare earths that both traders and government officials say have been blocked for the past month amid a territorial dispute between the two countries. The trade minister, Akihiro Ohata, also quoted a top Chinese official as acknowledging that customs officials had stepped up inspections of all rare earth shipments from China ... Mr Ohata said the Chinese vice minister of commerce, Jiang Yaoping, who was visiting Tokyo for an energy conservation forum, had told him that Chinese customs had strengthened checks of all rare earth exports as a 'counter-smuggling' measure. But Mr Jiang reiterated that there was no international trade embargo, Mr Ohata said ... As of Sunday afternoon Chinese customs officials were still blocking shipments of raw rare earths all over the world, industry officials said ... In July [2010] Beijing reduced its export quota for rare earths for the second half of the year by 72 per cent. Exporters had only six weeks' worth of quotas left when China imposed its unannounced embargo on shipments to Japan. Beijing has continued to deny that any embargo exists ... Mr Ohata said last week that Japan was seeking an agreement with Vietnam for the joint development of rare earth materials.

(www.iht.com, 24 October 2010)

As of Sunday afternoon [24 October] Chinese customs officials were still blocking all exports of raw rare earths, although there have been no restrictions on the export of value-added rare earth products like powerful magnets, computer screen components and special glass polishes, industry officials said.

(www.iht.com, 25 October 2010)

Japan's government has made a formal protest to Beijing after two Chinese fisheries boats were seen near a disputed island chain ... The Chinese boats were spotted by the coastguard late on Sunday [24 October]. Protests over the territorial row took place in both countries at the weekend. The islands in the East China Sea, known in Japan as Senkaku and in China as Diaoyo, are controlled by Japan, but claimed by China. They are uninhabited, but surrounded by rich fishing grounds and potentially significant oil and gas reserves. A top Japanese government spokesman said: 'Last night around 9 p.m. [12.00 GMT] our coastguard sighted them and afterwards the two [Chinese ships] left there and sailed north towards China. After the incident we launched a protest through diplomatic channels' ... On Sunday about 200 people took part in anti-Japanese protests in Lanzhou in north-west China, a day after a similar protest in Deyang in the south-west. In Japan 300 anti-China protesters rallied in Takamatsu city on Saturday [23 October].

(www.bbc.co.uk, 25 October 2010)

Demonstrations against Japan broke out in at least six Chinese cities over the weekend ... Calls for more protests tomorrow [26 October] also circulated widely and spread on the internet, including a planned march to the Japanese consulate in the western city of Chongqing. The Communist Party newspaper issued an editorial calling the protests 'understandable', but urging demonstrators to plunge into their work and studies rather than take to the streets ... In its editorial ... the *People's Daily* empathized with protesters but warned against actions that violate laws and regulations. The paper said: 'Expressing one's patriotic passions is understandable. We believe that the vast majority will turn their patriotic passions into concrete actions in their daily life and safeguard the bigger picture of reform, development and stability' ... Chinese protesters gathered yesterday [24 October] in a number of relatively small cities outside the major cities, including Changsha in the south, and Baoji and Lanzhou to the west. On Saturday [23 October] hundreds of protesters had rallied in the south-west city of Deyang. Japanese television footage showed Chinese police watching closely and in some cases ripping down banners and escorting people away from the demonstrations. There were several hundred reports of arrests or property damage ... Marchers carrying Chinese national flags chanted 'Love China' and 'Boycott Japanese goods'. But other signs touched on sensitive domestic issues ranging from freedom of speech to high housing prices. One displayed in Baoji called for multi-party democracy, a challenge that could confirm fears among the communist leadership that a protest movement, if left unchecked, could evolve into confrontation with the party.

(www.independent.co.uk, 25 October 2010)

Japan will add six submarines to its current fleet of sixteen during the next four years as it sees increased naval activity from China, according to news reports from Tokyo ... The new vessels will give Japan's Maritime Self-Defence Force [MSDF] its largest submarine fleet since it was established in 1976 ... The submarine building programme was revealed by MSDF and defence ministry officials on condition of anonymity. It will be formalized in December [2010] for implementation during 2011 to 2015. China maintains a fleet of about sixty submarines ... [It was reported] that China had recently sent three fishery patrol boats to the disputed islands. An official of China's agriculture ministry: 'Going to waters off the Diaoyu Islands and protecting [Chinese] fishing activities there is part of protecting national sovereignty and the legal interests of fishermen' ... Protesters targeted Japanese-owned factories and stores in demonstrations Saturday [23 October] through Tuesday [26 October] ... Security forces set up a protective cordon around the Japanese embassy in Beijing.

(www.cnn.com, 26 October 2010)

The United States and Europe should work together with industry to reduce dependence on China for crucial minerals because global trade bodies are ill equipped to solve the problem of withheld supplies, officials and executives at a high-level conference said Tuesday [26 October]. Germany has been the most vocal country in Europe in raising concerns about the potential economic impact of shortfalls of rare earth and other metals, and its economy minister was a featured speaker at the conference organized by the Federation of German Industries. The general consensus among attendees, who included representatives from industry as well as the EU, the WTO and the World Bank, was that existing trade rules were inadequate when it came to responding to China's decision to cut back export quotas of such materials ... Pascal Lamy, general secretary of the WTO, said the WTO had no remit to deal with raw materials as such. However, many broadly written international trade rules can be construed as applying to raw materials as well. The United States, the EU and Mexico brought a WTO trade case against China last year [2009] alleging that it had violated a ban of export restrictions by limiting exports of bauxite and a half-dozen other industrial minerals; an initial decision in that case is expected from a WTO panel next April [2011] ... German companies complained that the lack of rules gave China a free rein to do what it liked with its rare earth minerals. At the same time, flush with cash, it faces no constraints in access to other raw materials to feed its expanding economy ... Industry chiefs reiterated complaints that China was hinting that, if they wanted access to its rare earth minerals, then they should invest in China ... The chief executive of ... a [German] chemicals company said ... that Western companies like his were reluctance to do so for fear that they would lose control of their intellectual property rights.

(www.iht.com, 26 October 2010; *IHT*, 27 October 2010, pp. 17, 20)

China has said it will not use exports of so-called rare earth minerals as a diplomatic bargaining tool ... The United States and the EU asked Beijing to clarify its policy on mineral exports after China stopped shipping to Japan ... A Chinese spokesman: 'China will not use rare earths as a bargaining tool. We will have co-operation with other countries in the use of rare earths, because it is a non-renewable energy resource' ... [But the spokesman] did not answer a reporter's question about when normal exports of rare earth minerals would resume ... Meanwhile, US Secretary of State Hillary Clinton has called on China to clarify its policy on rare earth resources. She said recent Chinese restrictions served as a 'wake-up call' for the industrialized world which should drive it to look for other suppliers. Rare earth metals are scare minerals that have particular properties, such as being magnetic or shining in low light. This makes them particularly useful in some new technologies, such as solar panels or electric cars or lightweight batteries.

(www.bbc.co.uk, 28 October 2010)

China is expanding its fleet of naval surveillance ships amid maritime disputes with several neighbouring countries ... A new high-speed inspection ship was launched this week and thirty-six more would be added later ... Japan and China are locked in their worst dispute in years over ... islands both claim ... China has sent fisheries patrol vessels to the islands while reports in Japan say Tokyo plans to add six submarines to its navy ... Other disputed island claims include the Spratly and Paracel Islands in the South China Sea, which are claimed by China as well as Vietnam, the Philippines, Malaysia, Taiwan and Brunei.

(www.bbc.co.uk, 28 October 2010)

[On Thursday 28 October China vowed] not to use rare earth minerals as a bargaining chip in world trade discussions and not to cut exports any more next year, state-run media reported ... During a press conference Thursday in Beijing, a spokesman said ... [that China] would work with other countries and international bodies – including the WTO – as it sought to resolve 'disputes' over rare earth minerals, according to a report in the state-run *China Daily*. The spokesman said: 'China will not use rare earths as an instrument for bargaining. Instead, we hope to co-operate with other countries in the use of rare earths on the basis of win–win outcomes and jointly protect the non-renewable resource' ... [He] said that China was dealing with environmental problems tied to excessive mining of such rare earth minerals – a driving reason behind the drop in exports. Chinese officials said that at the current rate of production some reserves of medium and heavy rare earth minerals may run out after fifteen or twenty years, according to the *China Daily* article. The report said that China had cut its exports of certain rare earths, with smuggling even further cutting into already dwindling reserves ... [But the spokesman] denied reports that export quotas would be cut further next year [2011].

(www.cnn.com, 29 October 2010)

The United States and Japan ... said late Wednesday [27 October] that they would both need to find alternative sources of supply for ... rare earth minerals ... US Secretary of State Hillary Clinton said she planned to question Chinese officials this week about reports that China had halted shipments of the rare earth minerals, and she hoped Beijing would allow the shipments to 'continue unabated and without any interference'. But even if trade resumes, Mrs Clinton said, 'Our countries and others will have to look for additional sources of supply. That is in our interest commercially and strategically' ... Rare earth minerals are used to manufacture a variety of advanced products, ranging from cell phones and wind turbines to missiles ... Mrs Clinton said the episode had served as a 'wake-up call that being so dependent on only one source, disruption could occur for natural disaster reasons or other kinds of events could intervene' ... The day before Mrs Clinton left for Asia, the State Department hastily added a China stop to her itinerary, reflecting its sensitivities about Beijing. She will stop for two hours on Hainan, a resort island east of Vietnam, to meet with China's state councillor for foreign policy, Dai Bingguo ... Mrs Clinton said she and Mr Dai would discuss the preparations for a visit to the United States by President Hu Jintao next year [2011]. Mr Dai is also a key Chinese contact for Mrs Clinton on North

Korea. 'We have a long list of issues to discuss,' she said, though she noted that if the Chinese government offered reassurances on shipments of rare earths, it would 'shorten that discussion' ... Japan's foreign minister ... Sieji Maehara ... reiterated that the disputed islands ... known as Senkaku in Japan and Diaoyu in China ... fell under Japanese jurisdiction. He said he was encouraged that Mrs Clinton reaffirmed that the islands fell under the scope of the US–Japan Mutual Security Treaty, which guarantees the United States will come to the defence of any Japanese territory under attack ... Mr Maehara said: 'Japan and China are neighbours. Neither of the neighbours can move elsewhere.'

(www.iht.com, 28 October 2010)

The Chinese government abruptly ended on Thursday [28 October] its unannounced embargo of exports of crucial strategic minerals to the United States, Europe and Japan, although shipments to Japan still encountered some difficulties, four rare earth industry officials said. After blocking shipments of raw rare earth minerals to Japan since 21 September, and to the United States and Europe since 18 October, Chinese customs officials, without explanation, allowed shipments to all three destinations, said industry officials who insisted on anonymity because of the diplomatic sensitivity of the issue. Resumed shipments to Japan face additional scrutiny and some delay. The decision came a day and a half after US Secretary of State Hillary Clinton announced plans to visit China on Saturday [30 October]. She met on Wednesday in Honolulu [in Hawaii] with Japan's foreign minister, Seiji Maehara, and said afterwards that the suspension of shipments had been a 'wake-up call' and that both countries would have to find alternative suppliers ... Because China is on the opposite side of the international dateline from Honolulu, it was already mid-day on Thursday in China by the time Mrs Clinton spoke and rare earth shipments had resumed. Chinese customs officials allowed rare earth shipments to proceed starting Thursday morning China time, industry officials said ... Senior commerce officials have insisted repeatedly that they have not issued any regulations halting shipments. They have suggested at various times that the halt represented either a spontaneous and simultaneous decision by the country's thirty-two rare earth exporters not to make shipments because of a deterioration in Sino-Japanese relations or a greater thoroughness on the part of customs officials. Even with customs officials allowing containers of rare earths to leave China's docks, foreign buyers face a separate, serious problem. Chian has repeatedly reduced its export quotas for rare earths over the last five years so that they are now well below world demand. No more than a few thousand tonnes remain to be shipped under this year's quota, of of 30,300 tonnes of authorized shipments. World demand for Chinese rare earths approaches 50,000 tonnes a year, according to industry estimates. The value of the remaining quotas has soared to the point where to export a single tonne of raw earths from China now sells for about $40,000, including special Chinese taxes on the quota ... China only requires export quotas for shipments in which the material has a rare earth content of about 50 per cent or more ... The United States and Europe already buy mostly highly processed [magnetic] powders from China, so the expansion of the customs policy of blocking shipments of raw earths had a limited, mostly symbolic effect.

(www.iht.com, 28 October 2010; *IHT*, 29 October 2010, pp. 1, 19)

When Japanese mineral traders learned in late September that China was blocking shipments of a vital commodity, the word came not from a government announcement but from dock workers in Shanghai. And on Thursday [28 October] the traders began hearing that the unannounced embargo of so-called rare earth minerals was ending – again, not from any Chinese government communiqué, but through back-channel word from their distributors ... The export quotas China continues to impose on rare earths, even when ships leave the docks, are restricting global supplies and causing world market prices to soar far beyond what Chinese companies pay ... [China] has been willing to do dirty, toxic and often radioactive work that the rest of the world has long shunned ... Despite producing 95 per cent of the world's rare earths, China has only 37 per cent of proven reserves, Sizable deposits are known to exist in the United States, Canada, Australia, India and Brazil, among other places ... Across China rare earth mines have scarred valleys by stripping topsoil and pumping thousands of gallons of acid into streambeds.

(www.iht.com, 30 October 2010)

The foreign ministers of China and Japan have met on the sidelines of the Asean summit ... The Japanese foreign minister, Seiji Maehara, said he and his counterpart, Yang Jiechi, had agreed to make efforts to improve bilateral ties ... Seiji Maehara: 'The discussion took place in a good atmosphere. It was held calmly while both sides said what we should say. I believe it is likely that the leaders of China and Japan will hold a meeting here in Hanoi' ... There has been speculation over whether Chinese premier Wen Jiabao will hold direct talks with Japan's prime minister, Naoto Kan ... Mr Maehara also said he had asked Mr Yang to unblock the export of rare earth minerals and reopen talks on the joint development of a gas field in the East China Sea ... China suspended talks about the gas field last month ... The regional summit in Vietnam has so far been dominated by discussions about next month's elections in Burma.

(www.bbc.co.uk, 29 October 2010)

A summit involving Japan and China was in jeopardy Friday [29 October] after a Chinese foreign ministry official accused Japanese diplomats of making statements that violated China's sovereignty, according to the Chinese state-run news agency. China and Japan are participating in a summit of Asean in Hanoi, but Japanese representatives made 'untrue statements about the content of a meeting between the Chinese and Japanese foreign ministers held earlier in the day', the Xinhua news agency said. Chinese assistant foreign minister Hu Zhengyue said that 'the Japanese move ruined the atmosphere for leaders from the two sides to conduct talks in the Vietnamese capital' ... Earlier this week the Japanese government lodged a protest with the Chinese government after the Japanese navy spotted two Chinese patrol boats near the [disputed] islands. The boats did not cross into Japanese territorial waters but the vessels were in Japan's 'contiguous zone', according to Japan's Kyodo News Agency. The presence of Chinese patrol boats made the Japanese feel 'uncomfortable', Japan's chief cabinet secretary ... said in the protest message to China ... On Friday China's Hu Zhengyue accused Japanese representatives at the Hanoi summit of 'violating China's sovereignty and territorial integrity through statements to the media', the Chinese news agency reported. During the summit Chinese foreign minister Yang Jiechi met with his counterpart Seiji Maehara and told him that 'the Daioyu Islands had been an integral part of Chinese territory since ancient times', Xinhua reported. Hu Zhengyue then accused Japanese diplomats of 'making untrue statements about the content of the meeting', saying that they 'distorted China's stance in implementing the principled consensus between the two countries on the East China Sea', Xinhua said.

(www.cnn.com, 29 October 2010)

China has accused Japan of 'violating Chinese sovereignty and integrity' ... The renewed diplomatic tensions scuppered plans for a Sino-Japanese summit in Hanoi on Friday [29 October] ... China also rebuked US Secretary of State Hillary Clinton, saying it was 'strongly dissatisfied' with remarks she had made that appeared to take Japan's side in the argument over the [disputed] islands ... China earlier denied a report that it had agreed to restart negotiations on a deal jointly to exploit gas resources in disputed areas of the East China Sea. But Japanese officials dismissed suggestions they had ever made such a claim.

(*FT*, 30 October 2010, p. 5)

China issued scathing comments directed at Japan and the United States on Friday [29 October], a day after the two allies discussed a territorial dispute in the East China Sea. Chinese assistant foreign minister Hu Zhengyue said in Hanoi that Japan was making untrue statements and turning the contested islands ... into a 'hot topic' on the sidelines of an Asian regional summit by talking to the media and holding discussions with other countries before the meeting. Beijing also criticized Secretary of State Hillary Clinton for speaking out about the territorial dispute after holding meetings with her Japanese counterpart, Seiji Maehara, on Thursday in Hawaii, according to Xinhua, the official Chinese news agency.

(*IHT*, 30 October 2010, p. 5)

[Ahead of Hillary Clinton's] arrival Washington called on the nations to 'have a thoughtful, considered dialogue and resolve these issues [concerning the disputed islands]'. A State Department spokesman: 'We recognize that there is an open question of sovereignty, and we expect that to be resolved between Japan and China through dialogue' ... But China has already said it is 'strongly dissatisfied' with Mrs Clinton for speaking out on the dispute after meeting the Japanese counterpart Seiji Maehara in Hawaii on Thursday [28 October]. She said the islands fell within the scope of Japan's security alliance with the United States.

(www.bbc.co.uk, 30 October 2010)

China said Friday [29 October] that it would supply Japan and other countries with rare earth metals ... Prime minister Wen Jiabao of China made the vow during a trilateral meeting with leaders of Japan and South Korea, a spokeswoman for President Lee Myung-bak of South Korea said in Hanoi ... Mr Wen told the leaders that 'China will continue to supply rare earths to the international community' and that it would 'work with major buyers in expanding the source of rare earths and developing alternative minerals', she said.

(*IHT*, 30 October 2010, p. 12)

China has reassured the United States it has no intention of withholding rare earth minerals from the market, the US Secretary of State has said ... US officials said Hillary Clinton's Chinese counterpart, Yang Jiechi, told the US Secretary of State that his country would not use rare earths as a diplomatic, political or economic tool in dealing with other countries ... Representatives from China and Japan also held informal talks on the fringes of an Asean conference in Vietnam ... The United States has encouraged China to cool the row with Japan and, according to Reuters, has offered to host a trilateral meeting with China and Japan to resolve the dispute between the two.

(www.iht.com, 30 October 2010)

The premiers of China and Japan met at an Asian regional summit in a bid to defuse a territorial dispute on Saturday [30 October], while the United States urged Asia's two big economies to cool the stand-off and proposed three-way talks ... A Japanese official, however, said the two leaders subsequently held an 'informal' ten-minute meeting on the summit sidelines on Saturday ... US Secretary of State Hillary Clinton, who met her counterpart, Yang Jiechi, in Hanoi, urged calm on both sides, and offered to host trilateral talks to bring relations back on an even keel ... Hillary Clinton, in Vietnam for the first US participation in an East Asia Summit (EAS), also got assurances from China over its policy on exporting rare earth minerals that it wished to be a 'reliable supplier'. She said: 'Minister Yang clarified China has no intention of withholding these minerals from the market ... Although we are pleased by the clarification we have received from the

Chinese government, we still think that the world as a whole needs to find alternatives' ... The summit this year, the fifth since the group's founding in 2005, has been overshadowed by the row between China and Japan ... Four Asean members – Brunei, Malaysia, the Philippines and Vietnam – have long-running disagreements with Beijing over parts of the South China Sea.

(www.iht.com, 30 October 2010)

As the United States, Russia and sixteen Asian nations gathered in Hanoi to discuss regional co-operation, China's aggressive maritime and territorial claims were sowing unease with several of its neighbours ... Though it has no position on the sovereignty claims, Mrs Clinton said the United States viewed the islands as protected under the terms of its defence treaty with Japan, which means it would defend them from any foreign attack. That statement brought a rebuke from the Chinese foreign ministry spokesman ... who said China 'will never accept any word or deed that includes the Diaioyu Islands within the scope' of the treaty ... Prime minister Wen Jiabao of Chian refused to meet one-on-one with prime minister Naoto Kan of Japan, though [Chinese] foreign minister Yang Jiechi said China would consider Mrs Clinton's proposed trilateral meeting. In her formal remarks to the Asian leaders, Mrs Clinton reiterated that the United States stood ready to help resolve another territorial dispute: one that pits China against Vietnam, Malaysia and the Philippines over a string of strategically significant islands in the South China Sea. Mrs Clinton said: 'The United States has a national interest in the freedom of navigation and unimpeded lawful commerce. And when disputes arise over maritime territory, we are committed to resolving them peacefully based on customary international law.'

(www.iht.com, 30 October 2010)

'[The United States made a] 1972 decision to return the islands ... which Japan calls the Senkaku and China calls the Diaoyu ... to Japan' (www.iht.com, 1 November 2010). 'Leaders from eighteen countries gathered this weekend [in Hanoi]' (www.iht.com, 31 October 2010).

US Secretary of State Hillary Clinton (Saturday [30 October]): 'We've recommended to both that the United States is more than willing to host a trilateral where we would bring China and Japan and their foreign ministers together to discuss a range of issues. It is in all of our interest for China and Japan to have stable, peaceful relations' ... A senior US official told CNN that Clinton had raised the issue of three-way talks with Chinese state councillor Dai Bingguo on Hainan Island and foreign minister Yang Jiechi in Hanoi on the sidelines of the Asean summit. She also raised it with Japanese foreign minister Seiji Maehara in Hawaii earlier in the week ... On Friday China's foreign ministry spokesman showed some irritation over Clinton's claim that the Senkaku Islands fall within the scope of a US–Japan security treaty. Clinton said on Saturday: 'With respect to the Senkaku Islands, the United States has never taken a position on sovereignty, but we have made it very clear that the islands are part of our mutual treaty obligations, and the obligation to defend Japan. We have certainly encouraged both Japan and China to seek peaceful resolution of any disagreements that they have in this area or others' ... The Chinese foreign ministry spokesman said: '[China] will never accept any word or deed that includes the Diaoyu Islands within the scope of the US–Japan Treaty of Mutual Co-operation and Security.'

(www.iht.com, 31 October 2010)

Japan's prime minister, Naoto Kan, met his Vietnamese counterpart, Nguyen Tan Dung, in Hanoi on Sunday [31 October], after a series of Asean meetings. A joint statement read: 'Prime minister Nguyen Tan Dung announced that Vietnam has decided to have Japan as a partner for exploration, mining, development, and separation and production of rare earth minerals in the country' ... The Japanese government believes it will win exploitation rights for rare earth minerals in Vietnam's north-western Lai Chau province. The statement said Tokyo would provide financial and technical support for the rare earth development ... Japan and Vietnam have also agreed to work towards the early signing of a bilateral nuclear co-operation pact. The joint statement said: 'The Vietnamese government chooses Japan as a co-operation partner to build two nuclear reactors' ... Japan is the world's third biggest nuclear power generator, and the government is keen to develop nuclear plants in fast growing markets like Vietnam.

(www.bbc.co.uk, 31 October 2010)

Japanese prime minister Naoto Kan has stepped up his efforts to promote overseas trade by concluding an agreement to build two civil nuclear reactors for Vietnam and to co-operate with the Vietnamese government on the exploration and refining of rare earth minerals. Mr Kan met Nguyen Tan Dung, his Vietnamese counterpart on Sunday [31 October] after a summit of Asian leaders in Hanoi. A Japanese government spokesman said the two leaders held 'fruitful discussions encompassing political, security, economic and other issues', including development assistance and possible Japanese projects involving high-speed rail and metro systems. The civil nuclear reactor is a coup for the Kan administration and the first significant order since it embarked on a policy of supporting exports of Japanese technology overseas. The Kan administration has stated its goal on increasing infrastructure exports in order to support Japan's economic growth. It also wants to promote Japan's high-speed rail technology for use in Vietnam and other countries. The Japanese nuclear project, which will be located in Ninh Thuan province, is also the first order for the International Nuclear Energy Development of Japan Co., a public–private venture established last month designed to help export Japan's nuclear technology. Global competition to sell nuclear technology to power-hungry developing nations is heating up, with France, Japan, South Korea and the United States leading the way. France and South Korea have also been vying to secure nuclear power projects in Vietnam, which wants to generate as much as 20 per cent of its energy from nuclear by 2010. The United States concluded a memorandum of understanding on nuclear co-operation with Vietnam in March [2010] but Vietnam must sign a formal Section 123 agreement before it is allowed to import nuclear technology.

(*FT*, 1 November 2010, p. 9)

Vietnam has chosen Japan as a partner to mine rare earth minerals and develop nuclear power ... prime minister Naoto Kan of Japan said on Sunday [31 October] ... Vietnam has plans to build eight nuclear power plants by 2030 to meet rising energy demand. Currently hydropower contributes more than a third of the country's energy. Mr Kan confirmed that Japan would help Vietnam develop nuclear power. Also on Sunday President Dmitri Medvedev of Russia met with his Vietnamese counterpart, Nguyen Minh Triet, and witnessed the formal signing of a deal to build Vietnam's first nuclear power plant. The two countries agreed to the deal last year [2009]; construction is to start in 2014 and be completed in 2020. Russia's state atomic company, Roasatom, said in a statement that it would build two reactors at the plant with a total capacity of 2,400 megawatts. Japan and Russia are eager to gain a footing in Vietnam's fast-expanding nuclear power market ... [Rosatom said] that Moscow was negotiating with Vietnam to build two more reactors and was 'aware of worthy competitors from other countries'.

(www.iht.com, 1 November 2010)

Russia agreed to build Vietnam's first nuclear power plant in a ceremony in Hanoi on Sunday [31 October] presided over by President Dmitri Medvedev ... An accord [was signed] for building two reactors by 2020. Hanoi has picked four sites at which it will build at least four reactors each ... Meanwhile, the Russian bank VTB and BIDV of Vietnam signed a deal to start a $500 million fund to invest in energy and mining.

(*IHT*, 1 November 2010, p. 19)

China has rejected an offer from the United States to host three-way talks with Japan over the future of a group of disputed islands in the East China Sea. A Chinese foreign ministry spokesman said the dispute involved only two nations, not the United States. The spokesman said: 'I want to emphasize that this is only a US idea. It must be pointed out that the Diaoyu Islands are Chinese territory, and the territorial dispute between China and Japan over the Diaoyu Islands is the business of the two nations only. The United States has many times said the US–Japan security treaties can apply to the Daioyu Islands. This is totally wrong. The United States should immediately correct this mistaken position.'

(www.bbc.co.uk, 2 November 2010)

China's Marine Corps held a major naval exercise on Tuesday [2 November] in the South China Sea, state-run media reported on Wednesday [3 November], massing 1,800 troops and more than 100 ships, submarines and aircraft for a live-fire display of the nation's growing military power. The waters have been the scene of increased tensions between China and its neighbours this year over competing claims to islands and seabed mineral rights.

(www.iht.com, 3 November 2010)

'Japan's constitution renounces war and the country only has forces for defence' (www.iht.com, 3 November 2010).

At a meeting of regional leaders in Hanoi on 30 October ... China's prime minister Wen Jiabao ... [and his Japanese] counterpart Naoto Kan ... managed a mere ten minutes of chat ... At a gathering on 4 October of European and Asian leaders in Brussels ... Wen Jiabao spoke in a corridor with Naoto Kan for twenty-five minutes ... [Japan detained] a Chinese fishing boat crew on 7 September ... [There followed] the swift release of the crew, and on 24 September of their captain ... The Japanese say the [Chinese] skipper was steaming drunk. On 1 November thirty-odd Japanese politicians were shown a video they say left no doubt of a deliberate ramming of a Japanese coastguard vessel ... Yang Jiechi, China's foreign minister, apparently assured US Secretary of State Hillary Clinton in Hanoi that China would be a 'responsible supplier' of rare earths. At the height of the fishing boat dispute, China stopped exports to Japan of these minerals ... Still, an official in Tokyo says that Japan has not received a single shipment since the captain's release. He also says that the Chinese have even hinted to Japanese manufacturers that if they want rare earths, they should move their factories to China. To the Japanese that sounds like a menacing invitation to hand over their most valuable technologies ... Military types [in China] privately criticize the [Chinese] foreign ministry for wetness in dealing with Japan and the West ... Foreign minister Yang Jiechi is not even in the Politburo, let alone on the Standing Committee, pinnacle of Communist Party power ... [China rebuked US Secretary of State Hillary Clinton] on 27 October when she emphatically stated that the Senkaku are covered by America's security alliance with Japan ... The southernmost of the [four] Russian-occupied Kuril islands are so close to Japan's north-eastern tip that when the fog lifts, there they are ... In the days after Japan's surrender in 1945 Soviet forces seized the islands. Thanks to the dispute over what Japan calls its Northern Territories, Russia and Japan have never signed a peace treaty ending the Second World War ... On 1 November President Dmitri Medvedev became the first Russian [or Soviet] leader to visit the islands [visiting the second largest of the islands] ... The American administration says it is sympathetic to Japan's Northern Territories claims, but that defending them does not fall under the terms of the security alliance.

(www.economist.com, 4 November 2010)

A leaked video is circulating in cyberspace, showing a boat collision that sparked a recent diplomatic battle between China and Japan. The YouTube video shows the same collision that Japanese lawmakers watched on video last week, said legislator Hiroshi Kawauchi of the ruling Democratic Party of Japan. The Japanese coastguard shot the video, which is authentic and not doctored, said Kawauchi, who is a member of the House of Representatives in the Diet, Japan's legislature ... The crash video that Japanese lawmakers saw has not been released to the public. The video, posted on YouTube, shows what is thought to be the Chinese fishing trawler ramming into a ship, though to be a Japanese coastguard vessel. The Chinese government dismissed the video after Japanese lawmakers saw it, saying it had been edited and that it did not change the ownership of the islands ... Japanese prime minister Naoto Kan's office is investigating the leaking of the video, which has been shown on Japanese television. The man apparently doing the videotaping says on the video that the date is 7 September 2010. That matches the detaining of the fishing crew.

(www.cnn.com, 5 November 2010)

Japan's government is trying to find out how video clips, apparently shot by its coastguard during a confrontation with a Chinese trawler in September, ended up on YouTube this week. The clips, which have now been broadcast on Japanese television news programmes, appear to show the Chinese ship ramming two Japanese coastguard vessels during a stand-off in disputed waters ... Several edits of the material were posted online, including one featuring English titles, which appears to show the second clash between the two nations' vessels.

(www.iht.com, 5 November 2010)

The film ... appears to show the Chinese trawler deliberately ramming the Japanese boat *Mizuki* on two separate occasions. Plumes of black diesel exhaust are shown spewing from the rear of the Chinese ship, suggesting it may have been accelerating towards the other vessel ... The film appeared on YouTube, posted by a user registered as a twenty-five-year-old of Japanese nationality ... The Chinese foreign ministry said the video 'cannot change the truth, or cover up the illegality of Japan's actions'.

(*The Times*, 6 November 2010, p. 51)

An unusually broad coalition of business groups in North America, Europe and Asia has sent a letter to the heads of state of the G-20 major economies, asking them to make a commitment at their meeting this month in Seoul that trade in crucial rare earth minerals will not be interrupted because of industrial policies or political disputes. The range of countries and industries whose business groups signed the letter underscores the level of worry at companies around the world about recent restrictions place on rare earths by China ... Some of the groups signing the letter, like the United States Chamber of Commerce, also signed a letter last winter asking that the Chinese government not discriminate in favour of domestic companies in the purchase of high-tech equipment. But the letter on rare earths was also signed by business groups that have previously been wary of challenging an increasingly wealthy China, including the business federations of Germany and France and the *Keidanren*, a broad grouping of big Japanese corporations that has historically been extremely cautious on China issues. The letter was dated Wednesday [3 November] but not publicly released. It was obtained from an executive at one of the business groups that signed it. The Chinese government has collected export taxes of 15 per cent to 25 per cent on rare earths for years and has further restricted exports in the last two years with steep reductions in export quotas for rare earths. When China joined the WTO in 2001 it agreed to refrain from imposing export taxes and quotas. The Chinese government halted exports of raw rare earths to Japan on 21 September during a dispute over Japan's detention of a Chinese fishing trawler and expanded the interruption to all countries on 18 October. Chinese customs officials gave permission on 28 October for a resumption in shipments, but they have allowed some shipments to leave ports while continuing to block other shipments, industry executives said. Chinese officials have denied that they issued any official ban on rare earth exports and contend that export quotas and taxes are needed to conserve scarce supplies and protect the environment, which WTO rules allow.

(Keith Bradsher, *IHT*, 6 November 2010, p. 13)

American lawyers say that China would have a hard time winning the conservation case if another country challenges its policies before a WTO tribunal because China's own consumption of rare earths is soaring. China has pursued an industrial policy in recent years of forcing companies to move factories to China so as to have access to rare earths. The letter from the business groups objected to this, asking the G-20 leaders and their governments to commit themselves to 'refrain from export taxes, quotas or other market-distorting measures on rare earth elements that restrict global supply and unnecessarily contribute to price volatility, including through respect for the rules of the WTO and commitments resulting from its members' accession protocols'. The letter also called for the G-20 leaders and governments to 'renounce interference with commercial sale of rare earth elements, domestically or internationally, to advance industrial policy or political objectives'. Among the thirty-seven groups signing the letter were the Alliance of Automobile Manufacturers, the American Petroleum Institute, the Business Roundtable, the Consumer Electronics Association, the National Association of Manufacturers and the US Magnetic Materials Association, as well as the Brazil–US Business Council, Business Europe, the Canadian Chamber of Commerce, the Federation of Korean Industries and the Japan Electronics and Information Technology Industries Association.

(Keith Bradsher, www.iht.com, 5 November 2010)

A chronology of political developments

25 October 2010.

> This week US Secretary of State Hillary Clinton will visit Vietnam for the second time in four months, to attend an East Asian summit meeting likely to be dominated by the China questions. Next month [November] President Barack Obama plans to tour four major Asian democracies – Japan, Indonesia, India and South Korea ... In Hanoi in July Mrs Clinton said the United States would help facilitate talks between Beijing and its neighbours over disputed islands in the South China Sea. Chinese officials were livid when it became clear that the United States had lined up twelve countries behind the American position. With President Hu Jintao set to visit Washington early next year [2011], officials said Mrs Clinton would strike a more harmonious note in Asia this week. For now, they said, the administration feels it has made its point.
>
> (www.iht.com, 25 October 2010; *IHT*, 26 October 2010, p. 5)

26 October 2010.

> Nine Vietnamese fishermen returned home on Tuesday [26 October] after an ordeal at sea that included a month of detention by China and a week lost on stormy seas. The men had been at the centre of a diplomatic dispute between China and Vietnam, one of several territorial disputes recently in the region.
>
> (*IHT*, 27 October 2010, p. 6)

29 October 2010.

> The Vietnamese government has arrested several dissidents and several bloggers in the days before a visit to Hanoi by US Secretary of State Hillary Clinton, according to the US embassy and human rights groups. Washington has often voiced its concern over human rights issues in Vietnam, and the last actions drew sharp criticism from some members of Congress as well as a statement from the US embassy in Hanoi urging their release. Members of Congress and human rights groups urged Mrs Clinton to speak out in support of human rights while she is in Hanoi for a meeting of South-east Asian leaders. The convictions of three dissidents for causing public disorder and the arrests of three bloggers come at a time of increased pressure on critics that many analysts say is intended to silence debate ahead of a Communist Party congress in January [2011]. In addition, six Roman Catholics were tried and convicted Wednesday [27 October] in a case the Catholic News Agency said stemmed from violent clashes with the police over a parish's attempt in May to bury a woman in a cemetery that the local government had seized for a tourist resort. The arrests and trials 'contradict Vietnam's own commitment to internationally accepted standards of human rights', the US embassy said in its statement. The statement continued: 'We urge the government of Vietnam to release these individuals' ... According to the London-based rights group Amnesty International, Vietnam is holding

at least thirty people on political charges, including members and supporters of banned political groups, independent trade unions, bloggers, businessmen, journalists and writers ... The Vietnamese government ... insists that these are not political arrests and that all the accusations involve criminal activity ... The recent case against three labour activists, Nguyen Hoang Quoc Hung, Do Thi Minh Hanh and Doan Huy Chuong, involved charges of disrupting public order for distributing leaflets supporting workers' rights at a factory, according to Amnesty International. Their sentences were not officially announced. The bloggers are Le Nguyen Huong Tra, Phan Thanh Hai and Nguyen Van Hai. The last was rearrested after completing an earlier sentence for tax evasion. The government is particularly sensitive to blogs that touch on official corruption, relations with China and a Chinese-run bauxite mine that has prompted widespread controversy.

(www.iht.com, 29 October 2010; *IHT*, 30 October 2010, p. 5)

30 October 2010.

US Secretary of State Hillary Clinton's ... visit to Hanoi, the second in four months, illustrates the warmer ties between two former enemies. But she also chided the Vietnamese government for arresting a half-dozen dissidents and bloggers in the days before her arrival, saying Vietnam's economic success had to be matched by 'improvements in political freedom and human rights'.

(www.iht.com, 30 October 2010)

Internet

The net domain reserved for Vietnam has become a haven of cyber crime, suggests research. About 58 per cent of the sites using Vietnam's .vn domain harboured malware, found the McAfee [Labs] report. Those visiting the dangerous sites risk having sensitive data stolen or their computer being hijacked. In all, it found, 6.2 per cent of the 27 million live sites it tracks were found to be risky to visit, a figure up from 5.9 per cent in 2009. 'The web is getting trickier to navigate safely,' said the report, which tried to compile a global snapshot of the criminal activity perpetrated via the net ... Vietnam had only become a favourite with hi-tech criminals in 2010, said the report, as in 2009 the country's domain came thirty-ninth in the global risk ranking. By comparison, the UK is ranked as the forty-ninth riskiest domain... About 15,000 of the 24,000 websites sitting on the .vn domain were home to criminal activity, said the report. Many .vn domains are used as redirect points for other malicious sites or to control networks of hijacked computers or botnets.

(www.bbc.co.uk, 26 October 2010)

Demography

Sex ratios are becoming increasingly imbalanced in Vietnam, with far more boys being born than girls, the UN Population Fund [UNFPA] says. For every 100 females, 110.6 males were born – compared to a norm of 105. The situation was particularly worrying because of the rapid increase in the proportion of boys being born in the last years, it said. The UNFPA warned that the imbalance could lead to a number of social problems in the coming years. In May 2009 deputy prime minister Nguyen Thien Nhan warned that the gender imbalance in Vietnam could lead to about 3 million men having difficulty in finding wives by 2030. Bruce Campbell, the UNFPA's representative in Vietnam, said that other Asian countries with gender imbalances had developed these over much long periods. He said: 'Over thirty years China reached the ratio of 130 [males per 100 females] and Korea 116, and these are declining. Vietnam went from quite a normal level of 105 to 110.6 in the last five years' ... Vietnam banned foetal sex selection in 2003 in an effort to tackle this problem, but the practice is still going on. Mr Campbell explained: 'Three factors that contribute to the increase of an imbalanced ratio at birth are: firstly, son-preference, a very fundamental aspect of culture and society in many countries; secondly, the pressure of fertility to have a smaller family size, especially in a number of Asian countries; and, thirdly, the access to legal and affordable technology for son selection. And in Vietnam it's the combination of all three factors' ... Tran Van Chien, vice head of Vietnam General Office for Population and Family Planning (ministry of health), says that the biggest difficulty Vietnam was facing in tackling the problem was the 1,000-year-old tradition that favours men over women, where men carry on the family line and care for elderly parents. He says changing this will take years. But he said Vietnam was determined to learn from other countries' experience in raising awareness among its population with policies to enhance women's status in society.

(www.bbc.co.uk, 26 October 2010)

Direct foreign investment

TNK-BP, the Russian joint [fifty–fifty] venture [formed in 2003] between BP and a group of Russian billionaires, said on Monday [18 October] that it would acquire BP's production and pipeline assets in Vietnam and Venezuela for $1.8 billion. The company will use its own money to finance the acquisitions ... The deal comes as BP plans to sell $30 billion in assets to cover costs linked to the Gulf of Mexico oil spill, the worst such accident in American history.

(www.iht.com, 18 October 2010)

The transaction will leave half the assets' equity on BP's books but give the company an immediate flow of cash for the entire value of the sale ... BP will receive the cash and retain a 50 per cent stake in the reserves ... The agreement with TNK-BP is the first major deal for BP's new chief executive, Robert Dudley, an American who was appointed to run BP midway through the Gulf disaster. BP has said it will raise $30 billion to pay claims relating to the spill, which killed eleven workers and caused tens of billions of dollars in damages. BP has raised more than $11 billion, including the sales announced Monday. That includes $7 billion from the sale of fields in the United States, Canada and Egypt ... and $1.9 billion for the sale of assets in Colombia. For TNK-BP's investors, the sell-off comes at a good time. Taxes at home eat up much of the profits of Russian oil companies ... Until 2008 Mr Dudley had been chief executive of TNK-BP. When he took over from Tony Hayward as chief executive of BP after the Gulf spill, Mr Hayward went to a position on the board of the Russian company.

(www.iht.com, 18 October 2010)

BP has said it will create a $20 billion trust fund to pay claims from the explosion on 20 April on the *Deepwater Horizon* drilling rig ... The spill, which lasted three months, has been described as the largest accidental oil spill in history.

(*IHT*, 19 October 2010, p. 16)

TNK-BP ... will pay $1.8 billion to buy the UK oil group's assets in Venezuela and Vietnam, in a move that marks its most significant diversification outside Russia. The deal will boost BP's bid to raise $30 billion in cash by the end of 2011 to help pay for the costs of the Gulf of Mexico spill. But it also puts TNK-BP on the path of international expansion, propelling a longstanding aim of the company's Russian billionaire shareholders as opportunities for growth in their country diminish due to resource nationalism and a burdensome tax regime. The agreement will cement a peace deal that BP and its Russian partners reached just two years ago after a bruising shareholder battle over control of the company. During the dispute the Russian shareholders complained that BP was blocking the company's international expansion, and Bob Dudley, BP's chief executive, was forced to flee Russia over 'harassment' when he served as TNK-BP's chief. Mikhail Friedman, who leads the Russian shareholders as chairman of Alfa Group and also serves as TNK-BP's interim chief, called the deal 'a milestone in TNK-BP's strategic expansion in the global energy market' ... While the transaction will boost TNK-BP's reserves by only 2 per cent to 3 per cent, it will provide it with a key platform for international expansion as opportunities for growth in Russia decline. Only state-linked companies are reserved access to big new fields in the country, while the tax regime for upstream development 'takes away the impetus for investment', said Valeri Nesterov, oil and gas analyst at Troika Dialog ... Alfa–Access–Renova, the consortium via which the Russian shareholders hold their stake, said the company aimed to procure half of its production outside Russia's borders.

(*FT*, 19 October 2010, p. 21)

Russia is preparing to introduce a profit-based tax on new fields from 2012, Segei Shatalov, deputy finance minister, said, in a move that could quell fears of a production decline due to the current tax regime. The plan would also lower oil export duties and mineral extraction taxes, Mr Shatalov said. To compensate for the lower taxation on new fields, the ministry could raise export duties on oil products to equal 85 per cent to 90 per cent of the current crude export duty from 2011, he said.

(*FT*, 20 October 2010, p. 10)

The environment

Perhaps it is because most Asian economies are booming. Or perhaps it is because a series of recent weather-linked catastrophes and headline-grabbing pollution issues have hammered home the point. Either way, climate change and environmental issues have moved up Asia's list of worries, often topping any concerns about the global economy, according to opinion polls released over the past few weeks ... many of the world's developing economies – unlike those in Europe and the United States – are booming, allowing job prospects and the economy to become less of a concern than in the past ... Devastating floods have left millions homeless in Pakistan. Parts of China have experienced lingering heatwaves ... Hong Kong ... [has] an increasingly worrisome air quality problem ... The Asian Development Bank issued a report last month [October 2010] warning that Asian megacities 'will flood more often, on a larger scale, affect millions more people', if, as widely expected, climate change brings rising sea levels and more intense tropical cyclones. Of the ten most populous cities with heavy exposure to coastal flooding, five listed in 2005 were in Asia, the organization wrote: Calcutta, Guangzhou, Ho Chi Minh City, Mumbai and Shanghai. By 2070 nine of the ten cities in terms of population exposure are expected to be in Asian countries.

(www.iht.com, 7 November 2010; *IHT*, 8 November 2010, p. 18)

(There have been many reports of flooding in the area, including the following examples. 'The strongest cyclone to hit the Philippines in years has killed at least three people ... Super typhoon Megi could later hit Vietnam, where flooding has caused thirty deaths in recent days ... In central Vietnam, officials said five people were still missing after flooding unrelated to Megi ... A Vietnamese disaster official in Quang Binh province: 'Many people have not even returned to their flooded homes from previous floods, while many others who returned home several days ago were forced to be evacuated again': www.guardian.co.uk, 18 October 2010. 'Devastating floods spreading from north-eastern Thailand have left seventeen people dead over the past two weeks ... Officials describe the flooding, which follows deadly inundations in Vietnam and other nearby countries, as the worst in half a century': www.iht.com, 21 October 2010.)

Bibliography

Periodicals and reports

The *Vietnam Courier* was published in Hanoi until it ceased publication in 1992. Periodicals and reports mentioned in the text are abbreviated as follows:

CDSP – Current Digest of the Soviet Press (since 5 February 1992 *Post-Soviet*)
EIU – Economist Intelligence Unit
FEER – Far Eastern Economic Review
FT – Financial Times
IHT – International Herald Tribune

Note the following changes of title: *Soviet Economy* to *Post-Soviet Studies*; *Soviet Studies* to *Europe-AsiaSt udies*.

Books and journals

Andreff, W. (1993) 'The double transition from underdevelopment and from socialism in Vietnam', *Journal of Contemporary Asia*, vol. 23, no. 4.
Asian Development Bank (1996) *Asian Development Outlook 1996 and 1997*, Asian Development Bank: Manila.
Beresford, M. (1988) *Vietnam: Politics, Economics and Society*, London: Pinter.
Beresford, M. (1990) 'Vietnam: socialist agriculture in transition', *Journal of Contemporary Asia*, vol. 20, no. 4.
Beresford, M. (1992) 'Industrial reform in Vietnam' in I. Jeffries (ed.) *Industrial Reform in Socialist Countries: From Restructuring to Revolution*, Aldershot: Edward Elgar.
Bideleux, R. and Jeffries, I. (1998) *A History of Eastern Europe: Crisis and Change*, London: Routledge.
Bideleux, R. and Jeffries, I. (2007) *A History of Eastern Europe: Crisis and Change*, 2nd edn, London: Routledge.
Bideleux, R. and Jeffries, I. (2007) *The Balkans*, London: Routledge.
Brada, J. and Wädekin, K.-E. (eds) (1988) *Socialist Agriculture in Transition: Organizational Response to Failing Performance*, Boulder: Westview Press.
Crosnier, M.-A. and Lhomel, E. (1990) 'A first assessment of the Vietnamese economic reforms', CEDUCEE, Paris: paper presented to the IV World Congress for Soviet and East European Studies (Harrogate, July).
Dellmo, H., Granlund, J. and Gustaffson, A. (1990) *Vietnam's Economic Reforms and*

their Effects on State Enterprises, Stockholm: Swedish International Development Authority.

Dinh, Q. (1993) 'Vietnam's policy reforms and its future', *Journal of Contemporary Asia*, vol. 23, no. 4.

Dollar, D. (1994) 'Macroeconomic management and the transition to the market in Vietnam', *Journal of Comparative Economics*, vol. 18, no. 3.

Economist survey (1985) 'Comecon', 20 April.

Economist survey (1993) 'Asia', 30 October.

Economist survey (1995) 'Vietnam', 8 July.

Economist survey (2008) 'Vietnam', 26 April.

Elliott, J. (1992) 'The future of socialism: Vietnam, the way ahead?' *Third World Quarterly*, vol. 13, no. 1.

Fforde, A. (1987) 'Industrial development in the Democratic Republic of Vietnam', London: Birkbeck College Discussion Paper 2.

Fforde, A. (1988) 'Specific aspects of the collectivization of wet-rice cultivation: Vietnamese experience' in J. Brada and K.-E. Wädekin (eds) *Socialist Agriculture in Transition: Organizational Response to Failing Performance*, Boulder: Westview Press.

Fforde, A. (2005) 'Vietnam in 2004', *Asian Survey*, vol. XLV, no. 1.

Fforde, A. and de Vylder, S. (1988) *Vietnam – an Economy in Transition*, Stockholm: Swedish International Development Authority.

Fforde, A. and Paine, S. (1987) *The Limits of National Liberation: Economic Management and the Reunification of the Democratic Republic of Vietnam,* London: Croom Helm.

Financial Times (various surveys on Vietnam): 14 November 1991; 30 November 1993; 8 December 1994; 13 November 1995; 26 April 2008.

Fischer, S. and Gelb, A. (1991) 'The process of socialist economic transformation', *Journal of Economic Perspectives*, vol. 5, no. 4.

Fischer, S. and Sahay, R. (2000) 'Taking stock', *Finance and Development*, vol. 37, no. 3.

Gainsborough, M. (2003) 'Slow, quick, quick: assessing equitization and enterprise performance in Vietnam', *Communist Studies and Transition Politics*, vol. 19, no. 1.

Gelb, A., Jefferson, G. and Singh, I. (1993) 'Can communist economies transform incrementally? The experience of China', *Economics of Transition*, vol. 1, no. 4.

Goodkind, D. (1995) 'Vietnam's one-or-two-child policy in action', *Population and Development Review*, vol. 21, no. 1.

Gregory, P. and Stuart, R. (1990) *Soviet Economic Structure and Performance*, 4th edn, New York: Harper & Row (2nd edn 1981 and 3rd edn 1986).

Gregory, P. and Stuart, R. (1994) *Soviet and Post-Soviet Economic Structure and Performance*, 5th edn, New York: Harper Collins.

Hoen, H. (ed.) (2001) *Good Governance in Central and Eastern Europe: The Puzzle of Capitalism by Design*, Cheltenham: Edward Elgar.

Holzman, F. (1976) *International Trade under Communism*, New York: Basic Books.

Holzman, F. (1987) *The Economics of Soviet Bloc Trade and Finance*, Boulder and London: Westview Press.

Hussain, A. (1992) *The Chinese Economic Reforms in Retrospect and Prospect*, LSE: CP no. 24.

International Monetary Fund (IMF) (2010) Country Report came on line today (Sunday 12 September

Irvin, G. (1995) 'Vietnam: assessing the achievements of *doi moi*', *Journal of Development Economics*, vol. 31, no. 5.
Jeffries, I. (ed.) (1981) *The Industrial Enterprise in Eastern Europe*, New York: Praeger.
Jeffries, I. (1990) *A Guide to the Socialist Economies*, London: Routledge.
Jeffries, I. (1992a) 'The impact of reunification on the East German economy' in J. Osmond (ed.) *German Reunification: A Reference Guide and Commentary*, London: Longman.
Jeffries, I. (ed.) (1992b) *Industrial Reform in Socialist Countries: From Restructuring to Revolution*, Aldershot: Edward Elgar.
Jeffries, I. (1993) *Socialist Economies and the Transition to the Market: A Guide*, London: Routledge.
Jeffries, I. (1996a) *A Guide to the Economies in Transition*, London: Routledge.
Jeffries, I. (ed.) (1996b) *Problems of Economic and Political Transformation in the Balkans*, London: Pinter.
Jeffries, I. (2001a) *Economies in Transition: A Guide to China, Cuba, Mongolia, North Korea and Vietnam at the Turn of the Twenty-first Century*, London: Routledge.
Jeffries, I. (2001b) 'Good governance and the first decade of transition', in H. Hoen (ed.) *Good Governance in Central and Eastern Europe: The Puzzle of Capitalism by Design*, Cheltenham: Edward Elgar.
Jeffries, I. (2002a) *Eastern Europe at the Turn of the Twenty-First Century: A Guide to the Economies in Transition*, London: Routledge.
Jeffries, I. (2002b) *The Former Yugoslavia at the Turn of the Twenty-First Century: A Guide to the Economies in Transition*, London: Routledge.
Jeffries, I. (2002c) *The New Russia: A Handbook of Economic and Political Developments*, London: RoutledgeCurzon.
Jeffries, I. (2003) *The Caucasus and Central Asian Republics at the Turn of the Twenty-First Century: A Guide to the Economies in Transition*, London: Routledge.
Jeffries, I. (2004) *The Countries of the Former Soviet Union: The Baltic and European States in Transition*, London: Routledge.
Jeffries, I. (2006a) *North Korea: A Guide to Economic and Political Developments*, London: Routledge.
Jeffries, I. (2006b) *Vietnam: A Guide to Economic and Political Developments*, London: Routledge.
Jeffries, I. (2006c) *China: A Guide to Economic and Political Developments*, London: Routledge.
Jeffries, I. (2007) *Mongolia: A Guide to Economic and Political Developments*, London: Routledge.
Jeffries, I. (2010a) *Contemporary North Korea: A Guide to Economic and Political Developments*. London: Routledge.
Jeffries, I. (2010b) *Economic Developments in Contemporary China*, London: Routledge.
Jeffries, I. (2010c) *Political Developments in Contemporary China*, London: Routledge.
Jeffries, I., Melzer, M. (eds) and Breuning, E. (advisory ed.) (1987) *The East German Economy*, London: Croom Helm.
Le Duc Thuy, Luong Xuan Quy and To Xuan Dan (1991) 'The market mechanism in the new economic management system in Vietnam', in P. Ronnas and Ö. Sjöberg (eds) *Socio-economic Development in Vietnam: The Agenda for the 1990s*, Stockholm: Swedish International Development Authority.
Le Trang (1990) 'Renewal of industrial management policy and organisation', in P. Ronnas and Ö. Sjöberg (eds) *Doi Moi: Economic Reforms and Development Policies in Vietnam*, Stockholm: Swedish International Development Authority.

Marr, D. and White, C. (eds) (1988) *Postwar Vietnam: Dilemmas in Socialist Development*, New York: Cornell University Southeast Asia Program.

Nguyen Manh Hung (2000) 'Vietnam in 1999: the party's choice', *Asian Survey*, vol. XL, no. 1.

Nguyen Tuong Lai and Nguyen Thanh Bang (1991) 'A new development policy for human resources within the socio-economic strategy of Vietnam up to the year 2000', in P. Ronnas and Ö. Sjöberg (eds) *Socio-economic Development in Vietnam: The Agenda for the 1990s*, Stockholm: Swedish International Development Authority.

Nguyen Van Huy (1990) 'Renewal of economic policies and economic management organisation in Vietnam', in P. Ronnas and Ö. Sjöberg (eds) *Doi Moi: Economic Reforms and Development Policies in Vietnam*, Stockholm: Swedish International Development Authority.

Nguyen Van Linh (1987) *Some Pressing Problems on the Distribution and Circulation of Goods*, Hanoi: Foreign Languages Publishing House.

Nove, A. (1961) *The Soviet Economy*, London: Allen & Unwin.

Nove, A. (1981) 'The Soviet industrial enterprise', in I. Jeffries (ed.) *The Industrial Enterprise in Eastern Europe*, New York: Praeger.

Nove, A. (1986) *The Soviet Economic System*, 3rd edn, London: Allen & Unwin.

Osmond, J. (ed.) (1992) *German Reunification: A Reference Guide and Commentary*, London: Longman.

Phan Van Tiem (1991) 'Finance and capital mobilization policies in the socio-economic strategy 1991–2000', in P. Ronnas and Ö. Sjöberg (eds) *Socio-economic Development in Vietnam: The Agenda for the 1990s*, Stockholm: Swedish International Development Authority.

Pike, D. (1987) *Vietnam and the Soviet Union*, Boulder and London: Westview Press.

Pincus, J. and Anh, Vu Thanh Tu (2008) 'Vietnam: a tiger in turmoil', *FEER*, May.

Pingali, P. and Vo-Tong Xuan (1992) 'Decollectivization and rice productivity growth', *Economic Development and Cultural Change*, vol. 40, no. 4.

Pollack, J. (2005) 'The United States and Asia in 2004', *Asian Survey*, vol. XLV, no. 1.

Porter, G. (1990) 'The politics of "renovation" in Vietnam', *Problems of Communism*, May–June.

Post, K. (1988) 'The working class in North Vietnam and the launching of the building of socialism', *Journal of Asian and African Studies*, vol. XXIII, nos 1–2.

Pryor, F. (1991) 'Third World decollectivization: Guyana, Nicaragua and Vietnam', *Problems of Communism*, vol. XL, no. 3 (May–June).

Pryor, F. (1992) *The Red and the Green: The Rise and the Fall of Collectivized Agriculture in Marxist Regimes*, Princeton, NJ: Princeton University Press.

Riedel, J. (1993) 'Vietnam: on the trail of the Tigers', *World Economy*, vol. 16, no. 4.

Riedel, J. and Comer, B. (1997) 'Transition to a market economy in Vietnam', in W. Woo, S. Parker and J. Sachs (eds) *Economics in Transition: Comparing Asia and Eastern Europe*, London: MIT Press.

Riskin, C. (1987) *The Political Economy of Chinese Development since 1949*, London: Oxford University Press.

Ronnas, P. and Sjöberg, Ö. (eds) (1990) *Doi Moi: Economic Reforms and Development Policies in Vietnam*, Stockholm: Swedish International Development Authority.

Ronnas, P. and Sjöberg, Ö. (1991a) 'Economic reform in Vietnam: dismantling the centrally planned economy' *Journal of Communist Studies*, vol. 7, no. 1.

Ronnas, P. and Sjöberg, Ö. (eds) (1991b) *Socio-economic Development in Vietnam: The Agenda for the 1990s*, Stockholm: Swedish International Development Authority.

Roy, D. (1990) 'Real product and income in China, Cuba, North Korea and Vietnam', *Development Policy Review*, vol. 8, no. 1.
Spoor, M. (1987) 'Finance in a socialist transition: the case of the Democratic Republic of Vietnam (1955–64)' *Journal of Contemporary Asia*, vol. 17.
Spoor, M. (1988a) 'Reforming state finance in post-1975 Vietnam', *Journal of Development Studies*, vol. 4.
Spoor, M. (1988b) 'State finance in the Socialist Republic of Vietnam', in D. Marr and C. White (eds) *Postwar Vietnam: Dilemmas in Socialist Development*, New York: Cornell University Southeast Asia Program.
Tai, N. and Hare, P. (1995) *State Enterprise Ownership Transformation in Vietnam*, Discussion Paper no. 95/2, Edinburgh: Heriot-Watt University.
Thuy, Tran Le (2008) 'Defusing Vietnam's hidden detonator', *FEER*, May.
Tran Duc Nguyen (1991) 'Vietnam's socio-economic development to the year 2000: approaches and objectives' in P. Ronnas and Ö. Sjöberg (eds) *Socio-economic Development in Vietnam: The Agenda for the 1990s*, Stockholm: Swedish International Development Authority.
Tran Ngoc Vinh (1990) 'Renewal of financial and monetary policies, and the circulation of material and goods at home and foreign trade' in P. Ronnas and Ö. Sjöberg (eds) *Doi Moi: Economic Reforms and Development Policies in Vietnam*, Stockholm: Swedish International Development Authority.
Tsang, S. (1996) 'Against "big bang" in economic transition: normative and positive arguments', *Cambridge Journal of Economics*, vol. 20, no. 2.
Ungar, E. (1987–8) 'The struggle over the Chinese community in Vietnam, 1946–86', *Pacific Affairs*, vol. 60, no. 4.
United Nations (2006) *World Economic Situation and Prospects*, New York: United Nations.
Van Arkadie, B. (1991) 'Comment', in P. Ronnas and Ö. Sjöberg (eds) *Socio-economic Development in Vietnam: The Agenda for the 1990s*, Stockholm: Swedish International Development Authority.
Van Brabant, J. (1980) *Socialist Economic Integration*, Cambridge: Cambridge University Press.
Van Brabant, J. (1990) 'Reforming a socialist developing country – the case of Vietnam', *Economics of Planning*, vol. 23, no. 3.
Vo Nhan Tri (1988) 'Party politics and economic performance: the Second and Third Year Plans examined' in D. Marr and C. White (eds) *Postwar Vietnam: Dilemmas in Socialist Development*, New York: Cornell University Southeast Asia Program.
Wädekin, K.-E. (1982) *Agrarian Policies in Communist Europe*, Totowa, NJ: Rowman & Allanheld.
Wallace, W. and Clarke, R. (1986) *Comecon, Trade and the West*, London: Pinter.
Weitzman, M. and Xu, C. (1993) *Chinese Township Village Enterprises as Vaguely Defined Co-operatives*, CP no. 26, London: London School of Economics and Political Science.
Weitzman, M. and Xu, C. (1994) 'Chinese township-village enterprises as vaguely defined co-operatives', *Journal of Comparative Economics*, vol. 18, no. 2.
Werner, J. (1988) 'The problem of the district in Vietnam's development policy', in D. Marr and C. White (eds) *Postwar Vietnam: Dilemmas in Socialist Development*, New York: Cornell University Southeast Asia Program.
White, C. (1985) 'Agricultural planning, pricing policy and co-operatives in Vietnam', *World Development*, vol. 13, no. 1.

Wiles, P. (1968) *Communist International Economics*, Oxford; Blackwell.
Woo, W., Parker, S. and Sachs, J. (eds) (1997) *Economies in Transition: Comparing Asia and Eastern Europe*, London: MIT Press.
Wood, A. (1989) 'Deceleration of inflation with acceleration of price reform: Vietnam's remarkable recent experience', *Cambridge Journal of Economics*, vol. 13, no. 4.
Woodhouse, C. (1977) *Modern Greece: A Short History*, London: Faber.
Woods, W. (1972) *Poland: Phoenix in the East*, Harmondsworth: Penguin.
World Bank (1996) *World Development Report: From Plan to Market*, New York: Oxford University Press.
World Bank (2002) *The First Ten Years: Analysis and Lessons for Eastern Europe and the Former Soviet Union*, Washington: World Bank.
World Bank (2004) *From Transition to Development*, www.worldbank.org.ru.

Index

administrative probation 20
Agent Orange 53–4, 83–5
Anh Joseph Cao 33
AIDS 91–5
Arnold, W. 171
Article 79 of the penal (criminal) code 47, 50
Article 88, 23, 37, 50
Asean (Association of South-east Asian Nations) 49, 55, 82, 184–5, 216–19, 225
Asean Regional Forum 83
Asia-Pacific Economic Co-operation (Apec): summit, forum 14, 17–19, 86
Asian financial crisis 2, 16, 192

Ball, G. 54
bird flu 100–40
Bloc 8406 21–2, 29, 49
boat people 85, 153
Bowring, P. 58, 153
Bradsher, K. 224
Bui Thanh Hieu (Nguoi Buon Gio) 38, 38–9
Bui Tien Dung 12, 26
Bush, G.W. 14, 18–19, 25, 31, 59, 86, 189

Campbell, B. 227
Cao Dai (religion) 87
Cao Sy Kiem 202
chaebol 172–3, 180–1
Chiang Mai initiative 163
China Plus One 181
Chinese model 16
Clinton, B. 14, 19, 54–5
Clinton, H. 54–5, 57, 213–19, 222, 225–6
Comecon (Council of Mutual Economic Assistance) 1
Cong Thanh Do 23

Dao Dinh Binh 12, 26

Decree 31 20
de Rhodes, A. 86
Diaoyu Islands (China's name) *see* Senkaku Islands (Japan's name)
Dinh Van Huynh 32–3
Do Ba Tan 52
Do Thi Minh Hanh 226
Doan Huy Chuong 226
doi moi (renovation) 1, 11, 31, 154, 169–70
Dong Thu Huong 49

East Asia Summit (EAS) 82, 218
environment 229

free trade area (zone) 184–5

G-20 economies 223
Gates, B. 14–15
Gates, R. 77, 79–82
global financial crisis 2, 154, 207
Greve, K. 206
grupos 173
Gulf of Tonkin: incident, crisis 54

Hanoi (1,000th anniversary) 78–9
Hanyok, R. 54
Ho Chi Minh 1, 11, 21
Hoang Minh Chinh 28–9
Hoang Trung Hai 26, 199
Huynh Nguyen Dao 23
hyperinflation 6–7, 166–7, 170

internet 33–4, 38, 89–90, 226

Jackson–Vanek Amendment 189
Jeffries, I. 153
Johnson, L. 54

keiretsu 172

Kim Anh Kim 49
Konglomerat 173
Kuril Islands (Russia's name) (Northern Territories: Japan's name) 222
Kwakwa, V. 165
Kyoto Protocol 192

Lamy, P. 213
Le Cong Dinh 37, 40, 46–8, 50–1
Le Hoang 35
Le Kha Phieu 15
Le Nguyen Huong Tra 226
Le Nguyen Sang 23
La Thang Long 48
Le The Tiem 18, 36
Le Thi Cong Nhan 20, 23–4, 37
Lehman, J.-P. 154
Liang Guanglie 79–82

Mai Chi Tho (General) 12
Manifesto for Freedom and Democracy 22
market economy with socialist orientation 11
market-orientated socialism with Vietnamese characteristics 153
McAfee [Labs] report 226
Mehta, N. 201
Mydans, S. 15

Negroponte, J. 31
Nguyen Ai Quoc 28
Nguyen Bao Truyen 23
Nguyen Cong Khe 35
Nguyen Hoang Hai 31 (Dieu Cay) 31, 37
Nguyen Hoang Quoc Hung 226
Nguyen Hong Truong 180
Nguyen Minh Triet 10, 13, 16–18, 20, 23–6, 36, 53, 221
Nguyen Nghia 46
Nguyen Ngoc Nhu Quynh (Me Nam) 38–9
Nguyen Phu Trong 17, 26
Ngyuen Sinh Hung 26
Nguyen Tan Dung 10, 13, 16–18, 26, 31, 37, 46, 81, 86, 157, 169, 171–2, 175, 180, 183, 194–5, 197, 199, 206, 220
Nguyen Thien Nhan 26, 227
Nguyen Tien Trung 40, 48, 51
Nguyen Tung Van 181
Nguyen Van An 14, 17
Nguyen Van Bo 184
Nguyen Van Dai 20, 23–4, 37
Nguyen Van Giau 26, 158
Nguyen Van Hai 32, 35–6, 226

Nguyen Van Ly 20–2, 48, 88–9
Nguyen Viet Chien 32–3, 35–6
Nguyen Vinh Trong 26
Nguyen Viet Tien 26
Nguyen Vu Binh 24
Nhat Hanh *see* Thich Nhat Hanh
Nong Duc Manh 10, 13–15, 17, 27, 38–9, 169, 201–2
non-market economy 188
nuclear power plant 221

Obama, B. 36, 59, 225
Olympic torch (Chinese) 30
Orange Day 84

Paracel islands (Paracels: Hoang Sa) 28, 31, 38–9, 49, 53, 55–7, 77, 80, 82, 214
Paulson, H. 19
Pham Doan Trang 38–9
Pham Gia Khiem 26, 54, 171
Pham Hong Son 18, 89
Pham Thanh Binh 180
Pham Thanh Nghien 51
Pham Van Tra 16
Pham Xuan Quac (Major General) 32–3
Phan Thanh Hai 226
Phan Van Ban 23
Phan Van Khai 13–14, 16, 18, 30
Phung Quang Thanh (General) 79
Pincus, J. and Ahn, Vu Thanh Tu 10, 157, 173
Pope Benedict XVI 86
Project Management Unit 18 (PMU18) 12, 26
Putin, V. 19

rare earths 60–76, 81, 210–24
Rice, C. 31
Rumsfeld, D. 16

SARS 95–9
Senkaku Islands (Japan's name) (Diaoyu Islands: China's name) 63–75, 211–25
Spratly Islands (Spratlys: Truong Sa) 28, 31, 34–5, 39, 49, 53, 55, 57, 80, 82, 214
swine flu 141–52

Thayer, C. 180
Thich Huyen Quang 20, 31
Thich Nhat Hanh 88
Thich Quan Do 20
Thuy, Tran Le 3, 157
Tran Anh Kim 48, 50

Tran Duc Luong 13–14, 17
Tran Duy Thuc 50
Tran Huynh Duy Thuc 48, 51
Tran Huynh Thuc 40
Tran Khai Thuy 52
Tran Quoc Hien 23–4
Tran Van Chien 227
Truong Van Cam (known as Nam Cam) 17
Truong Vinh Trong 26

Viet Kieu 2, 85
Viet Tan 48, 50
Vietnam War: human toll 16, 53, 83–5

Vo Nguyen Giap (General) 12, 15, 35, 89, 198–9, 201
Vo Van Kiet 30–1
Vu Duc Long 29–30
Vu Tien Loc 179

WTO (World Trade Organization: Vietnam joined on 11 January 2007) 2, 17, 22, 66, 70, 72–3, 186–91, 210, 213–14, 224

Yang Jiechi 56–7

Zoellick, R. 52

eBooks – at www.eBookstore.tandf.co.uk

A library at your fingertips!

eBooks are electronic versions of printed books. You can store them on your PC/laptop or browse them online.

They have advantages for anyone needing rapid access to a wide variety of published, copyright information.

eBooks can help your research by enabling you to bookmark chapters, annotate text and use instant searches to find specific words or phrases. Several eBook files would fit on even a small laptop or PDA.

NEW: Save money by eSubscribing: cheap, online access to any eBook for as long as you need it.

Annual subscription packages

We now offer special low-cost bulk subscriptions to packages of eBooks in certain subject areas. These are available to libraries or to individuals.

For more information please contact webmaster.ebooks@tandf.co.uk

We're continually developing the eBook concept, so keep up to date by visiting the website.

www.eBookstore.tandf.co.uk